Freedom from Prejudice

Freedom from Prejudice

An introduction to the Australian Collection
in the National Gallery of Victoria **Brian
Finemore**

Selected and compiled by
JENNIFER PHIPPS

Consulting editor:
STEPHEN MURRAY-SMITH

National Gallery of Victoria 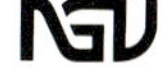

First Published 1977
National Gallery of Victoria
180 St Kilda Road, Melbourne, Australia 3004
Copyright this collection the National Gallery of Victoria 1976

Typeset in Monotype Baskerville at The Dominion Press
Colour separations by Eastern Studios Pty Ltd
Printed by The Dominion Press
Designed by Vane Lindesay

This publication has been assisted by the Visual Arts Board of the
Australia Council

Finemore, Brian.
  Freedom from prejudice.

  Index.
  Bibliography.
  ISBN 0 7241 0031 8.

  1. Painting, Australian.   2. Paintings,
  Australian — Exhibitions.   I. Phipps, Jennifer,
  comp.   II. Murray-Smith, Stephen, ed.   III. Title.

759.994

Acknowledgements

We are grateful to the many people who granted permission to reproduce paintings and offered assistance. These include the Art Gallery of New South Wales (Conder *Departure of the Orient—Circular Quay*, and Streeton *Redfern Station*); the Art Gallery of South Australia (Roberts *Breakaway*); and the National Library of Australia (Roberts *Bourke Street*). The following copyright holders kindly granted permission to reproduce works in the collection: Mr J. Balsaitis (*Metron II*); Mr W. P. Balson (Ralph Balson *Constructive Painting*); Mr Tony Coleing (*Untitled*); Mrs Grace Crowley (*Girl with Goats* and *Painting 1950*); Sir William Dobell Art Foundation (*Portrait of Helena Rubinstein*); Mr Michael Fizelle (Rah Fizelle *Portrait of Betty Collings*); Mr James Gleeson (*We Inhabit the Corrosive Littoral of Habit*); Mr David Heysen (Sir Hans Heysen *A Summers' Day*); Mrs Maurice Lambert (George Lambert *A Sergeant of the Light Horse*); Mr Jack Manton (Sir Arthur Streeton *Grey Day on the Hawkesbury River*); Mr Paul Partos (*Quantum*); Mr John Passmore (*Harbourside*) and Mr Oliver Streeton (Sir Arthur Streeton's paintings and watercolour). Every effort has been made to contact known copyright holders and the Gallery would be interested to receive information about copyright holders who have not been approached.

We also wish to thank the Country Women's Association of Victoria for permission to quote from articles published in their magazine *Country Crafts*; Cheshire-Longman Publishing Pty. Ltd. for permission to reproduce the text of the booklets *Australian Painting* and *Australian Impressionists*; and the National Gallery Society for permission to quote extracts from their Bulletin. Mrs I. Phipps kindly gave permission to publish the photograph of Mrs Louis Abrahams and Mr John Gilheany gave much time to sorting documents and catalogues.

Many members of the Gallery staff co-operated in the preparation of this book and not all can be mentioned by name. Mrs Lee White (Editor) Mrs Patricia Forster (Librarian), Mr Philip Jago (Publications Officer) and Mrs Daphne Hewlett, the installation staff under the direction of Mr Ben Holzhausen and the Gallery photographer, Mr George Mehes, all assisted in the work.

Finally, thanks are due to the designer, Mr Vane Lindesay, who worked to a demanding and difficult schedule in order to complete the design work.

The Plates

Brian Finemore, whose death inspired the production of this book, and to whom it is dedicated, will always remain in the memory of his friends a man of quicksilver wit and fierce and sometimes bitter honesty, a man with a capacity for deep despair, affectionate loyalties, labile twists of mood, and whose intellectual stance towards the art to which he dedicated his life was one of utter integrity and incorruptibility.

He was a sharp, mocking enemy, and perhaps seldom an easy friend. He worked under many bureaucratic constraints—as he saw them—and at a modest salary to establish new insights and new standards in Australian art criticism. He brought new meaning and a new respect to the word "curatorship", though he was fortunate to have some distinguished predecessors and colleagues in collateral fields.

Finemore was born on 8 October 1925 at South Yarra, which was about as far from the centre of Melbourne as he ever cared to wander: he was very much a city man, and Gordon Thomson once called him "the last of the boulevardiers". When forced to leave his flat near Spring Street a few years before his death, and to make a new home in East Melbourne, the flat in fact in which he was murdered on 23 October 1975, he was heard to remark "Imagine a man of my age and position being forced to live in the suburbs", and his derision for the pretentious and parochial found expression in his *mot*, "Camberwell is not so much a suburb as a state of mind". "Beneath these sallies", as a colleague has written, there was "some distant apprehension that the encircling gloom of mediocrity and banality, of intellectual death, lurked constantly at hand, and that a conscious act of will was needed to keep it at bay". Yet balancing this was his deep enjoyment and affection for the countryside (or, as he liked to say, the "landscape"), evident in his work on the Australian impressionists and in his love of the peace and beauty of a place such as Mount Macedon.

Brian attended Saint Patrick's College in East Melbourne and enrolled in the Fine Arts course at the University of Melbourne in 1948, the year that course was inaugurated. It was an initially stormy passage—"I hated Robert the Bruce for being conned by that spider"—and Joseph Burke, his professor, ascribes Brian's failure in first year to his wide-ranging interests in literature, music, the theatre and ballet, and to his gift for making friends. Eventually he graduated with distinction, and in 1959 joined the staff of the National Gallery of Victoria, to the service of which he devoted the rest of his life, and which will always bear the impress of his mind. He was responsible, for a start, for collecting one-third of the entire Australian collection.

Brian's insights, his capacities for gathering and interpreting data, and for organizing it into a form persuasive to his trustees and eventually of benefit to the people of his country, are amply apparent in this book. Indeed it is the point of this book, for while Brian the man was important to his friends, and while his personality of course throws light on his professional approach, his lasting public importance rests on the evidence presented in his own words.

Shortly after his appointment Brian Finemore was necessarily deeply involved, together with his colleagues and the architects, in the creation of the new National Gallery of Victoria. His special interest in the art of the nineteenth century, and the interactions of English, French, American and Australian art in that period, was balanced by his commitment to the art of his own time and his sympathy for those involved in the mastering of new visions. It was extremely fortunate that the first curator of Australian art in Australia should have had these qualities, and they were reflected in Finemore's spirited collecting, his avoidance of the parochial outlook—an outlook which had seriously affected what collecting of Australian art had been done in the past—and his concern to build up a balanced collection so far as limited funds would allow.

In the opinion of those best able to judge, however, there seems to be a large measure of agreement that Brian's major contribution was of a more evanescent nature. As Joseph Burke has written, "He put his main scholarly and creative energies into exhibitions, to the challenge of which he had a love-hate relationship". During his short career with the National Gallery he organized the considerable total of twenty exhibitions, including four major synoptic showings: Australian Landscape Painting (1964), The Field (1968), Heroic Landscape (1970) and Object and Idea (1973). The second and fourth of these have been called by Finemore's colleagues "the most important exhibitions of contemporary art to date . . . not surveys but definitive statements, bold and controversial".

It would be a pity, Ursula Hoff has remarked, to make Brian Finemore into a cult figure: "he had great and real faults and, professionally, never did himself justice, but he was unforgettable". It is likely that Finemore's full potential, perhaps as a great gallery director, was never realised; one of those best qualified to judge has referred to "cruel pressures towards senseless conformity". Outside these, Brian could be, another colleague has written, "irritating, unpunctual, vague and chaotically disorganized". Enormously patient with those in whom he discerned an interest and capacity to learn, he would not suffer fools gladly. "Dear Madam, No" was his most famous letter; on another legendary occasion, being badgered for an opinion over the phone, he told his caller to "hold it closer to the instrument so I can see the signature". He was beloved of the attendants, would happily scream "Hullo Dolly!" to a friend at the far end of a solemn hall filled with startled gallery-goers, frequently advised that the answer to the Gallery's problems was to burn it down and was happy to advertise his sexual nonconformity. He was *not* a corporation man.

Yet those like I who knew him loved him not only for his style and wit and for that voice of two generations ago—"the old-fashioned educated Australian speech of Robert Menzies and my grandfather", Jennifer Phipps described it—

but will also remember the pain and the strain that lay behind the gaiety and perhaps sustained it. And we will want remembered that, although under criticism for not producing a catalogue of the entire Australian collection, he worked steadily on it although it was beyond the capacity of an overworked department of three persons; we will want remembered that he frequently paid his own way to Sydney so that he should not become a curator of Melbourne art; that he paid out hundreds of dollars of his own money to exhibiting artists rather than break faith with them; that, perhaps rarest of all, he had little or no sense of professional jealousy and shared his ideas with all; that underneath the cultivated *snobbisme* and elegant ennui lay a mind of startling speed and depth of perception.

Brian Finemore was, in the fullest sense of the phrase, a public servant. "Here am I. Where are you?" he once wrote on a postcard to a friend from Assisi, paraphrasing the Auden he loved to quote. It was a good question, and may serve as his epitaph.

STEPHEN MURRAY-SMITH

In compiling this brief memoir I have relied heavily on letters from a number of Brian Finemore's friends and associates, sometimes using without acknowledgement their actual words. These letters will be lodged in the archives of the National Gallery of Victoria. I wish to acknowledge with deep gratitude this help from Alex Crawford, Ursula Hoff, Jennifer Phipps, Elizabeth Summons, Lina Bryans, Graeme Sturgeon, Ruth McNicoll, George Fairfax and Frances McCarthy.

During the fifteen years that he was in the Department of Australian Art, the late Brian Finemore shaped the Gallery's Australian collection into one of the finest and most comprehensive in the country. From the thoughts and ideas which supported the paintings, this book has emerged: published and unpublished articles and notes, Trustees' reports, lectures and talks. These diverse sources have been compiled and edited by Jennifer Phipps, Geoffrey Burke and Frances McCarthy to form an introductory history of Australian art based on the National Gallery's collection. Some of the entries were first written by the editors during the period when they worked under Mr Finemore and reflect the discussions they had with him at the time. Additional factual information has been added in footnotes.

Freedom from Prejudice, in addition to presenting a history of the art of this country, deals with the nature of collecting for a public gallery. It offers, therefore, an intimate approach to the study of Australian art dealing with the material itself and the role of the institution involved in evaluating, collecting and displaying it. The book is not a critical catalogue. It gives a personal insight into the cultural development of Australia as reflected upon by a man deeply concerned to see this development as clearly and impartially as was humanly possible.

The National Gallery of Victoria is deeply grateful to many individuals and institutions for their help in preparing this book. Dr Stephen Murray-Smith gave most generously of his time to act as consulting editor for the publication. Miss Jennifer Phipps, whilst extremely busy as Associate Curator of Australian Art, devoted many weeks to the selection and organization of the text. We also wish to thank Mr Daniel Thomas for reading the manuscript, the staff of the La Trobe Library and art room at the State Library for their assistance in the documentation of the text, and Ms Christine Simons who helped with measuring the works of art.

Finally, although it is a wholly inadequate tribute, the Gallery through the publication of this book, hopes to acknowledge to some degree its gratitude to Brian Finemore who gave almost a third of his life to the National Gallery of Victoria and thereby enriched not only this institution but the perceptions of everyone interested in the art of this country.

Eric B. Rowlison
Director, National Gallery of Victoria

EXPLANATION OF CODE

All measurements in centimetres in order of height, width, depth.
Recto—front.
Verso—back.
u.l.—upper left.   u.r.—upper right.   c—centre.
l.l.—lower left.   l.r.—lower right.   ex.—exhibited

A.B.	*Art Bulletin of the National Gallery of Victoria*
A.L.P.	*Australian Landscape Painting* 1964. Catalogue of Exhibition by Brian Finemore
A.P.	*Australian Painting* by Brian Finemore, Longmans, 1961, Melbourne
A.R.A.	Associate of the Royal Academy, London
B.F.	Brian Finemore
C.C.	*Country Crafts*
C.M.G.	Commander of St Michael and St George
G.B.	Geoff Burke, Assistant, Australian Art, National Gallery of Victoria
F. Mc.	Frances McCarthy, Assistant Curator of Australian Art, Art Gallery of New South Wales
J.P.	Jennifer Phipps, Associate Curator of Australian Art, National Gallery of Victoria
N.G.S.B.	*The National Gallery Society of Victoria Bulletin*
O.B.E.	Order of the British Empire
P.R.I.	President of the Royal Institute of Painters in Watercolours, London
R.A.	Member of the Royal Academy, London
R.I.	Member of the Royal Institute of Painters in Watercolours, London.

Articles without code were written by the late Brian Finemore, Curator of Australian Art, National Gallery of Victoria, 1962 to 1975.

Among the prejudices which prevail strongly at the present time is the belief that reason and the arts are incompatible companions; such statements as "there is no disputing about tastes" or "I don't know anything about art but I know what I like" show that those who say these things refuse to consider the case for art rationally. People seem to fear that knowledge might hurt the imagination and that the exercise of the artistic faculties both in the artist and in the spectator might be weakened by the use of reason. This fear of reason and knowledge is a very recent phenomenon as the Slade Professor at Oxford, Dr Wind, pointed out in his recent series of Reith Lectures. The great painters of the past were often able to absorb a great deal of philosophy and knowledge without weakening their aesthetic imagination. Michelangelo's ceiling of the Sistine Chapel, for example, illustrates a complicated programme but it is also one of the most original and imaginatively creative works in the history of painting. Michelangelo did not feel hampered by a scholarly theme, which, concerned with the salvation of the human soul, used biblical narrative for symbolic purposes. The literary content assured Michelangelo the understanding of a large number of spectators, to whom old truths appeared as a fresh revelation through the new and daring forms which Michelangelo created.

The modern lack of belief in the possibility of a rational approach to art has had an influence of long standing on the writing of art in this country. When in 1916 the first number of the journal *Art in Australia* was published, the editorial stated that it aimed to publicise the work of Australian painters by means of good reproductions. The magazine also contained articles but no programme was drawn up to say what these should be; most of the early articles contained no more than some biographical information and some appreciative comments. The scope of the journal and its illustrations improved over the years; the nature of the written contributions however did not differ essentially from the earlier ones; they became perhaps even more subjective and emotional.

The result of this attitude is that the journal *Art in Australia,* which continued to be published for over twenty years and should be a veritable mine of ideas and information on Australian art, is not as useful as it might be. When disputes arise on the art front today, it is little use turning over the page of most of the publications of the past: they yield no information. "What did Tom Roberts know of French Impressionism?" "Was he an Impressionist like the French painters of that name?" "Did Australian Impressionism arise at Heidelberg or at Box Hill?" We should be able to answer such questions. Again: "Which were the leading modern groups in Australian art before the war?" "What is the correct critical assessment of expressionism in Australian art?" "Was it decadent fourth-rate hillbilly expressionism as some have claimed, or has it had qualities of lasting value?" Material for discussion of these latter questions is to be found in the journal *Angry Penguins* which for a few years devoted itself to criticism and ideas, even if those of a small faction of artists only. But *Angry Penguins* also fostered an irrational approach to art, which was eventually exposed by the famous hoax of Ern Malley. The achievements of the Fine Arts Chair at Melbourne University, and the fine scholarly books on Australian art subjects by Dr Bernard Smith, are based on a rational and historical approach; but these have engendered little public zest for knowledge and ideas in relation to the arts.

The prejudice against a connection between reason and the arts has left in its wake a great misunderstanding between the artist and the spectator. Since the late nineteenth century artists everywhere have rejected literary subjects and have insisted on absolute originality and independence. Their art which was to exist only as art for art's sake, has in recent years also lost its subject. Artists are inclined more and more to draw on the unconscious and to concentrate on art as a freely creative activity. Abstract personal images and half conscious thoughts are reflected in modern painting. The spectator may feel that the colours are beautiful or disturbing, that the shapes are harmonious or discordant, but his mind is not stirred very deeply.

This subjective and withdrawn nature of much of modern art has led to a gulf between artist and patron; it has contributed much to the isolation of the artist. When Pope Julius II commissioned the Sistine Ceiling from Michelangelo, he engaged in argument with the painter; Michelangelo obtained permission to change the first simple plan to the complex programme which we now see there; nowadays such understanding relations between artist and patrons are a rarity. Mural commissions are given, but the results rarely make one feel that the artist and those who commissioned him have understood each other. What is needed, it seems, is a common ground on which artists and patrons can meet, a ground which permits an articulate interchange of ideas. But prejudice against content in art, and prejudice in favour of the irrational make such meeting very difficult.

This prejudice against knowledge also affects the services to art supplied by Australian galleries. In England, on the European continent and in America, galleries aim at being learned institutions as well as places of display. A striking example of this was the great Poussin exhibition at the Louvre in Paris in 1960, to which the Melbourne Gallery lent its fine picture, **The Crossing of the Red Sea.** This exhibition was put off for a whole year because the scholarly preparations, which eventually appeared in a superbly informative catalogue, had not been finished in time. The Melbourne painter Arthur Boyd recently held a retrospective show at the Whitechapel Art Gallery in London, for this the greatest care was taken in the selection so that every phase of his life was represented by the best possible example. The beautifully produced catalogue will remain an indispensable reference book for anyone who will want to know this Australian artist.

Something of this kind has only very occasionally been done in Australia.

Many of the shows assembled at the Adelaide Festival, for example, had no catalogue. The reason for this is not far to seek—there is usually no one available to do it.

Australian galleries have only very recently graduated to having professional officers. Until 1927 the Melbourne gallery was run by a Director and attendants; the only other professional officer was the drawing master. Nowadays enlightened government has resulted in nine full time curatorial officers in Melbourne, by far the largest number in any Australian gallery, but well below that of even the smaller American galleries. The number of officers has increased in recent years in other State galleries as well, but is still too small everywhere to allow Australian galleries to play the role in the community which is played by their sister institutions elsewhere.

The role which art galleries are encouraged to play in Australian life differs greatly from that of other countries. On the European continent, for example, art galleries are often generously state-endowed because their "draw" as tourist attractions makes them a vital factor in the nation's economy. In America, art galleries are privately financed and placed highly as symbols of community spirit. In each case galleries flourish as learned institutions.

In Australia, art galleries have only very limited support from state and public. People who admire the great collections overseas sometimes do not even know that there is something of this kind in their midst back home. As the galleries' educational work with children increases such awareness should spread. But how is the education service to function if there is no systematically prepared information on the works in the collections? How is the lecturer to know about this piece of eighteenth century glass, that fifteenth century statue, this group of nineteenth century paintings, that example of the latest modern work? Information does not come to the lecturer by sudden inspiration. The assumption is often made that art is merely a matter of appreciation and that anyone can appreciate once he is put into the right frame of mind.

Enthusiasm is regarded as important, knowledge is not. This we have seen in an attitude fostered by many twentieth century artists themselves. Such merely emotional reactions tend to create misunderstandings. Those who wish for reasoned understanding of the arts have to have some reference material. And the preparation of such references is, in overseas gallery practice, the job of curatorial officers. American galleries in particular place their pride in providing a great variety of brochures and guides for their visiting public; English galleries, such as the Victoria and Albert Museum, turn out the most delightfully produced small-scale publications so that the interested visitor can take away something to read about objects in the collection that have appealed to him. Only in Melbourne have the Trustees generously engaged in such publishing. Public

3

prejudice against the written word in connection with art still stands in the way of success of such a venture.

I have discussed a number of instances in which the prejudice against knowledge and learning has in my opinion become a serious hindrance to a free interchange of views between the artist, art galleries and the spectator. How can we rid ourselves of prejudice which threatens the free use of the imagination and art? How can we reach a common ground on which artists and spectators can meet and co-operate?

In my opinion a good step in this direction could be taken by the institutions that teach art. Art schools at present teach a varying range of techniques and crafts; they instil formal ideals, aesthetic response in their pupils, but the artist of the future should be worthy of the kind of education which was often enjoyed by his great forerunners in the past. To quote the example of Michelangelo once more. This artist in his youth was a pupil at the academy founded by the great Florentine prince Lorenzo di Medici; here Michelangelo studied not only art but came in touch with the leading philosophers and writers of his day. Why should the young twentieth century artist not be brought into touch with the leading scientific, literary and sociological ideas of our day? Would this not provide the common ground on which he could meet with some of his spectators?

Secondly, I think that those who are engaged in the publicising of art should introduce their hearers not only to praise of the present but to a true understanding of the art of the past. It is false and dangerous to claim that what the previous generation did is *ipso facto* out of date and useless, like last year's hat. One thing that a study of the history of art can teach us is that no art movement of any importance has ever arisen merely from the artists' subconscious. It is just the struggle between the demands of a new period and the traditions established by past generations, the re-interpretation of old means to suit new ends, that was at the core of the artistic development of such artists as Michelangelo and Picasso. Michelangelo not only absorbed and mastered the art of his immediate forerunners but went back beyond them, to his spiritual grandfather Masaccio and to classical antiquity, in the endeavour to bring his own original ideas to the perfection which still overwhelms us. Picasso was a complete master of the academic manner of the artists among whom he grew up before he ventured on his daring innovations; at no time however did he lose touch with tradition— indeed the transformation of tradition is one of the main subjects of his art. Knowledge and learning are the tools of our mental freedom; do not let prejudice prevail against them.

Brian Finemore
(October, 1962)

Early Art in Australia

In the earliest productions of that period of Australian art which is known as the colonial we may explore those most subtle and delicate relations between experience and imagination, between reality and ideality, between this ancient antipodean land and its discoverers and settlers. This period is generally dated from about the time of Captain Cook's first voyage to observe at Tahiti the solar transit of Venus in 1769. Its conclusion is about 1880, though many of its distinctive features had waned by the 1860s. European pictorial art first came to the Pacific as the handmaiden of science. The resolution of the conflict between the desire to record for the emergent classificatory sciences and the accepted traditions of artistic representation is one of the fascinations of this art. And the period is permeated by the nineteenth century artist's romantic desire to illumine a personal response to this strange new land and its novel features.

There is no such thing as one reality in art. As André Malraux has written "All art is stylized, that is to say humanized. As man would have made it had he been God". The exploratory voyages in the Pacific of the French, Russians, British and Americans from the late eighteenth century until the middle of the nineteenth century have left a wealth of absorbingly interesting drawings and paintings. In many, the historic and ideological content is of prime importance and these works may be studied in our fine historical libraries, notably the La Trobe in Melbourne and the Mitchell in Sydney; while for those intrepid travellers who still go on voyages of exploration, the National Library at Canberra is becoming a great treasury. In other works the balance between historical record and artistic quality is either equal, or is tipped in favour of the artistic. These works one must seek out in the various State art galleries.

It is difficult for us to recapture imaginatively the immense curiosity and hunger for information aroused in European cultivated and scientific society by the discoveries in the Pacific.

It is to this enthusiasm that we owe our records of the "nondescript" productions of New Holland, that is, of objects previously not described by the then dominant classificatory sciences of botany, zoology, geology, meteorology and geography. We owe these earliest records to a curious assortment of professional artists assigned to voyages, and also to governors, surveyors, military officers, anonymous convicts and others. But we owe the desire to record to the tradition of the Royal Society established in 1645 when "Divers worthy persons, inquisitive into natural philosophy, and other parts of human learning did, by agreements meet weekly in London on a certain day, to treat and discourse of such affairs". We owe also a great debt to the naval tradition of keeping diaries and records. Even in 1588 English explorers were officially instructed to keep diaries and records of anything of interest they observed.

A great many persons of artistic talent between 1750 and 1850 were engaged in scientific recording, on voyages and journeys of exploration as topographical and botanical artists. The name Joseph Banks suffices to explain the ideology underlying this practice. The collection of evidence was essential for the sciences of classification, but as the scientist and the artist were both interested in the structure, vegetation, life and atmosphere of this planet, they gradually incorporated portraits of rocks, of native peoples, of flora and fauna into topographical landscape paintings combining these subjects. Ecological relationships were essential for the proper understanding of any one specific field of study, while the classical tradition of the Royal Academy inspired the artists to create paintings as one harmonious whole. The portrayal of objects and peoples in their native habitat led to the creation of a particular type of landscape painting which is why I entitle this essay "Figures in a landscape".

The conflicting ideals of art and science often led to strange results. For example, one sees Australian Aboriginals portrayed as Graeco-Roman figures in the poses of Neoclassical painting—witness the engraving, **Two of the natives of New Holland advancing to combat,** in Sydney Parkinson's published journal of 1784. But in fairness to the artist endeavouring to reconcile art and science on the spot, many of the engravers of their published volumes added academic embellishments to make the simpler drawings acceptable to English taste.

It would be idle to pretend that the Melbourne Gallery has an important collection of these earliest works, but it has some. The tradition continues well into the settlement of Victoria. The natural impetus created by the novelty of the countryside was reinforced by the prevailing tide of European art with its absorption in landscape painting. The tradition then begun continues in various forms to this very day. Of Australia's period of settlement and booming growth the Melbourne Gallery has some splendid pictures. Among these is a fine group of works by Conrad Martens (1801–78), who arrived in Sydney in 1835 via Valparaiso, where he left H.M.S. *Beagle,* upon which he was topographical artist. **Looking East over Circular Quay (1)** is a water-colour of about 1838. In the foreground, high on the area known as The Rocks, a European couple look down the wide sunfilled harbour dotted with sailing vessels. On the shore line are some substantial warehouses, storing the imports and exports of the colony, but basically this is an idealized Turnerian landscape, a study of sun, sea and hazy atmosphere. In **Natives at Rose Bay (2)** we see two Aboriginals spearing fish in the shallows as the sun sets; the foreground blue and cool, the horizon a blaze of crimson and gold against which the figures of the already dwindling and dispossessed natives of this country are romantically silhouetted. This is a picture of beauty and poignancy. Martens earned most of his living, however, by portraying the estates and mansions of the landed rich in the eighteenth century English tradition of paintings of the country seats of the nobility and gentry.

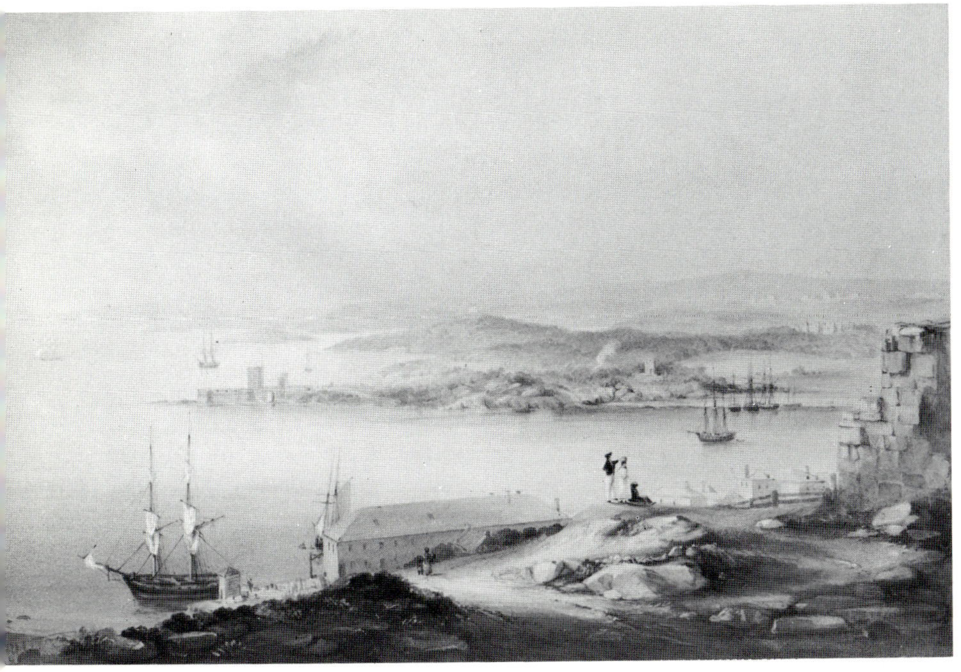

1
Conrad Martens
b. England, 1801–78
**Looking East over
Circular Quay From
Miller's Point**
Watercolour
44 × 65.8 cm
Felton Bequest 1950
2236.4

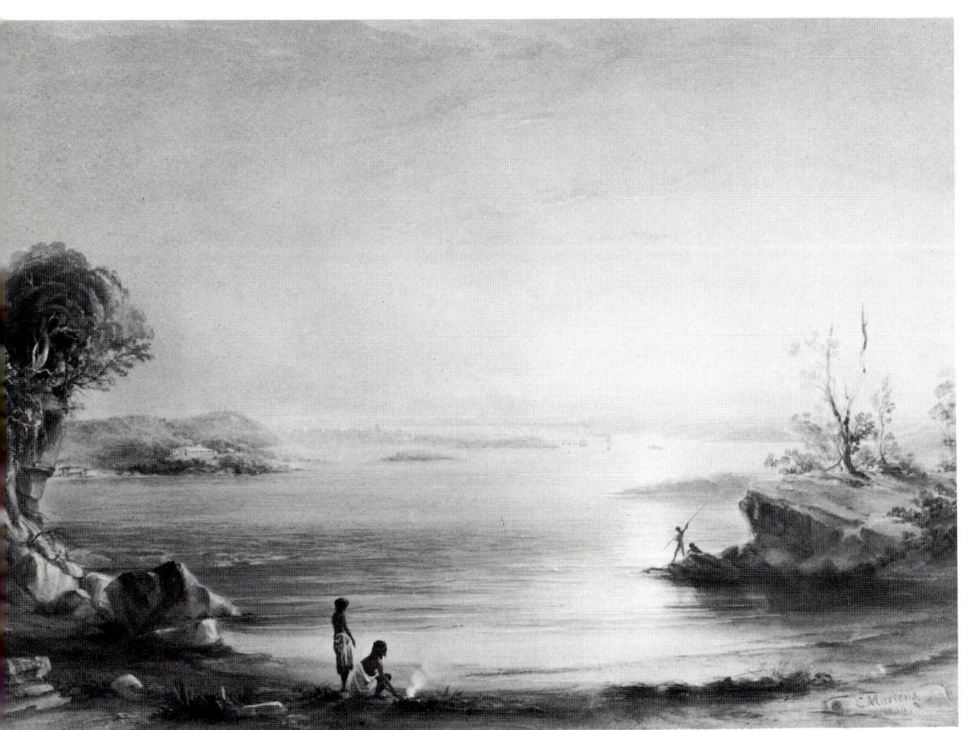

2
Conrad Martens
b. England, 1801–78
**View of Sydney
From Rose Bay
(With Native
Figures)** 1836
Watercolour
46.2 × 66.6 cm
Inscriptions. Recto: l.r.
"C. Martens 1836"
Felton Bequest 1950
2230.4

Contrasting with Martens's works is a painting of 1837, **The River Nile Van Diemen's Land (Plate I)** by John Glover (1767–1849). Glover arrived in Hobart Town in 1831, already a mature and prosperous English artist. He took up a grant of land and lived as a patriarchal squire while continuing to paint landscapes both of Tasmania and of England. It is interesting that most of his English views were required by the nostalgic settlers, while his paintings of Van Diemen's Land found their way to Europe. **The River Nile** is a very beautiful picture in verdant greens and palest blues, lying half way between topography and the picturesque. In the translucent waters of the foreground stream the Aboriginals bathe in the poses of noble savages, while others hunt upon the shores, and the foreground is abloom with flowers. The concept is idyllic, and the composition derives from the ordered classical landscape of Claude Lorraine. This is, indeed, both a traveller's tale and figures in a landscape.

Another picture of superb quality but of more grim and moving content is Robert Dowling's **Tasmanian Aborigines (3).** Dowling arrived in Tasmania in 1830 at the age of three, and his life there coloured his best work. After George Augustus Robinson had "conciliated" the few remaining Tasmanian Aboriginals, they were placed on Flinders Island where most gradually pined away and died. The annihilation of a human species, the Tasmanian Aboriginal, is for ever to the shame of European settlement of the Pacific. This happening made a lasting impression upon Robert Dowling, and his two major pictures are upon the theme of the last survivors of that unhappy race. Against a romanticized but still recognizably local landscape, beneath a large overshadowing tree trunk, are grouped the last survivors, as in the frieze of a sarcophagus. Classicized and formalized though they be, each figure is an individual portrait of a race lost for ever. Upon the reverse of the canvas in Dowling's hand are inscribed their names. Among them is Trugernana, then a young woman, the last survivor of her race who died in 1876. The dark subdued tones of this painting combined with its stately composition make it one of the most impressive colonial paintings.

Not even the briefest talk on Australian colonial art would be complete without reference to the last and most popular of those artists—he whose figures in a landscape were those of the migrant diggers of the 1850s goldrushes. S. T. Gill arrived in Adelaide in 1839 aged twenty-one. He joined Horrock's expedition, thus continuing the tradition of topographer/explorer artists. But it is his portrayal of the life of the gold fields, of the diggers and the city of Melbourne in its period of explosive growth, which enshrine his fame **(6).** The Melbourne Gallery and above all the La Trobe Library show fine examples of his work. In remarkably sensitively observed landscapes he portrayed the diggers and their life of toil. In others he shows the rumbustious life of those who struck it rich, as in **Diggers' Wedding, Melbourne,** where the bride and groom drive in a carriage through the streets riotously drinking champagne.

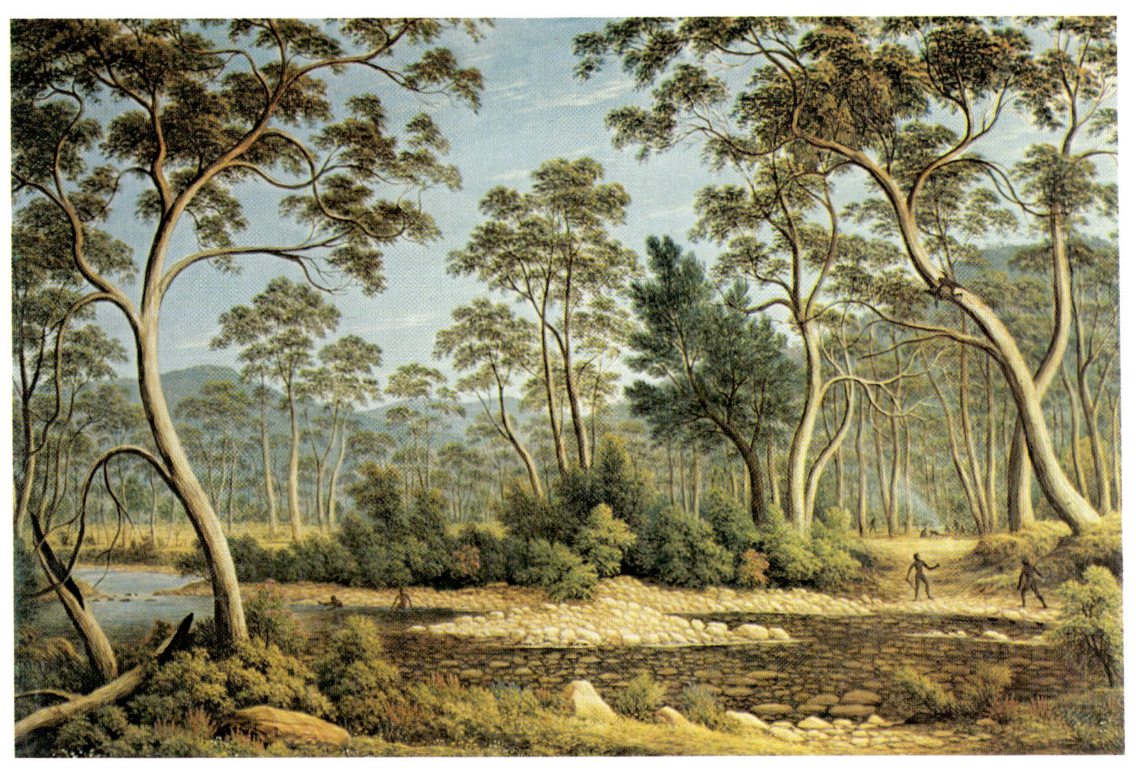

Plate **I**
John Glover
b. England, 1767–1849
The River Nile, Van Dieman's Land 1837
Oil on canvas
76.2 × 114.3 cm
Inscriptions. Verso: on label of P. & D. Colnaghi & Co. Ltd. in writing: "Inscribed, signed and dated 1837 on back of canvas before relining." "The River Nile, Van Dieman's Land From Mr Glover's Farm"
Felton Bequest 1956
3359.4

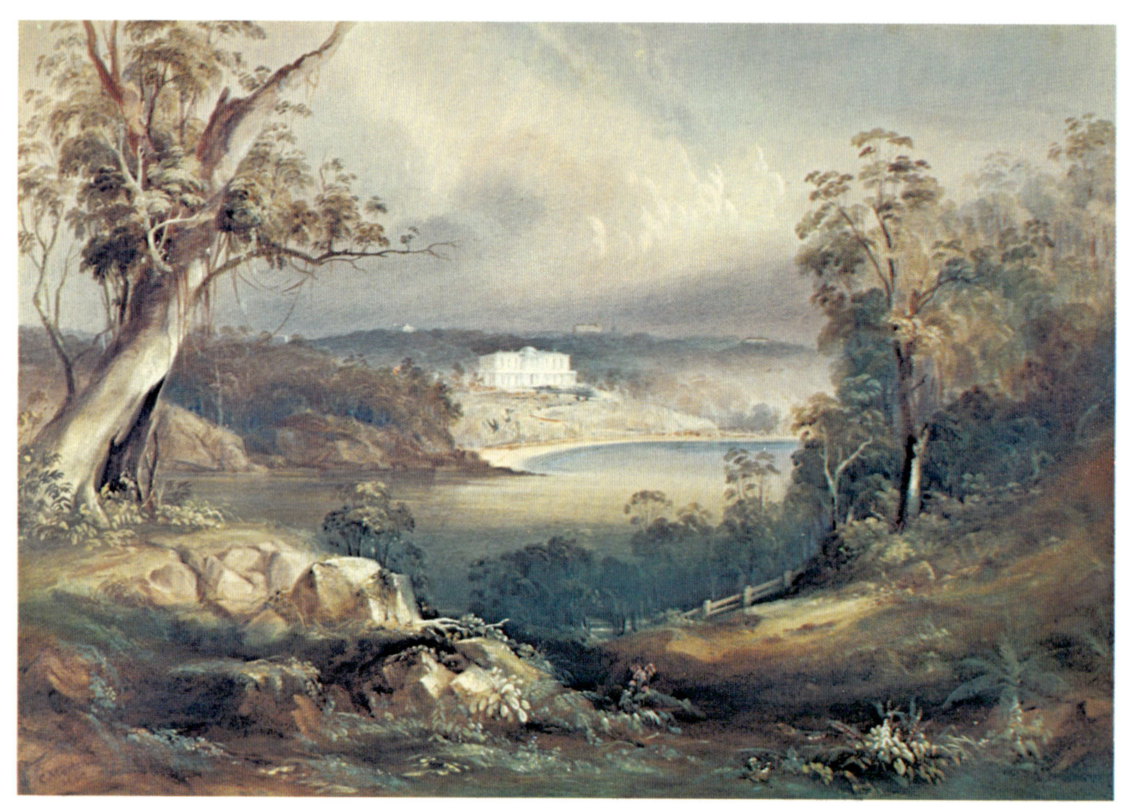

Plate **II**
Conrad Martens
b. England, 1801–78
Elizabeth Bay and Elizabeth Bay House 1839
Watercolour
46 × 66 cm
Inscriptions. Recto: l.l. "C. Martens 1839"
Felton Bequest 1950
2231.4

Plate **III**
Thomas Clark
b. England, 1814–83
The Coast near St Kilda 1853
Oil on canvas
48.2 × 94 cm
Inscriptions. Recto: l.l. "Thos Clark 1853"
Purchased 1969
95.6

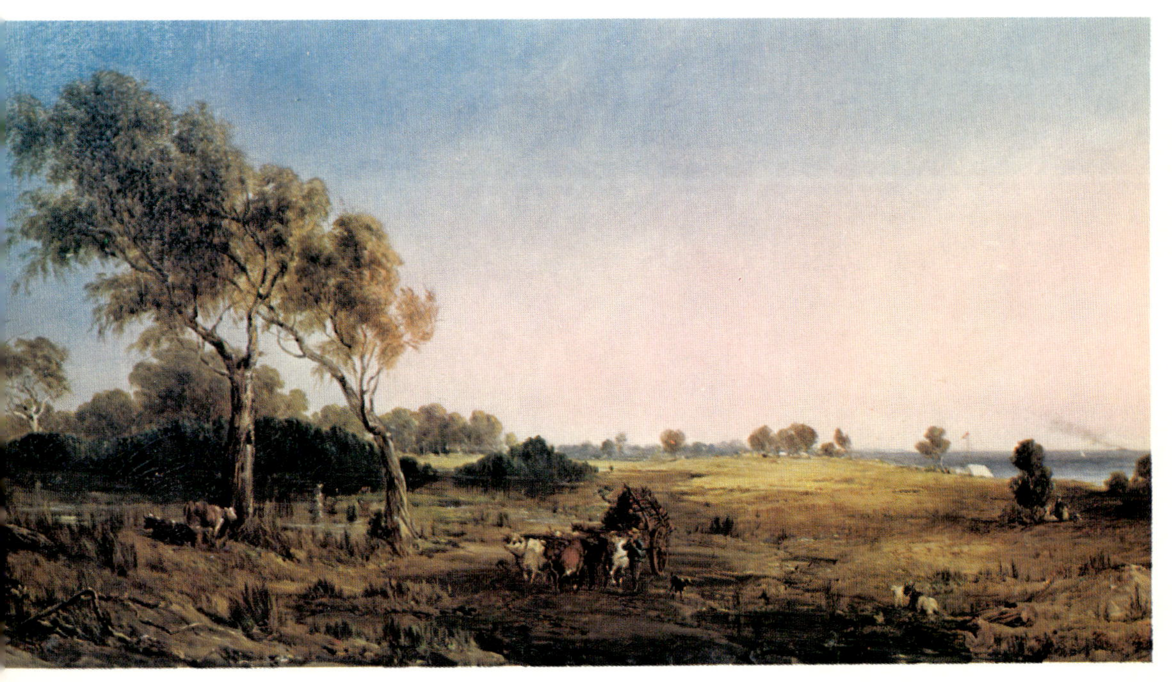

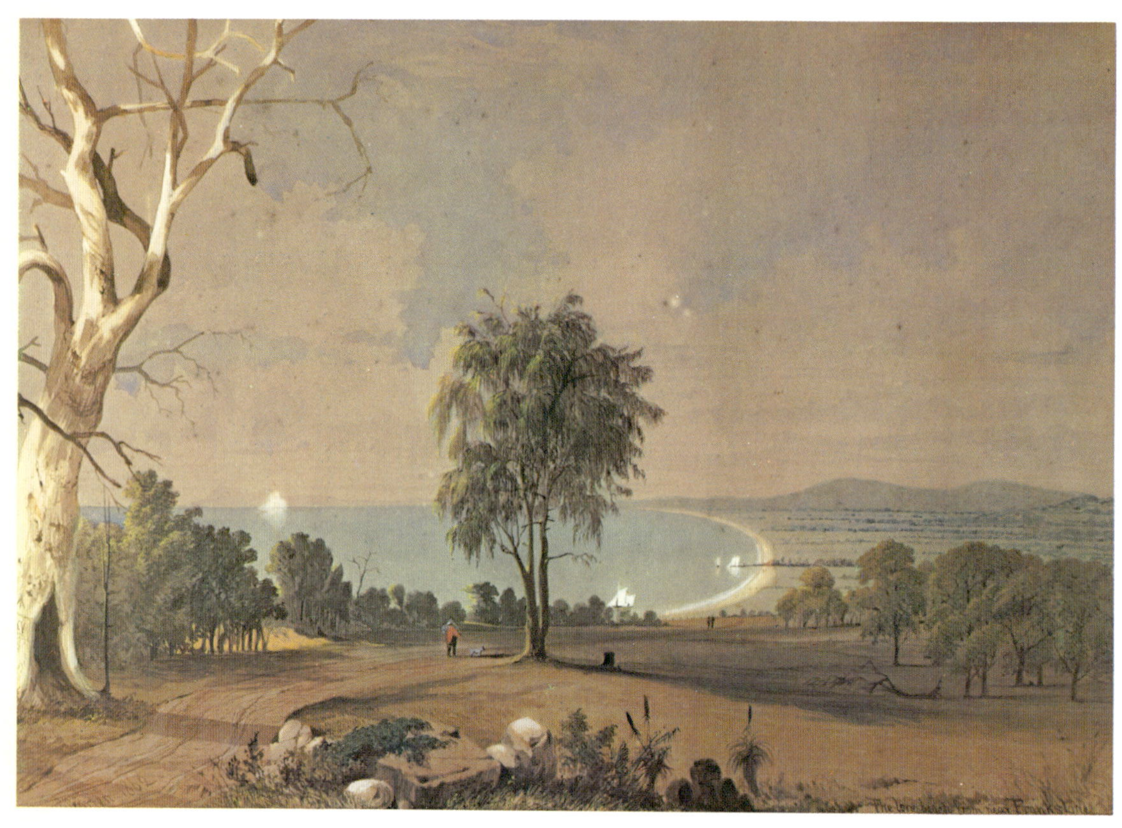

Plate **IV**
George O'Brien
b. Ireland 1821–88
The Long Beach from near Frankstone 1862
Watercolour
28.4 × 40.5 cm
Inscriptions. Recto: l.l. " 'G. O'Brien 1862'. Surveyors mark on tree 'CXXV' "
l.r. "The Long Beach near Frankstone"
Purchased 1974
A1/1974

3
Robert Dowling
b. England, 1827–86
Tasmanian Aborigines
Oil on canvas
66 × 121 cm
Inscriptions. Verso: names of Aborigines. Inscribed in the artist's hand (standing, right to left):
"Jimmy, Hampshire Hills. V.D.L.; Jack, Cape Grim V.D.L.; Timmy, East Coast, V.D.L."
(Seated, right to left): "Manalargenna, Chief, East Coast; Jinny, Port Sorell; Woureddy, Bruni
Island, V.D.L.; Trugernana, Recherche Bay, V.D.L.; Jinny, West Coast, V.D.L." (Figure with
back turned not named.)
Purchased from Mr J. B. Dowling, descendant of the artist, 1949.
2102.4

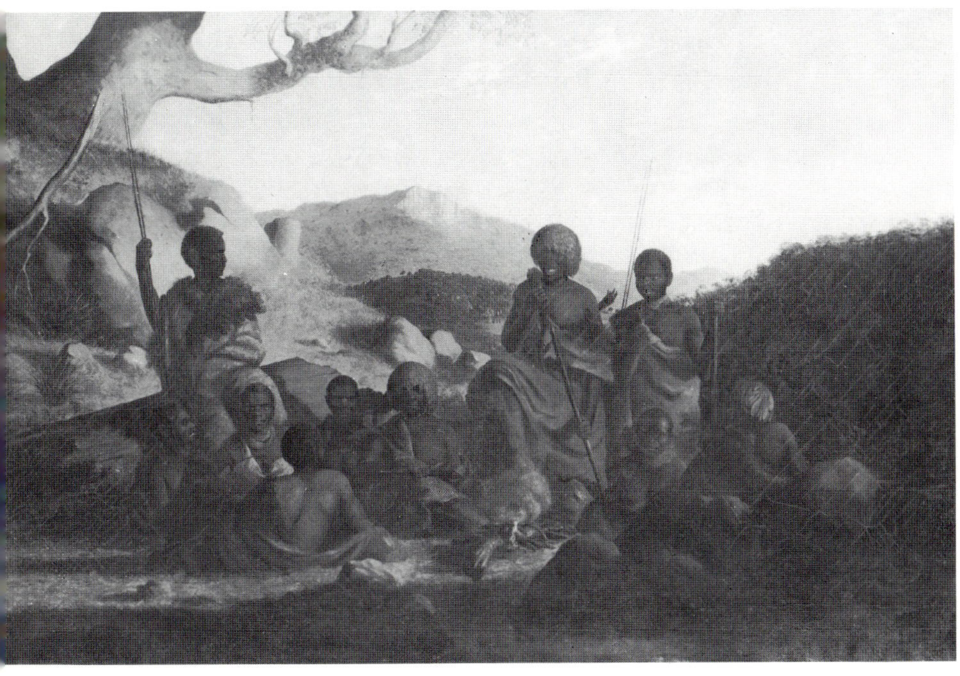

Innumerable artists, amateur and professional, have left a massive record of
our beginnings. All interested in their study are indebted to the work of Dr Bernard
Smith, notably his books *European Vision and the South Pacific*, and *Australian Painting*.

In conclusion may I quote T. S. Eliot

> We shall not cease from exploration
> And the end of all our exploring
> Will be to arrive where we started
> And know the place for the first time.

May his words be prophetic of the future of Australian Art.

(c. 1964)

Plate II
Conrad Martens, b. England, 1801–78
Elizabeth Bay and Elizabeth Bay House, Sydney. 1839

We are all fascinated by glimpses of our colonial past—even the most amateur sketch of early Sydney or Melbourne has an appeal to the historically-minded. But the views of Sydney by Conrad Martens are works of considerable aesthetic merit. Doubtless he is the first artist of quality in our history. The story of his journey to Australia is typical of the early nineteenth century Pacific world. Born in London, the son of a German merchant, he studied under the renowned English water-colourist Copley Fielding (1787–1855). In 1832 he went to Rio de Janeiro and then to Montevideo, at which port he succeeded Augustus Earle as artist on H.M.S. *Beagle* on its surveying voyage. Two years later he left the vessel and came to Sydney via New Zealand, arriving in 1835. There he died in 1878 after a career involving much vicissitude, leaving behind a now much-prized record of the early colonial scene.

Sydney in 1839 was a small town. At various distances from the township were numerous large estates which, with their owners, retainers and servants, were almost complete worlds in themselves. With these country seats New South Wales repeated the English eighteenth century scene. Artistically these pictures also reflect the art of eighteenth century England; the topographical painting of an estate has its origin there. The conventions of its picturesque presentation belong to Martens's English training, but it is untrue to say that he saw Australia through English eyes. Rather did he portray the world he lived in within the conventions of English watercolour art. All representation is a convention: Conrad Martens used the conventions of his training with great artistry.

C.C.
(February, 1960)

Plate III
Thomas Clark, b. England, 1814–83
The Coast near St Kilda. 1853

Thomas Clark came to Melbourne with his family in 1852. He had been director of the Nottingham School of Arts; headmaster of the government School of Design, Birmingham, (Edward Burne-Jones was a pupil), and drawing master at the King Edward's School of Design, Birmingham.

Within the year of his arrival Clark painted **The Coast Near St Kilda.** It is a delightful picture in which landscape and genre are harmoniously wedded. Presumably the site is near St Kilda swamp, now the Albert Park Lake area.

This splendid tract of bushland, from beach to St Kilda Road, was once reserved as a public park, a pioneer foresighted vision later betrayed by greed as have been many other such visions.

The landscape is portrayed with a subtlety of tone in the summer sky, and an airiness of atmospheric effect. The man leading the bullock team lights his pipe with a natural casualness, while on the right a party picnics beside a tree, and the tent with its fluttering pennant on the distant foreshore may be a naval or military encampment.

Thomas Clark achieved success in Victoria and was briefly instructor at the Carlton School of Design. He was one of the campaigners for the creation of an art school, and in 1870 he was appointed drawing master at the newly created School of Design at the National Gallery. Von Guerard was head of the painting school. Both Roberts and McCubbin were his students in 1875 and it was Clark who encouraged Roberts to study abroad. He died in 1883 at South Yarra after a long illness, and rather shabby treatment by the Trustees and Government.

(1969)

4
Marshall Claxton, b. England, 1812–81
An Emigrant's Thoughts of Home. 1859

Claxton was a painter of historical and genre subjects. He exhibited at the Royal Academy from 1832–76. In 1843 he won a prize in the cartoon competition for the decoration of the new Westminster Hall. However, the emigration fund of the time lead him to visit Australia about 1850. It was his intuition to exhibit his own works, deal in the work of other British artists, and found a school. Historically he is a most interesting figure as he came to this country as an artist, not as an artist in search of gold or landed estate. His Australian venture failing (it was a time of economic change), he returned to England via India, Egypt and the Holy Land. This picture is a studio painting made almost immediately on his return to England.

The fact of emigration underlies the history of Britain in the nineteenth century and is the basis of Australia's existence. There is a vast verbal literature on the subject and also an extensive pictorial record. The most famous British painting is Ford Maddox Brown's **The Last of England.** The visual records of shipboard life are extensive. In America those of George Wright are typical of this specific genre of the nineteenth century. When one visits the great galleries of American painting it is pictures of this sort which humanize the collections. The Melbourne collection of Australian colonial painting is almost entirely topographical, and this painting enlivens that area.

4
Marshall Claxton
b. England, 1812–81
An Emigrant's Thoughts of Home 1859
Oil on board
60.5 × 46.8 cm
Inscriptions. Recto: 1.1. "M. Claxton 1859".
Verso: (label) "No. 1 Emigrants Thoughts of Home Marshall Claxton".
Presented by the National Gallery Women's Association 1974.
A8/1974

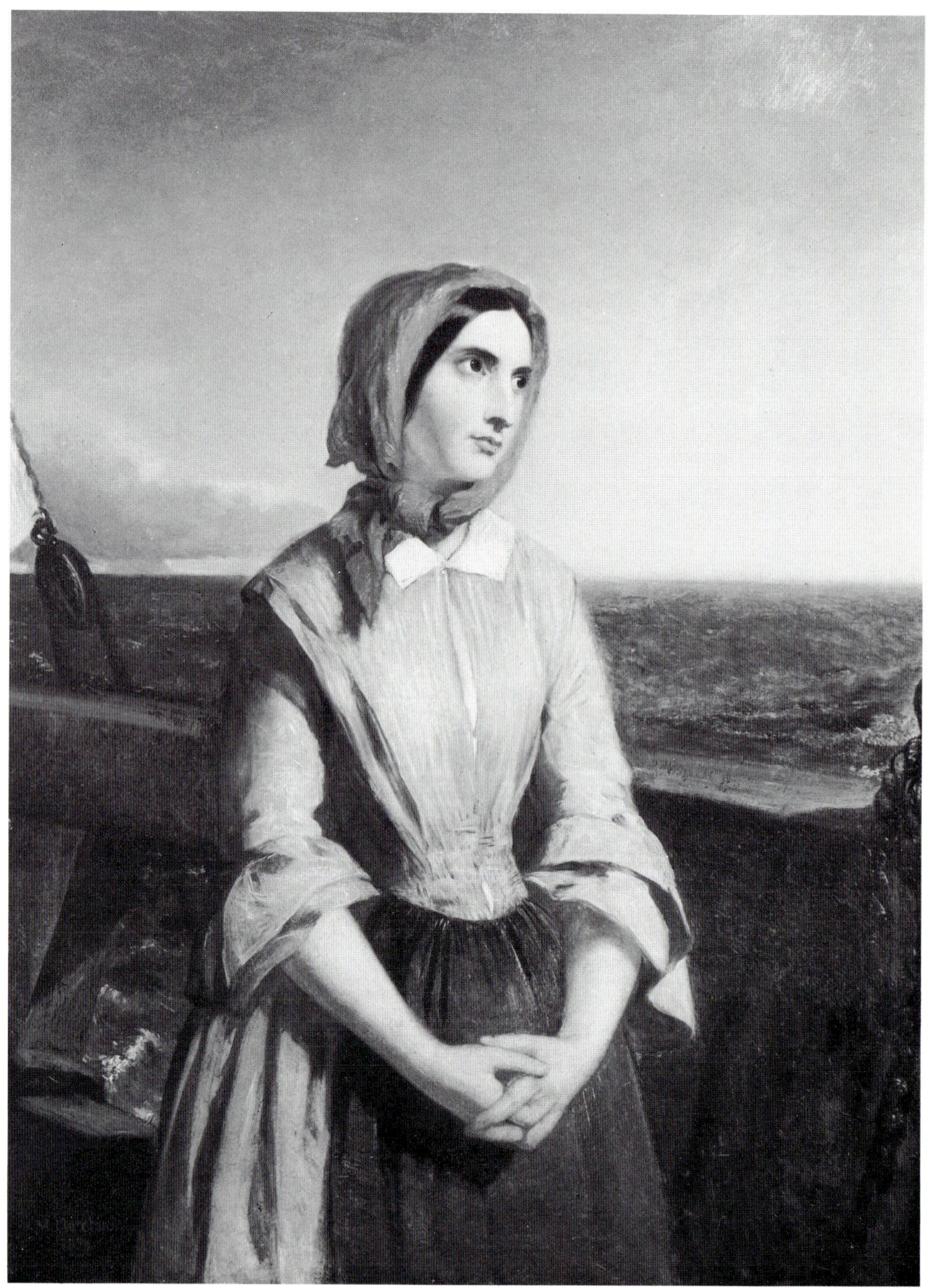

It precedes Tom Roberts's **Coming South (11)** by nearly thirty years, and makes an interesting contrast. I do not compare the technical excellence as Roberts obviously owes so much to Tissot's later painting of shipboard life.

As for the element of nostalgia underlying the settlement of Australia and America by British and Irish emigrants, I can only refer to a vast literature. In Australia, Geoffrey Serle's work has thrown much light on the subject, as do the diaries and letters in the La Trobe and Mitchell Libraries. I may quote only Henry Parkes's description of feelings "The other side of the hill is in a state of nature little different from the time when it was only trodden by native blacks; being invitingly green and thinly studded with trees, it has much the appearance of a nobleman's park in the old country . . . burst like a vision of delight on my eyes which have not seen such a sight since I left England."

(1974)

Plate IV
George O'Brien, b. Ireland, 1821–88
The Long Beach from near Frankstone. 1862

George O'Brien was born in 1821 at Dromoland Castle, County Clare. The descendant of a distinguished family, his father was Admiral Robert O'Brien and his grandfather was Sir Lucius O'Brien. Nevertheless, at eighteen he was in Melbourne, where in 1854 he was made an associate of the Victorian Institute of Architects. The La Trobe Library has drawings of this period. In the mid-sixties he went to New Zealand where he became a major topographical artist of the Dunedin School of the "Settlement Period", the equivalent of our "Colonial".

This watercolour is an elegant example of the picturesque tradition.

(1973)

5
Nicholas Chevalier, b. Russia, 1828–1902
The Buffalo Ranges. 1864

Nicholas Chevalier was born in St Petersburg, Russia, the son of Louis Chevalier, a Swiss, and his Russian wife. In 1845 at the age of seventeen he returned with his father to Switzerland. During the next six years Nicholas studied painting in Lausanne and architecture in Munich, where he helped with plans for the palace of Ludwig the First at Berchtesgaden. He moved to London in 1851 and achieved some success in lithography and watercolour; whilst there he designed a fountain for Queen Victoria at Osborne and the setting of the famous Koh-i-noor diamond. He then spent some months studying in Rome. The family falling on financially evil days Nicholas came to Victoria to join his brother Louis who had come out to the goldfields. Nicholas arrived in 1855, visited the goldfields, attended to various business interests of his family and prepared to return to Europe. But the newspapers, Melbourne *Punch* and *The Illustrated Australian News*, found his talents useful and he decided to stay, introducing chromolithography to Melbourne. He travelled widely in Victoria and New Zealand and returned to England with the Duke of Edinburgh in 1869, dying in London in 1902.

(1970)

In 1864, Nicholas Chevalier painted the rugged and picturesque terrain in The Buffalo Ranges, Victoria. Here are recollections of the romantic wilderness of Salvator Rosa, but modified by the evidence of pioneer civilisation in the slab hut and bullock team in the foreground. It is interesting to remember that this was the first Australian painting to enter the Melbourne collection and to recall the words of Marcus Clarke, who saw in it "The Sylvan sunlight peculiar to our clime".

A.L.P.
(1964)

6

Samuel Thomas Gill, b. England, 1818–80
The New Rush. 1865

S. T. Gill, the man who recorded the vigorous turbulent life of Victoria's goldrush of the 1850s, was born in England, the son of Reverend Samuel Gill, headmaster of a school at Plymouth. In the year 1839, aged twenty-one, he arrived in Adelaide with his parents. In 1880 he fell dead in the street in Melbourne, penurious and forgotten, to be buried in a public grave. But during his stay in Australia he had travelled extensively and recorded the life of his times in innumerable sketches and watercolours.

In 1846 he was a member of the ill-fated Horrocks' expedition exploring the Flinders Ranges. In 1849 he published *Heads of the People:* twelve lithographic caricatures of South Australian colonists; and in 1851 he set out for the Victorian goldfields. The following year he published in Melbourne *A Series of Sketches of the Victoria Gold Diggings and Diggers as they are.* In 1854 he published an excellent collection of coloured lithographs of views of Melbourne; these are delightful

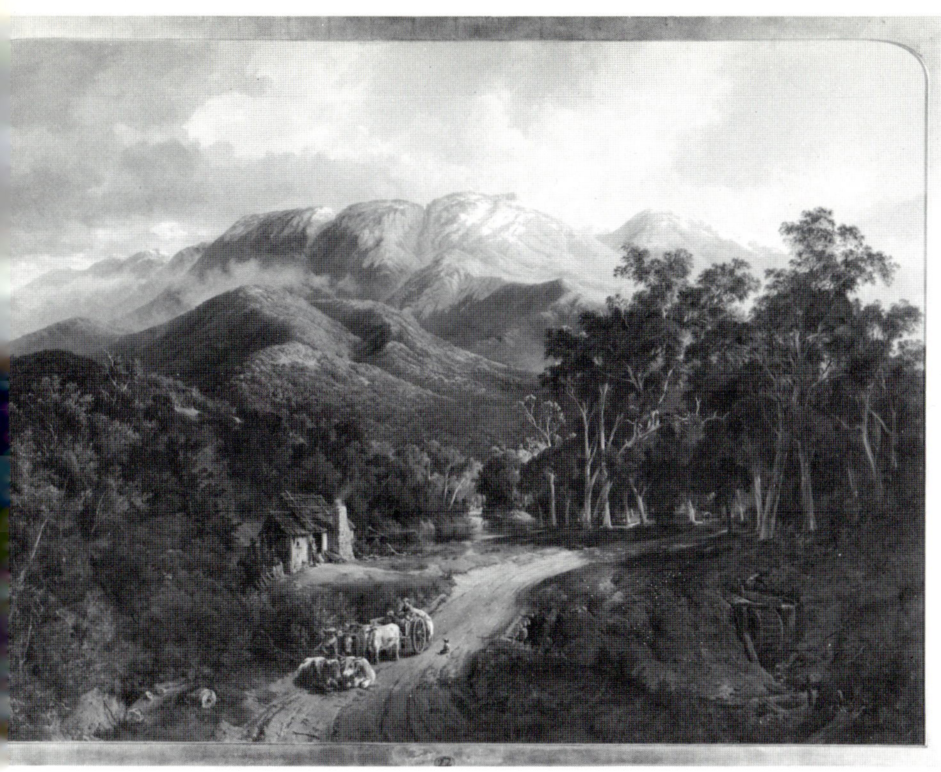

5
Nicholas Chevalier
b. Russia, 1828–1902
The Buffalo Ranges
1864
Oil on canvas
129.5 × 180.3 cm
Inscriptions. Recto: l.l.
N. Chevalier Dec. 1864
Backed
Ex. Inaugural
Exhibition of National
Gallery of Victoria
1864–5
Purchased 1864
P. 300.1

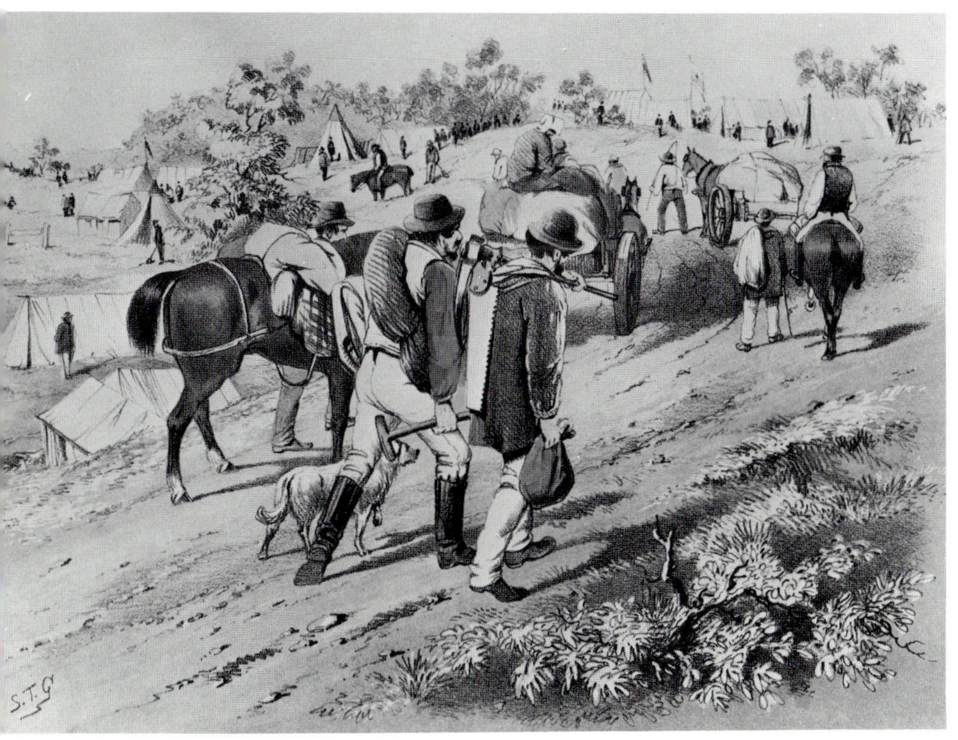

6
S. T. Gill
b. England, 1818–80
The New Rush 1863
Handcoloured
lithograph
28.8 × 42.6 cm
pl. 20 from *The
Australasian Sketchbook*,
Hamel & Ferguson,
Melbourne, 1863
Purchased 1954
3049.4

and now much sought after. But the vein of racy robust humour descending from the art of Thomas Rowlandson is best seen in his studies of the diggers.

In 1865 *The Australian Sketchbook* was published from which this illustration comes. The National Gallery print room has a complete folio. They lack the vividness of his on-the-spot sketches, but record most attractively typical characters and occupations of the colonial life of his day. Always a *bon viveur* and wit his later life was spent in obscurity and darkened by drunkenness. His last work of real interest was a commission to execute forty watercolours for the Melbourne Public Library. Though not a great artist he made a refreshing and candid record of an exciting time in our brief history. We do well to cherish his work and remember his name.

C.C.
(April, 1960)

7
Louis Buvelot, b. Switzerland, 1814–88
Summer Evening near Templestowe. 1869
When Louis Buvelot came to Melbourne in 1865 the city was at the height of its first period of adolescent growth. The goldrushes which began in 1851 had transformed Melbourne from village to city. In 1856 the Public Library was opened, and on Christmas Eve, 1864, the Picture Gallery held its first exhibition. Both these cultural events had occurred under the enthusiastic guidance of Sir Redmond Barry who reported happily of the opening of the picture Gallery: "Nearly five hundred visitors inspected the paintings, a goodly number, considering it was a mail day and wet". In short, Buvelot arrived when the pioneer colonists were seeking to recreate here the cultural environment of Europe.

Buvelot had a distinguished career. He trained first in his native Switzerland, then in Paris whence he emigrated to Brazil. There he won the patronage of the Emperor Don Pedro II. After eighteen years he returned to Switzerland. However, finding the severe winters injurious to his health he came to Melbourne. For the first few months he practised as a photographer in Bourke Street, while his wife helped finances by giving lessons in French. However he soon acquired some patrons and devoted himself entirely to painting. In 1869 the National Gallery acquired three of his Victorian landscapes, one of them **Summer Evening near Templestowe.** Buvelot painted these large pictures in the studio but he based them on pencil sketches and watercolour studies which he made on the spot.

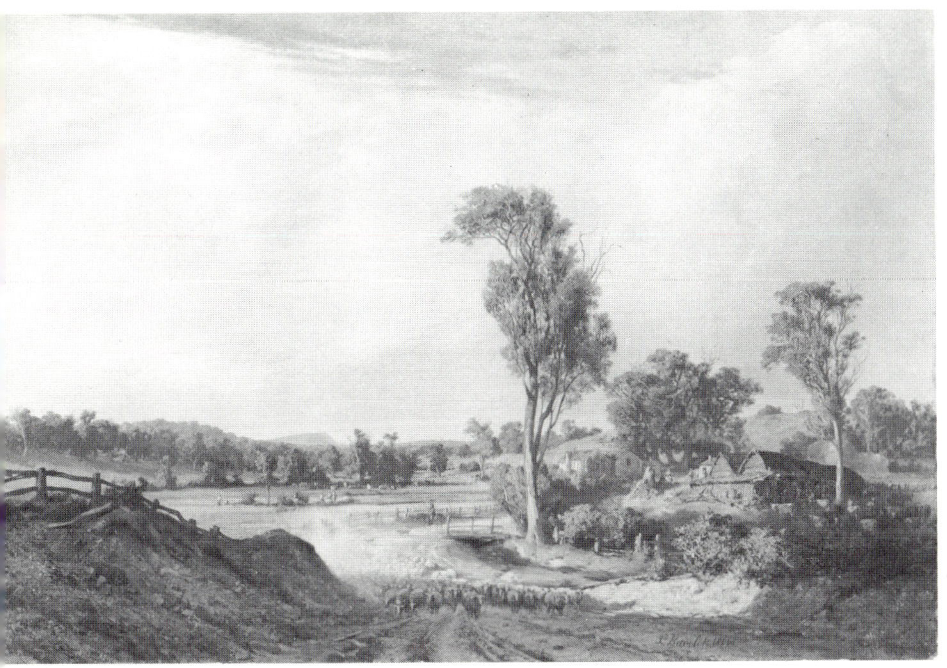

7
Louis Buvelot
b. Switzerland,
1814–88
**Summer Evening
near Templestowe**
1866
Oil on canvas
76.2 × 118 cm
Inscriptions. Recto:
l.r. "Ls. Buvelot, 1866"
Backed
Purchased 1869
P. 300.1

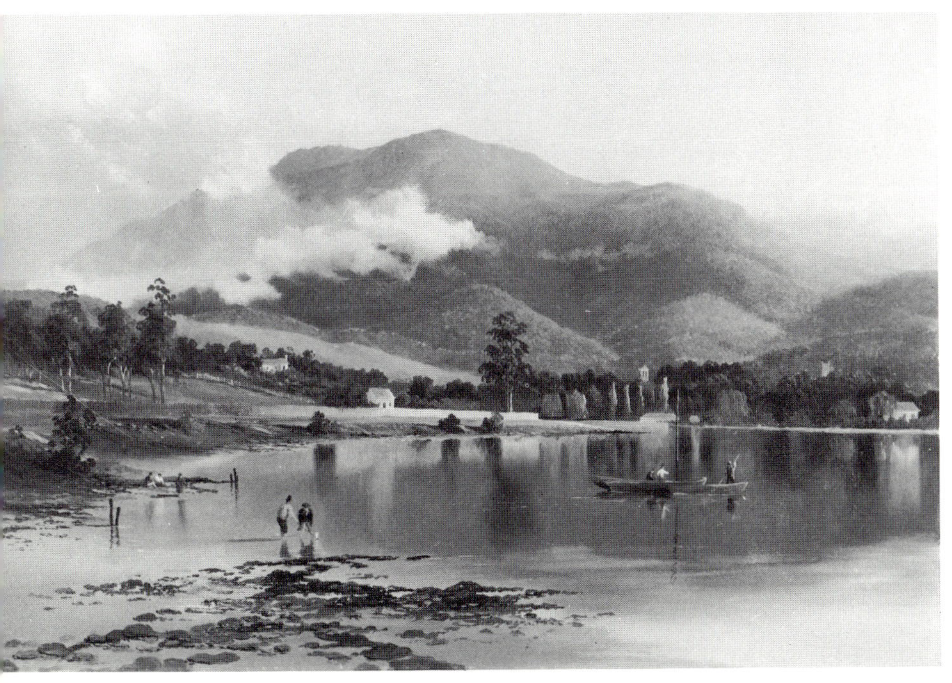

8
W. C. Piguenit
Australian, 1836–1914
**Mount Wellington
From New Town
Bay** 1879
Oil on canvas
46.4 × 69.2 cm
Inscriptions. Recto: l.l.
"W. C. Piguenit 1879"
Purchased 1972
A4/1972

The founders of the Australian impressionist school of landscapists freely acknowledged the inspiration his work and advice had given them. We owe him a profound debt for his beautiful pictures and for his influence upon the development of a native landscape tradition.

(1970)

8

William Charles Piguenit, Australian, 1836–1914
Mount Wellington from New Town Bay. 1870
"The first Australian born landscape painter of any consequence"—Bernard Smith. William Charles Piguenit was born in Hobart, Tasmania, in 1836 and died in Sydney, New South Wales, in 1914.

Piguenit, Von Guerard and Chevalier are the triumvirate of the romantic landscapists who sought subjects of mountain grandeur and extensive plains, enhanced by the light and shade of misty or brilliant heavens.

This painting is a fine example of his more serene subjects. Mount Wellington is seen from New Town Bay, enhanced by a veil of cloud and reflected in the tranquil waters. In the centre middle ground is seen the Romanesque-revival Congregational church, and to its right, the tower of St John's church, New Town.

This painting is an excellent example of one aspect of Piguenit's work. Like Von Guerard he was a great traveller and the Gallery still seeks one of the dramatic and picturesque subjects he chose in the primeval country.

(1972)

Largely self-taught, Piguenit worked as a draftsman in the Tasmanian Lands Department, but he resigned in 1873 in order to paint full-time. He won a bronze medal for photography at the 1870 Intercolonial Exhibition, Sydney. In 1880 he moved to Sydney, where he died in 1914.

J.P.
1976

In the boom years of the 1880s the most expansive period of Victoria's history, when wealth and advanced ideas poured into "Marvellous Melbourne" whose rapid growth was amazing the world, there emerged that school of painting affectionately known as the "Heidelberg School", but more accurately described as "Australian Impressionists".

Looking back in 1920, Tom Roberts, the inspiring leader of the group, succinctly described its birth. "Then I came back to Australia, and our little circle, McCubbin, Conder, Streeton and myself set to work and made the beginning of the modern Australian movement—open air and go to nature without any immodesty."

This study is largely concerned with the achievement of those artists: Tom Roberts (1856–1931), Fred McCubbin (1855–1917), Charles Conder (1868–1909) and Arthur Streeton (1867–1943). Building on the foundations laid by Louis Buvelot (1814–88) and Julian Ashton (1851–1942), and stimulated by French Impressionism, these artists created the first Australian national school of painting.

After training at the National Gallery School, Melbourne, Roberts spent a further four year term of study and travel in Europe from 1881. On a walking tour of Spain in 1883 with three Australian friends, including the Sydney artist John Russell, he met two young artists from Paris, Laureano Barrau and Ramon Casas. From them Roberts gained his most immediate contact with the style and principles of impressionism. Returning to Melbourne in 1885 with a doctrine of painting directly from nature in the open air, of seeking momentary effects of light, of studying the modifications of local colour in sunlight and shadow, in short, a doctrine of "Truth to Nature", he joined forces with Fred McCubbin. Together they set up a painting camp at Housten's Farm, Box Hill **(Plate VI)**. This was the first of those artists' camps which are part of the legend of the era. Mentone 1886 **(9)**, Charterisville 1890, Curlew Camp on Sirius Cove, Sydney (1891) followed. But the most famous, and influential was Eaglemont near Heidelberg (1888) **(10)** where Roberts, McCubbin, Conder and Streeton for a brief while worked and lived together. The memory of those last youthful summers of 1888–90 with their friends at Heidelberg coloured the remainder of the artists' lives; while the district gave its name to the group.

In August 1889 the young artists challenged the prevailing taste of press and public. Together they held the now legendary "9″ x 5″ Exhibition of Impressions" at Buxton's Rooms, Swanston Street, Melbourne. It was so-called because many of the pictures were painted on cigar box lids. Roberts, Streeton and Conder were the main exhibitors, McCubbin and others making a token contribution. Conder designed the catalogue which carried a manifesto to the public. Like so many revolutionaries before them, the artists felt it necessary to expound their novel attitude. It read thus:

"To the Public. An effect is only momentary: so an impressionist tries to find

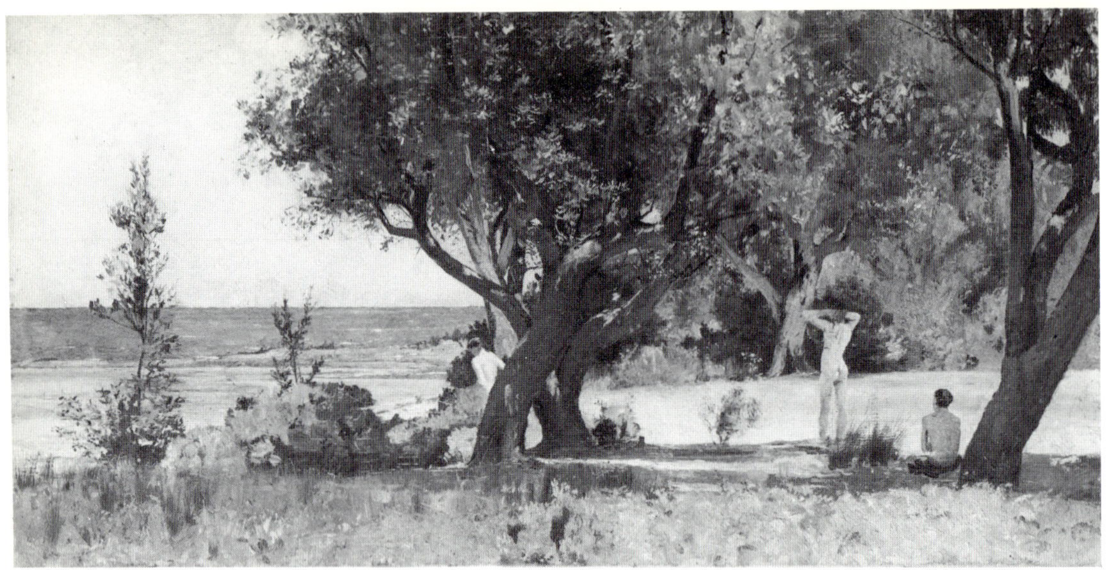

9
Tom Roberts
b. England, 1856–1931
**Sunny South. (Boys
Bathing.)** 1887
Oil on canvas
30.8 × 61.2 cm
Inscriptions. Verso:
"Tom Roberts,
59 William Street"
Felton Bequest 1940
1078.4

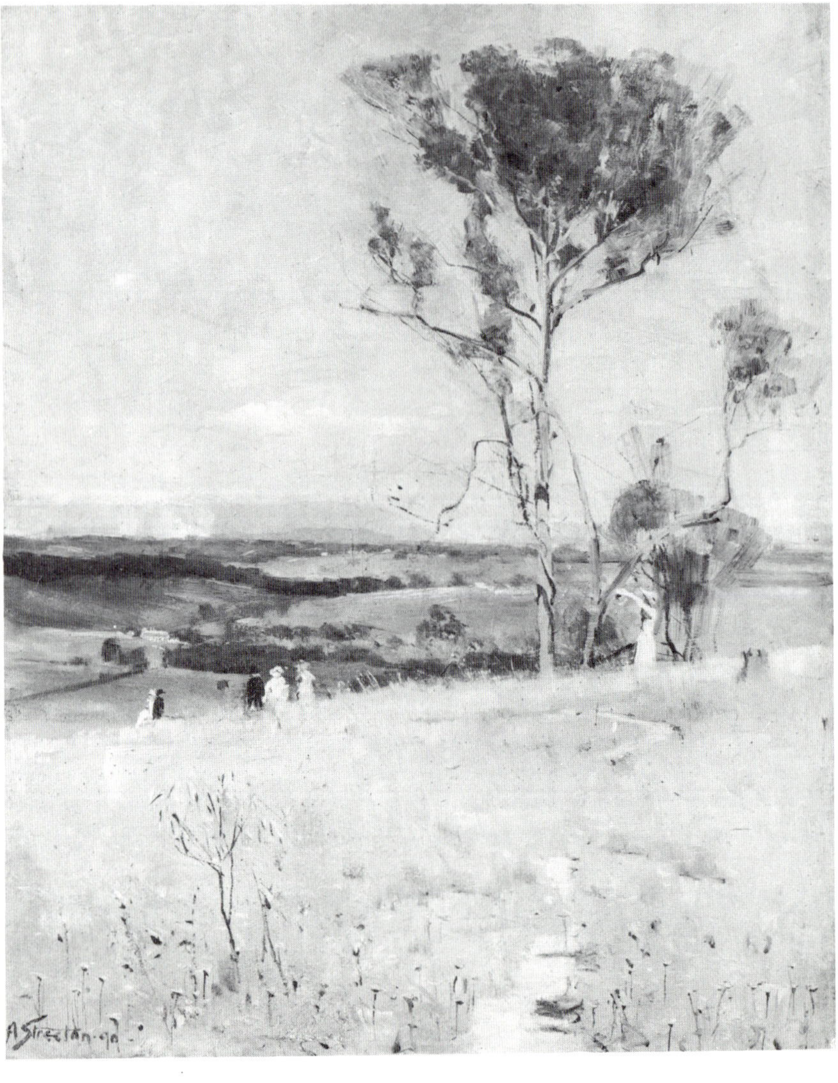

10
Sir Arthur Streeton
Australian, 1867–1943
Near Heidelberg 1890
Oil on canvas
52.1 × 39.5 cm
Inscriptions. Recto:
l.l. "Streeton '90"
Backed
Felton Bequest 1943
1223.4

20

his place. Two half hours are never alike, and he who tries to paint a sunset on two successive evenings must be more or less painting from memory. So, in these works, it has been the object of the artist to render faithfully, and thus obtain first records of effects widely differing and often of very fleeting character."

The reaction was immediate and unfavourable. James Smith of *The Argus* wrote

"Of the 180 exhibits catalogued on the present occasion four-fifths are a pain to the eye. The exhibition viewed as a whole would leave a very painful feeling behind it, and cause one to despond with regret to the future of art in this colony, did we not believe with Mr W. P. Frith, R.A. that 'Impressionism is a craze of such ephemeral character as to be unworthy of serious attention'."

Happily both Mr Frith and Mr Smith were wrong. The artists pinned the abuse to the poster at the door, and the public came to see this odd work, and these odd artist chaps. But they had their supporters, notably Theodore Fink of the *Herald* newspaper, G. W. L. Marshall-Hall, the brilliant Ormond Professor of Music, Carl Pinschof, the hospitable Austro-Hungarian Consul General, and Sir Baldwin Spencer, the anthropologist. The exhibition marked a turning point. From this time the star of the impressionists rose until it dominated the firmament of Australian art.

To compress into the traffic of a few pages the personalities of the men, the tides of taste, the social, economic and historic changes which influenced the development of this school is well-nigh impossible. When Roberts returned to Melbourne, the National Gallery School under George Folingsby (1830–91) was sending out its young artists into a community of ever increasing wealth and sophistication. Already artists were working out of doors, seeking a more accurate portrayal of the landscape. Looking back in old age Julian Ashton recalled his first years in Melbourne after his arrival in 1878 thus:

"Besides the water colours of the Yarra, I had done a fairly large canvas of Merri Creek [Art Gallery of New South Wales] which I think is the first picture painted entirely out of doors in the Commonwealth. I had but lately come from France with all the enthusiasm of the plein airists who denounced any picture that was not painted out of doors."

This changing tide in the mode of depicting the landscape was led by Louis Buvelot who is sometimes described as the Father of landscape painting in Australia.

The soil was prepared, the climate favourable for the growth of an impressionist school, and Tom Roberts was to be its creator. But the style that developed was not simply a modified version of French impressionism. The Realism of Manet, the Naturalism of Constable and Corot, the Romanticism of Turner, the Aestheticism of Whistler, the theory of history painting and the informality of photography played their part within the framework of the emerging colonial culture as the colonies moved towards Federation, in a ferment of nationalism. Each artist made his differing contribution, each drew on varying sources of inspiration in developing his own talent. By examining some individual paintings in the heritage of the "Heidelberg School", their style and their origins, a pattern in the various strands which interwoven made the tradition, may be discerned.

It is difficult to overestimate the importance of Louis Buvelot as a precursor of the Australian Impressionists. He was a Swiss-born artist of great ability and sensitivity who, from the time of his coming to Melbourne in 1865 at the age of 51 until his death in 1888, introduced a new poetic concept, a new tonal accuracy to the depiction of the countryside. **Coleraine and a Waterpool** 1871 **(Plate V)** well exemplifies his style. He favoured simple rural scenes in the manner of the French "Barbizon School", so known from a group of painters who worked at that village in the forest of Fontainebleau during the mid-nineteenth century, their aim being the naturalistic presentation of peasant life and scenery. This deceptively humble farming subject of geese paddling in a pond at twilight is informed by a subtle poetry and a remarkable accuracy of vision. The two great gums which quite fill the central plane of the picture stand silhouetted against the sky suffused with the light of the setting sun. The sky, the trees, the reflecting pool, the cattle and geese all are unified into a tranquil tonal harmony of russets, tans and gold. When Buvelot came to Melbourne, settlement had already tamed the wilder aspects of the primitive Antipodean landscape. Thus he found plentiful subjects congenial to his artistry in the environs of Melbourne. Nor was his work overlooked. Roberts, Streeton and McCubbin freely acknowledged their debt to Buvelot's example; and in 1916 Fred McCubbin wrote in moving and perceptive terms of his influence.

"Where Von Guerard and Chevalier went in search of mountains and waterfalls for their subjects, Buvelot interested himself in the life around him; he sympathized with it and painted it. There was no one before him to point out the way. He possessed therefore in himself the genius to catch and understand the salient living features of this country. In a sense he was a forerunner: all his pictures are reminiscent of Australian life as we know it. Incidents by country roadsides, weather worn farm houses, familiar farm yards, fields in which men are working, fences and wayward gum trees, the effect of sunlight on a tree, or shadow in a forest glade. I remember as if it were yesterday standing one evening a long time ago, watching the sunset glowing on the trees in Studley Park, and it was largely through Buvelot that I realized the beauty of the scene."

Tom Roberts's personality and vision was the catalyst in the creation of the impressionist school. He was, without question, the most influential and perhaps also the finest painter Australia has produced. He was equally accomplished as landscapist, portraitist and painter of "history pieces" with a national contemporary flavour. His art was built on the dual bases of impressionism and realism. That is, the intention remained to express appearances as seen at first sight, not as known to the intellect. But his art is not confined to the impressionist absorption in pure appearance at a fleeting glance. That technique he subordinated to the realistic statement of generalized themes of landscape, sentiment, or history, in compositions of great complexity.

His younger followers of the Heidelberg School, Streeton and Conder, drew inspiration mainly from his outdoor landscape sketches which are the most impressionist of his work. The diversity of his artistic vocabulary and intention may be seen in the works here illustrated.

Coming South 1886 **(11)** portrays a continuing part of our national life. It is a scene re-enacted daily and some such story lies embedded in every Australian family. Roberts was himself an immigrant, coming to Melbourne at the age of thirteen with his widowed mother and family. His life is a classical example of poor migrant boy makes good. Once, looking back in the days of his fame, he commented "Well, this was begun at two bob a day at the School of Design. Australia gave me my first real chance." Working as a photographer's assistant by day, studying at night, Roberts learnt enough and saved enough to return to Europe in 1881 seeking to enlarge his training. This tenacity of purpose which later earned him the nickname "Bulldog" enabled him to return to Melbourne, the most highly trained and wide-ranging artist of his generation.

It was on his voyage back to Australia on board the *Lusitania*, the Orient Line's first mail steamer, that Roberts made the studies for **Coming South.** It is the first of his works, which, taking a scene from contemporary life, makes it both particular and universal. The heroic history pictures of later years—**Shearing the Rams, The Breakaway, Bailed Up**—are presaged by this elegant and tender study of varied humanity on the long voyage to the new land.

This early work, more realist than impressionist, shows Roberts still close to his studies at the Royal Academy School. However, the choice of a subject from everyday experience derives ultimately from Edouard Manet (1832–83), most probably via the example of the French artist, James Tissot (1836–1902), the most charming illustrator of Victorian life, who settled in London after 1870. Yet there are tentative impressionist features in the high, blond tonality of the

11
Tom Roberts
b. England, 1856–1931
Coming South 1886
Oil on canvas
63.8 × 50.5 cm
Inscriptions. Recto: l.r.
"Tom Roberts 1886"
Presented by Colonel
Aubrey H. L. Gibson,
1967 in memory of
John and Anne
Gibson, settlers, 1887
1738.5

12
Tom Roberts
b. England, 1856–1931
**Bourke Street,
Melbourne** c. 1886
Oil on canvas
51.5 × 76.6 cm
Inscriptions. Recto:
l.r. "Tom Roberts"
National Library of
Australia, Canberra

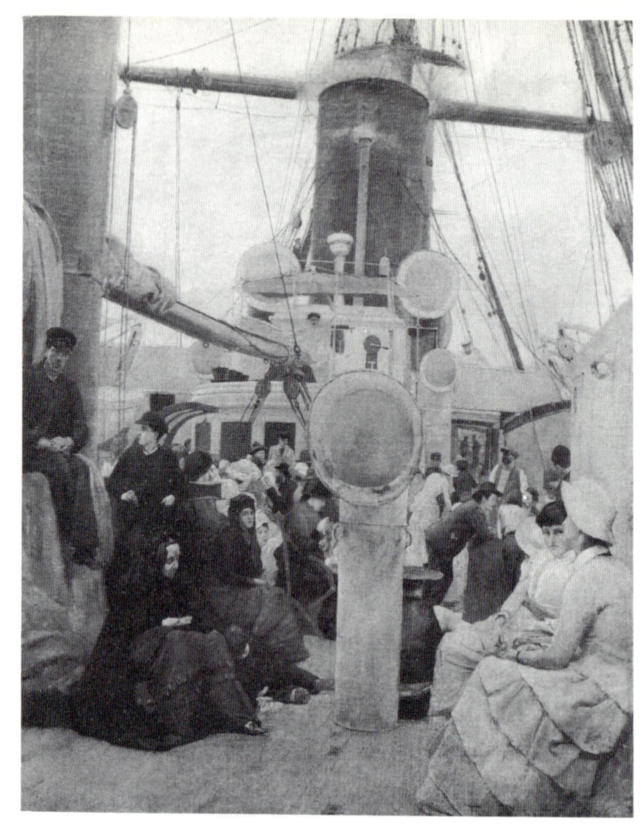

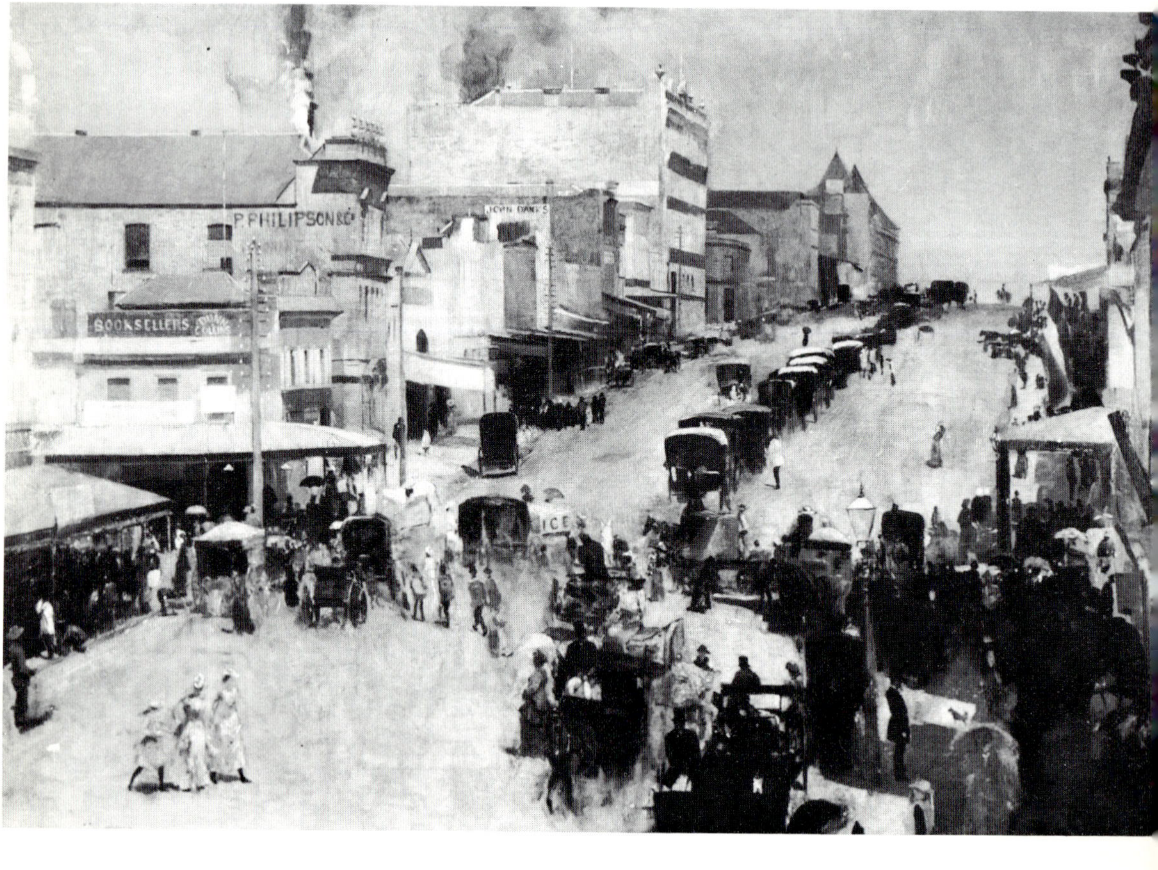

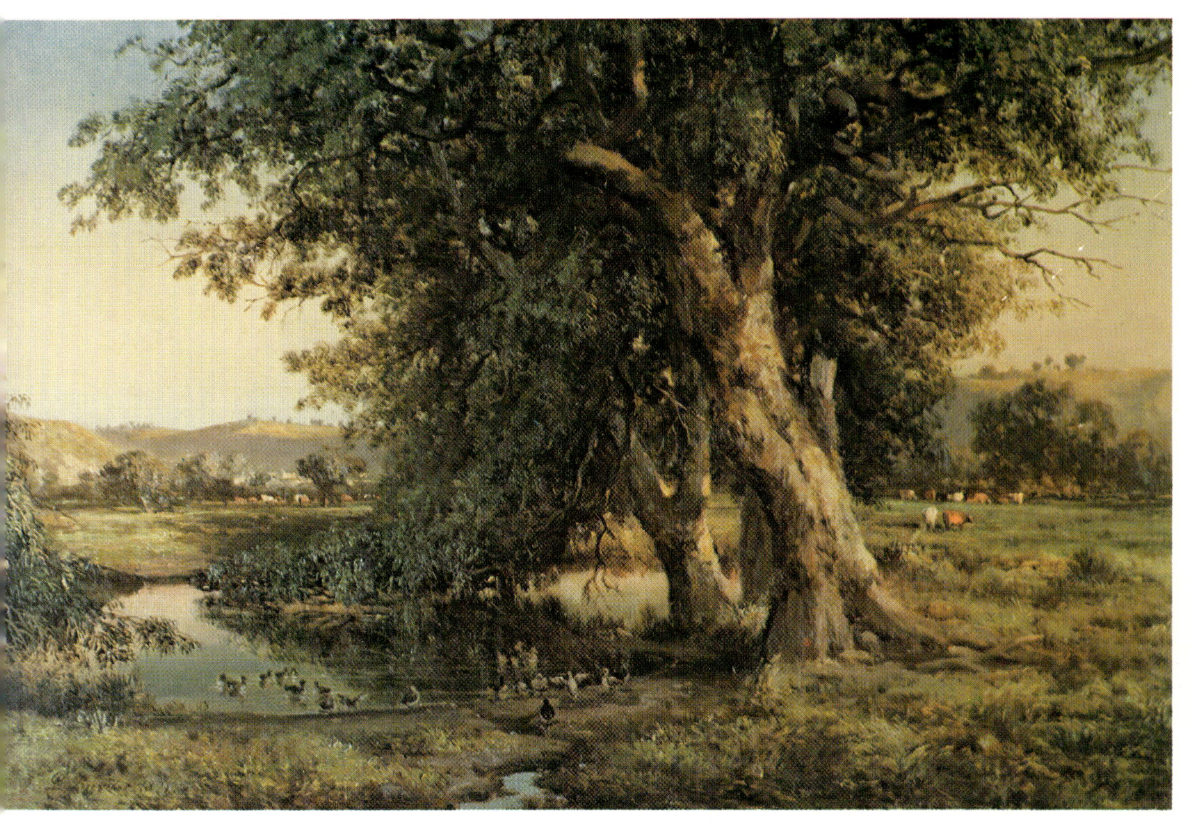

Plate **V**
Louis Buvelot
b. Switzerland, 1814–88
Coleraine and a Waterpool 1871
Oil on canvas
39.4 × 61 cm
Inscriptions. Recto: l.l. "Lˢ. Buvelot 1871"
Verso: "Waterpool at Coleraine, painted by Lˢ. Buvelot, 1871"
Collier Bequest 1955
3231.4

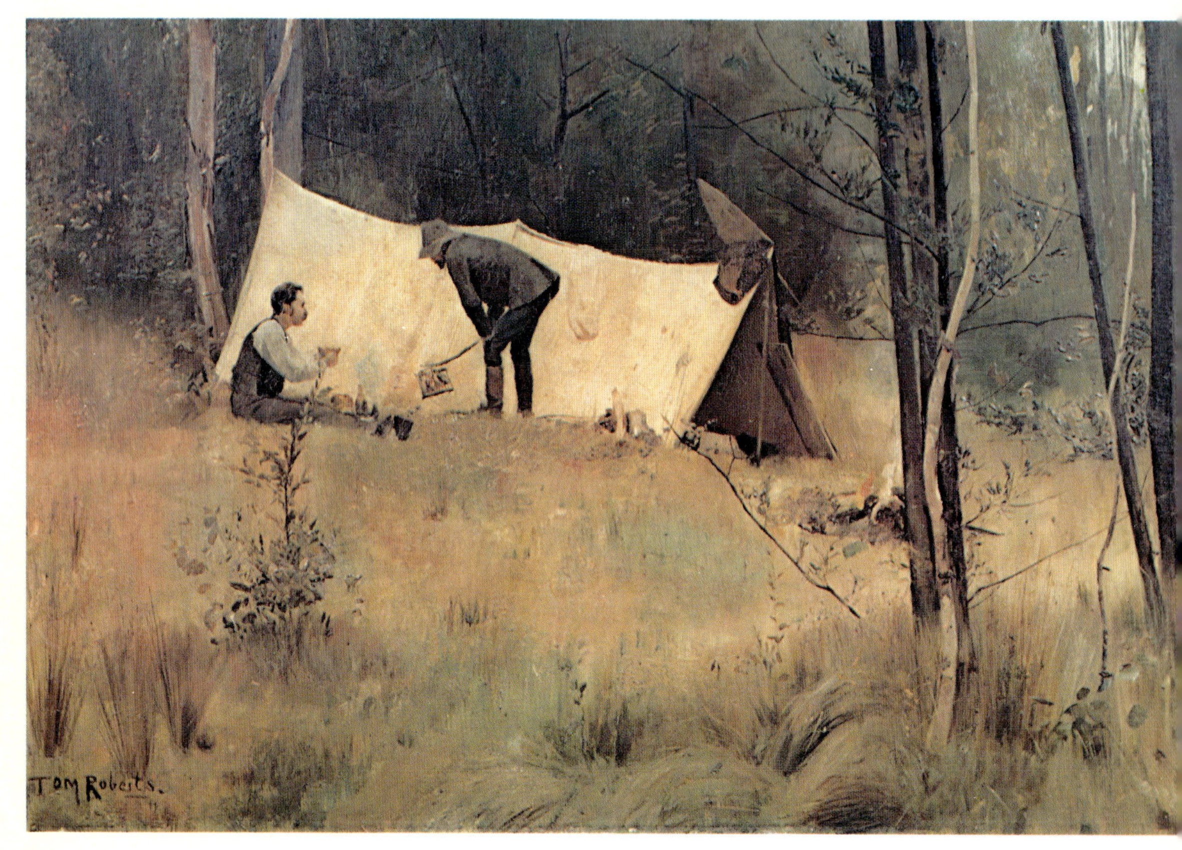

Plate **VI**
Tom Roberts
b. England, 1856–1931
The Artists' Camp c. 1886
Oil on canvas
45.7 × 60.8 cm
Inscriptions. Recto: l.l. ''Tom Roberts''
Backed
Felton Bequest 1943
1224.4

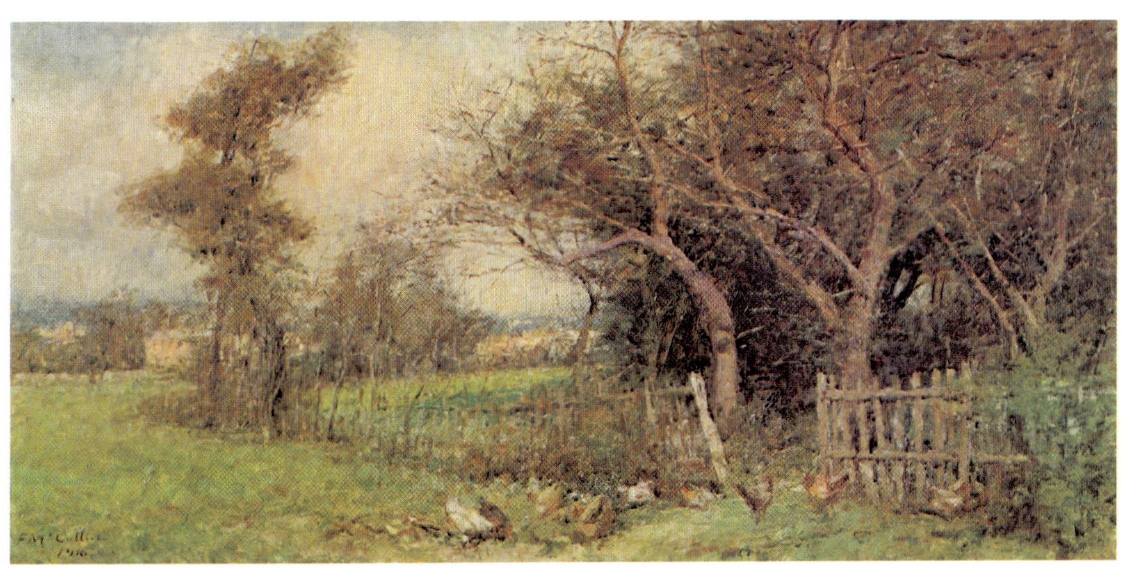

Plate **VII**
Fred. McCubbin
Australian, 1855–1917
Autumn Morning, South Yarra 1916
Oil on canvas
70 × 137.5 cm
Inscriptions. Recto: l.l. "F. McCubbin 1916"
Purchased 1955
3164.4

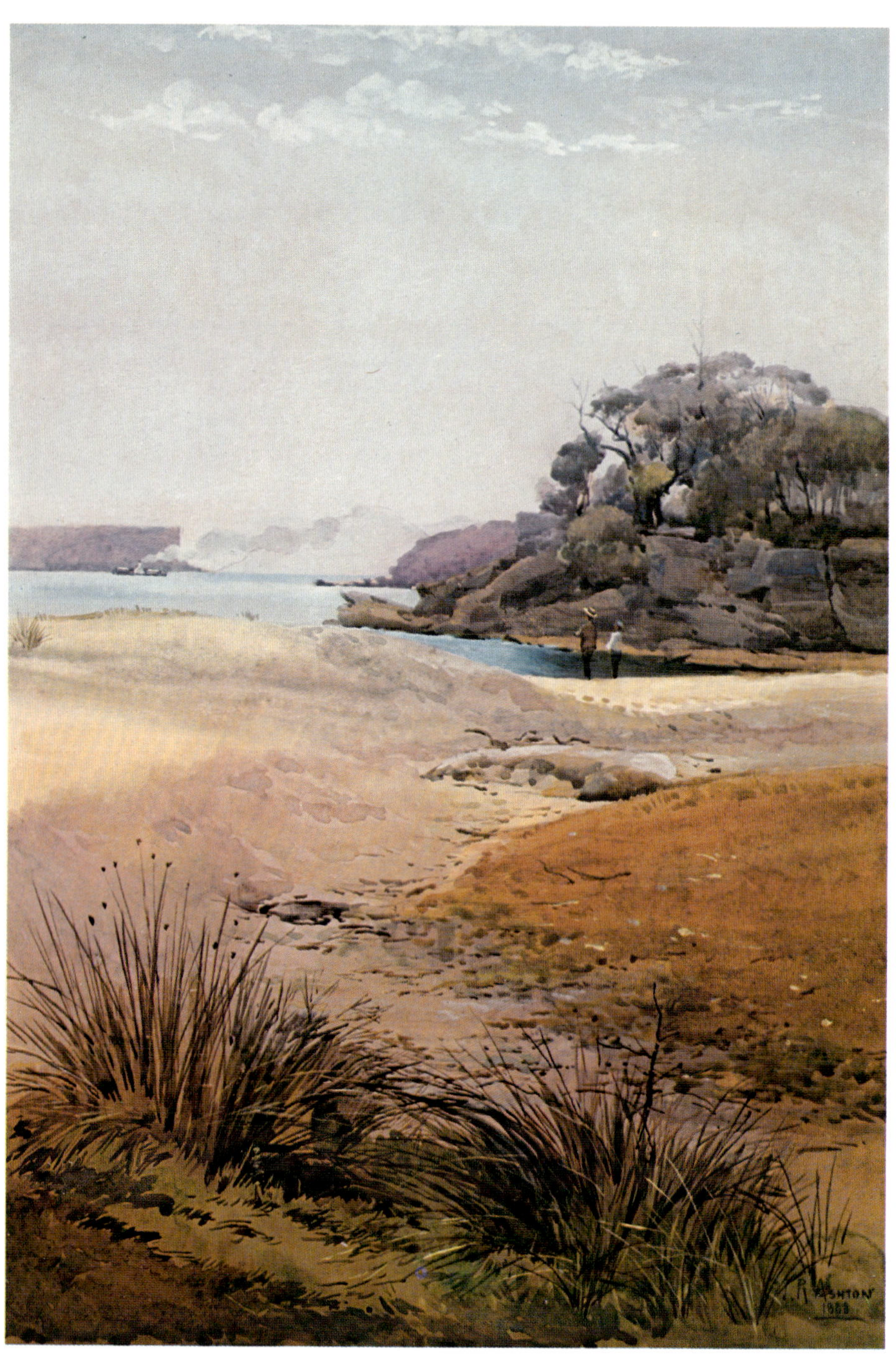

Plate **VIII**
Julian Rossi Ashton
b. England, 1851–1942
View of the North Head, Sydney Harbour 1888
Watercolour
35.5 × 24.9 cm
Inscriptions. l.r. "J. R. Ashton 1888"
Purchased 1965
1523.5

picture, and the search for more exact analysis of the play of light, in the use of complementary colour in the shadows.

The Artists' Camp 1886 (**Plate VI**) which was painted when the artists were camped near Housten's Farm, Box Hill, is more broadly treated. Avoiding a too detailed definition of form, Roberts has suggested the soft light of morning amidst the enveloping bush emphasized by the more careful rendering of the foreground saplings. A small picture in a low-keyed palette of softly modulated browns and greens, it is reminiscent of the compact evocative naturalism of the Barbizon painters. The casual subject of the two artists preparing breakfast may owe something to the informality of the "snapshot" in photography.

During the winter the artists painted at Box Hill; in the summer they moved to the camp at Mentone where Roberts painted **The Sunny South** 1887 (**9**), a similarly informal subject. The handling is more painterly, more lively in its contrasts of light and shade, more impressionist in the violet hue of the sky than is **The Artists' Camp.** But it is a mistake to seek a strict chronological development in Roberts's style. Throughout his life he moved the emphasis of his work from realism to impressionism and back as the subject prompted.

Bourke Street, Melbourne 1885–6 (**12**) is a wonderful little painting of the most intense immediacy. Here indeed is the "first record of an effect of very fleeting character" of the 9″ x 5″ manifesto. One feels that looking away for a moment, the whole scene might change. The bustle of traffic, the hastening figures in the streets of boom-time Melbourne are caught in an enveloping atmosphere of heat and light. The parked carriages throw uncompromising mauve shadows on the pavement. The blue of the sky is drained out by the fierce summer light, and the suggestions of semi-opaque, basically evanescent substances, puffs of smoke, wisps of cloud, rising dust, the whole painted in the highest key, make this painting one of the most essentially impressionist in Roberts's oeuvre.

The reputation of Tom Roberts would rest secure on the faithful naturalism of his landscape and the sensitive percipience of his portraiture, had he painted nothing else. But it is the achievement of his great "history pictures" which places him high above his fellows. In them, under the inspiration of a deeply felt nationalism and love for the outback life of his adopted country, the twin forces of his art, realism and impressionism reach equilibrium. Two of those masterworks were painted at Brocklesby Station near Corowa, New South Wales; **Shearing the Rams** 1890 (**13**) and **The Breakaway** 1891 (**14**). Each is an elaborate formal composition which takes an aspect of Australian pastoral activity and by condensation, makes it heroic. Yet each is based on realistic observation, both of visual appearances and the typical behaviour of men and beasts in such activities.

Twice Roberts went to Brocklesby for the shearing season, making innumerable

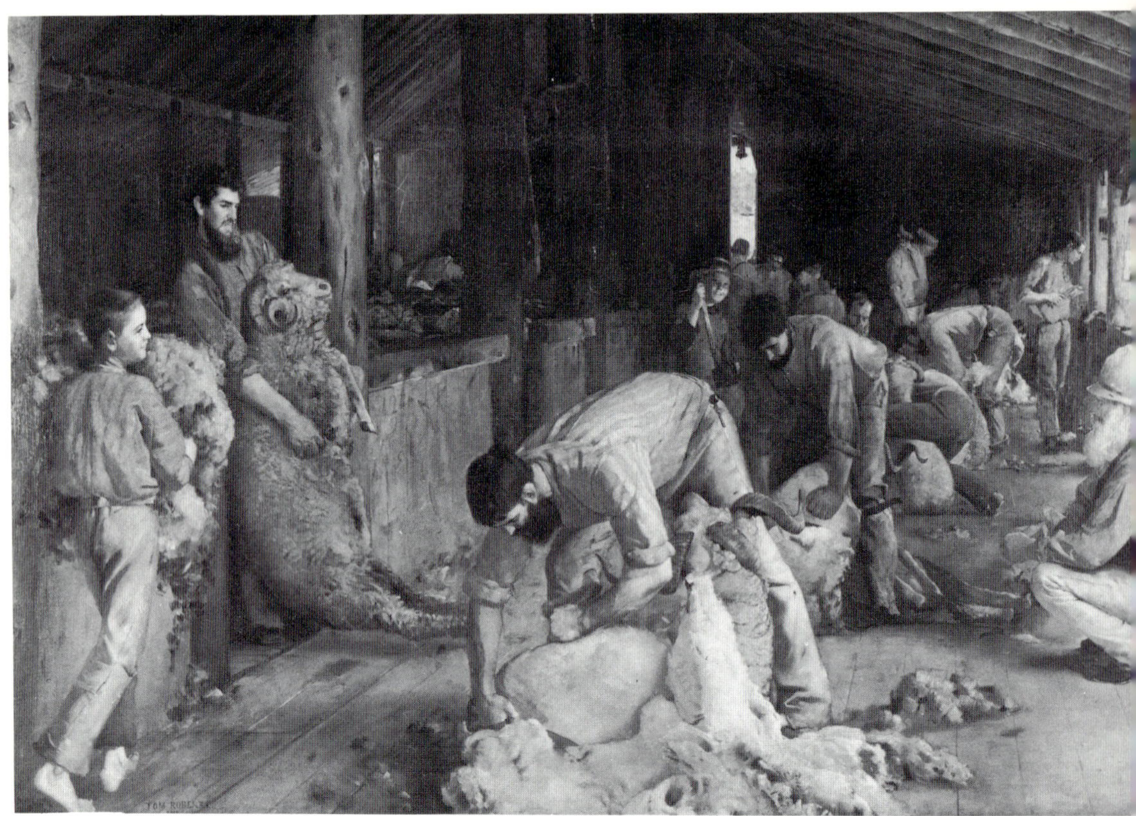

13
Tom Roberts
b. England, 1856–1931
Shearing the Rams
1890
Oil on canvas board
121.9 × 182.6 cm
Inscriptions. Recto: l.l.
"Tom Roberts 1890"
Backed
Felton Bequest 1932
4654.3

studies before setting up his canvas in the woolshed with the actual participants as his models. Before painting **The Breakaway** he painted studies of a chock and log fence under fierce overhead sunlight. In the completed picture the diagonal of this fence dividing the foreground emphasises the direction of the breakaway sheep. Nevertheless, this concentration on visual accuracy of detail, in no way detracts from the unity of these paintings. Indeed the artist's skill gives these highly considered compositions an appearance of effortless spontaneity.

In a letter to *The Argus* defending his choice of a mundane subject like **Shearing the Rams** for a noble painting, Roberts described his intention to honour "strong masculine labour" and "the patience of the beasts whose year's growth is being stripped from them for man's use". Inside the shadowy woolshed one is conscious of the blazing sunlight outside. This is superbly conveyed by the strictly impressionist glimpse of burnt golden landscape through the rear entry of the shed, and the enchanting reflected light on the smiling face of the tar-boy in the middleground. The careful viewer will find infinite pleasure in the various poses and expressions of the labouring men and youths, and in the subtle modulations of colour in the painting of their attire. At no point in making its tribute to this country's great pastoral life does this painting lose its artistic or human interest.

In the dynamic composition of **The Breakaway** Roberts leaves the ordered

26

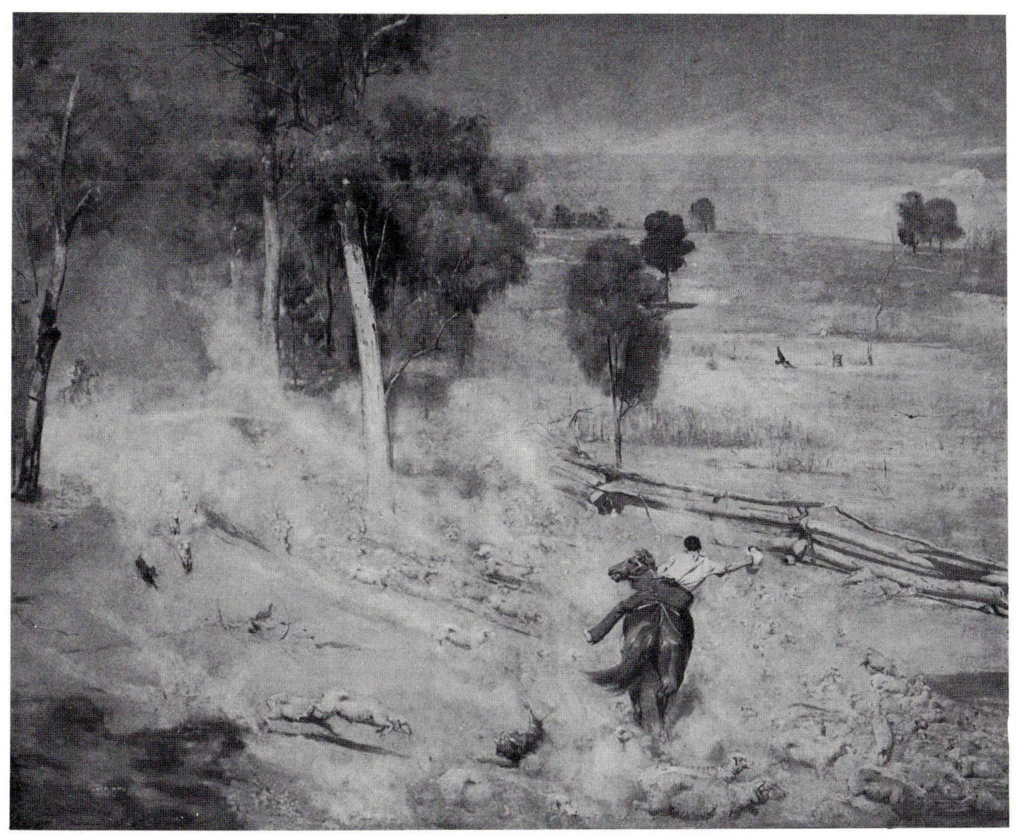

labour of the woolshed for dramatic action. There is an overpowering sense of blinding light and heat in this painting. Into a sky of intense blue, from which the sun beats directly overhead, there rises on the horizon a distant swirl of dust. In the foreground, as thirst-crazed sheep, scenting water, breakaway towards a still-standing waterhole, a stockman strives to cut them off. The impetuous straining energy of the horseman and his mount displays Roberts's draughtsmanship at its finest. No one looking at the picture can be but stirred by this drama played out in the brilliance of high summer. Roberts's industrious months in the Riverina were rewarded. The painting bears the stamp of truth.

The sources of the "history" pieces of both Roberts and McCubbin are multiple. Artistically, the example of Bastien Lepage (1848–84), painter of scenes of peasant life and labours, whom both admired, is paramount. Intellectually, there is a burgeoning of the nationalist myth, the ethos of the outback, of the pioneer, mateship and of the establishment of the labour movement, displayed in the writings of the *Bulletin* of "Banjo" Paterson and Henry Lawson. While the vigorous talk of the ebullient Marshall-Hall urging the artists to forsake the "suburban bush" for the outback, and the philosophising discourse of McCubbin himself ("The Proff") on the need to paint scenes of specifically Australian character also played their part.

Fred McCubbin, born in Melbourne 1855, was but a year older than Roberts.

14
Tom Roberts
b. England, 1856–1931
The Breakaway
1890–1
Oil on canvas
135.9 × 166.4 cm
Inscriptions. Recto:
l.l. "Tom Roberts"
Art Gallery of South
Australia, Adelaide

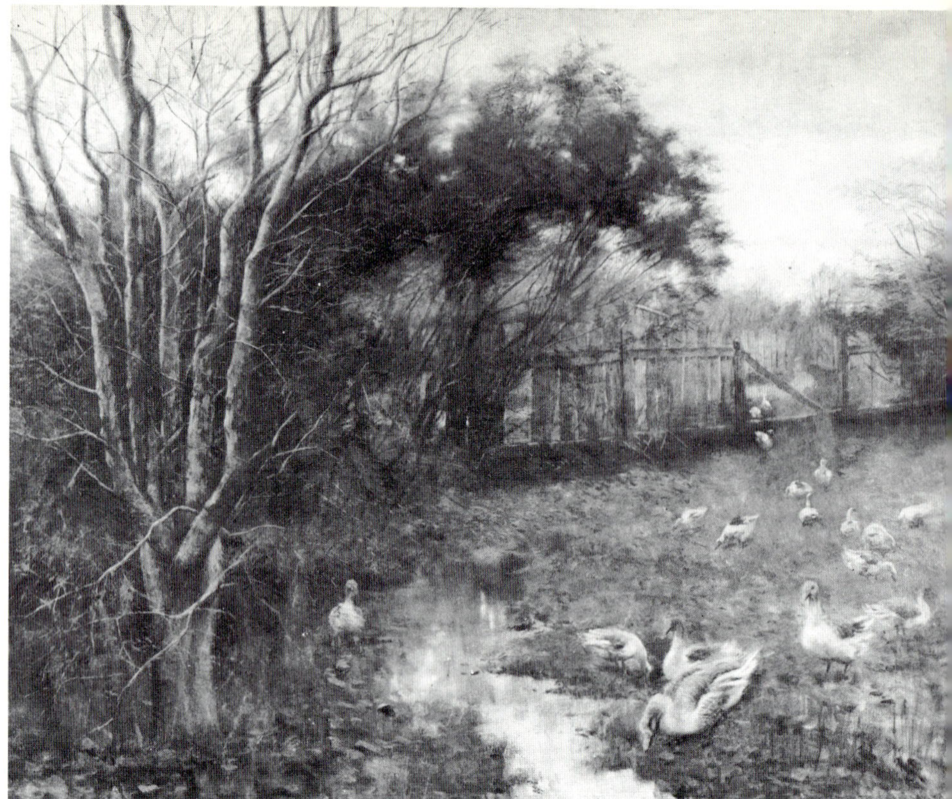

Yet in the writings and reminiscences of the period he plays something of a sympathetic fatherly role to the group. Perhaps this was due to his appointment as drawing master of the National Gallery School from 1886. He certainly did not hesitate to make constructive and friendly criticism of his colleagues' work, even that of Roberts. Though his meeting with Roberts and their shared painting expeditions were influential to his development, McCubbin followed his own course, never becoming slave to a doctrinaire impressionism. Indeed, his contribution to the 9″ x 5″ Exhibition was five works only, as against Roberts's sixty-two. McCubbin's work is various and falls naturally into at least three phases. **A Winter Evening** of 1897 **(15)** reveals McCubbin's innate lyricism; and the choice of his humble subject shows his affinity to Buvelot. It is a most delicately seen study, the misty gloaming given strength by the thorough draughtsman's analysis of the anatomy of the leafless tree in the left foreground.

McCubbin's "history" paintings of pioneer themes **The Lost Child** 1886 **(27)** (National Gallery of Victoria) and **Down on his Luck** 1889 (Western Australian Art Gallery) antedate those of Roberts. Here illustrated is the later triptych **The Pioneer** of 1904 **(16).** Against a sensitively realized bushland scene the pioneers are carefully portrayed in typical narrative poses. The inspirational example of Bastien Lepage may be confirmed by viewing that artist's **The Potato Gatherers** of 1874 in the National Gallery of Victoria. While the closely related tone colours of the background owe something to Whistler's subtle studies in that field, McCubbin had a true insight of the modest haunting beauty of the sapling country of the foothills. He did not favour open vista pictures; instead he became

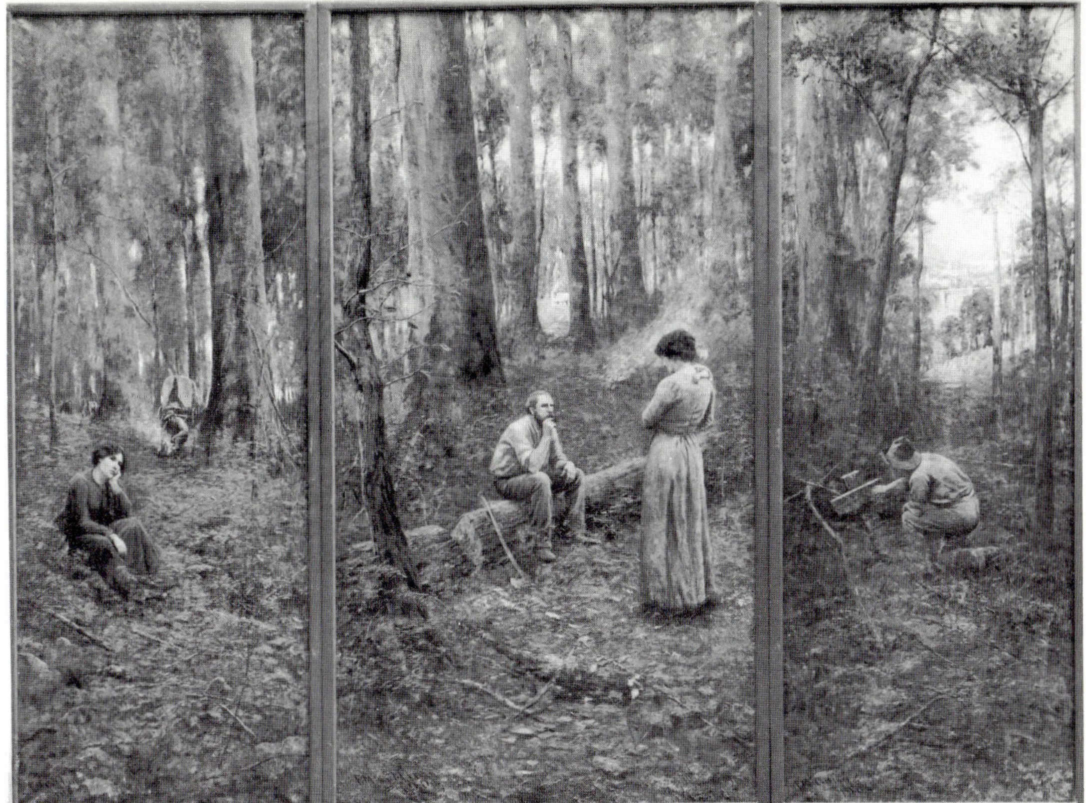

unrivalled in suggesting with a palette of related pale grey, blue and green, the surrounding enveloping, almost subaqueous, light of the bush.

McCubbin was very conscious of the artistic problem in these story pictures of a dichotomy between the impressionist vision of the landscape setting and the realist figures drawn from posed models. Indeed, McCubbin more often than not cajoled his wife, children and friends into posing for hours while completing these large paintings. However, to overcome this sense of a lack of unity in the artistry of these works, McCubbin gradually adopted a freer mode of paint handling, inspired by the English Romantic artist, J. M. W. Turner (1775–1851), of breaking up the surface into flecks of colour, often applied with the palette knife.

In the late years of his life, more particularly after a visit to England in 1906, his manner became very free and more impressionist in the French tradition than any others of the group. A fine example of the sparkling, painterly quality of this late period is the colourful **Autumn Morning, South Yarra** of 1916 **(Plate VII)** painted a year before his death.

McCubbin is a painter for whom many collectors have a special affection, both for the tranquil lyricism of his work and in admiration of his unceasing quest for new achievement which never abated throughout his whole life. The volume of the sketches, studies and completed painting that he left makes one think that he hardly ever had a paintbrush out of his hand. Indeed, painting was for him his natural and necessary element.

It is after Roberts met Arthur Streeton at Mentone in 1886, and in the following year, visiting Sydney, met Charles Conder, who followed him to Melbourne in

16
Fred. McCubbin
Australian, 1855–1917
The Pioneer 1904
Oil on canvas
3 panels:
Left panel 223.5 ×
86 cm
Centre panel 224.7 ×
122.5 cm
Right panel 223.5 ×
85.7 cm
Inscriptions. Recto:
l.l. on each panel:
"F. McCubbin 1904"
Verso on each panel:
"F. McCubbin,
Woodend"
Felton Bequest 1906
253.2

17
Charles Conder
b. England, 1868–1909
**Cove on the
Hawkesbury** c. 1888
Oil on cardboard
37 × 22 cm
Inscriptions. Recto:
l.r. "Conder"
Backed
Bequeathed by Mary
Helen Keep, 1944
1392.4

October 1888, that the Heidelberg School came into being; and its full flowering was in the summers spent at Eaglemont camp. The youthful talent of the two artists, Streeton and Conder, in 1888 respectively twenty-one and twenty, made novel contributions to the emerging style. At that time their talents, at once diverse and similar, interacted profoundly. It is an idle task to champion one, as the greater influence on the other. The fairest judgement seems to be that Streeton contributed the greater technical virtuosity and Conder the greater decorative and imaginative innovations. Blamire Young wrote of Conder at the Heidelberg camp.

"The Heidelberg camp was a quarrelsome one and under the leadership of Tom Roberts, it was more robust than intellectual. Conder's was the difficult role of peace maker and he introduced what there was of refinement and delicacy."

Charles Conder spent only six years of his life in Australia arriving, a boy of fifteen in June 1884, and departing in April 1890. Yet his achievement was of such intrinsic quality and his example of such influence, that he ranks equal with his confreres. A mingling of sources may be seen in Conder's art; most clearly, the initial time spent painting with Julian Ashton on the Hawkesbury, the example of Girolamo Nerli's direct sketches, the impressionist attitude of Tom Roberts and the decorative aestheticism of Whistler. But these are absorbed and transmuted by his remarkably sophisticated personality. His wide reading in poetry, his dreaming contemplation of the visual world as symbol of emotional states, an element of the exotic in his passionate makeup, mesmerized his friends and made his paintings individual and unmistakably "Conder".

A comparison of Julian Ashton's **North Head, Sydney Harbour** 1888 **(Plate VIII)** with Conder's **Cove on the Hawkesbury** (17) reveals a common interest, not merely in description but in decorations. It was with Julian Ashton that Conder, as a youth in New South Wales, made his first painting expeditions to Richmond and to the Hawkesbury River districts. There is no doubt that prior to Conder's meeting Roberts, Ashton was the major influence on his artistic training. Ashton has been given less than his due for his role in the emergence and encouragement of a national school of landscapists. Possibly the fact that he lived to the great age of ninety-one has prompted writers to judge him only from his late work, and on the products of his school of painting in Sydney after 1900. The watercolour of 1888 here illustrated is a fine example of his work of that period. Its delicacy of colour, informality of subject, and decorative composition illustrate his affinity with the early movement. In **Cove on the Hawkesbury** Conder's daring placement of the girl with scarlet parasol beneath the triangle of blue water is masterly, owing something to Whistler and to the Japanese

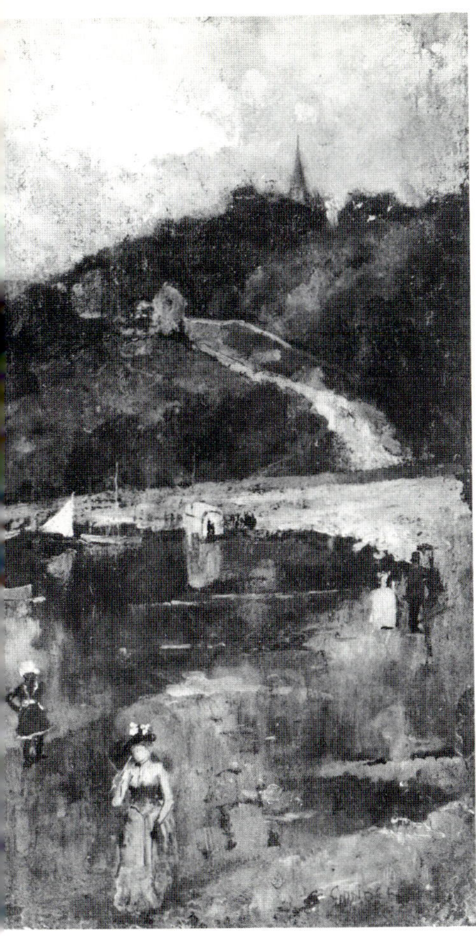 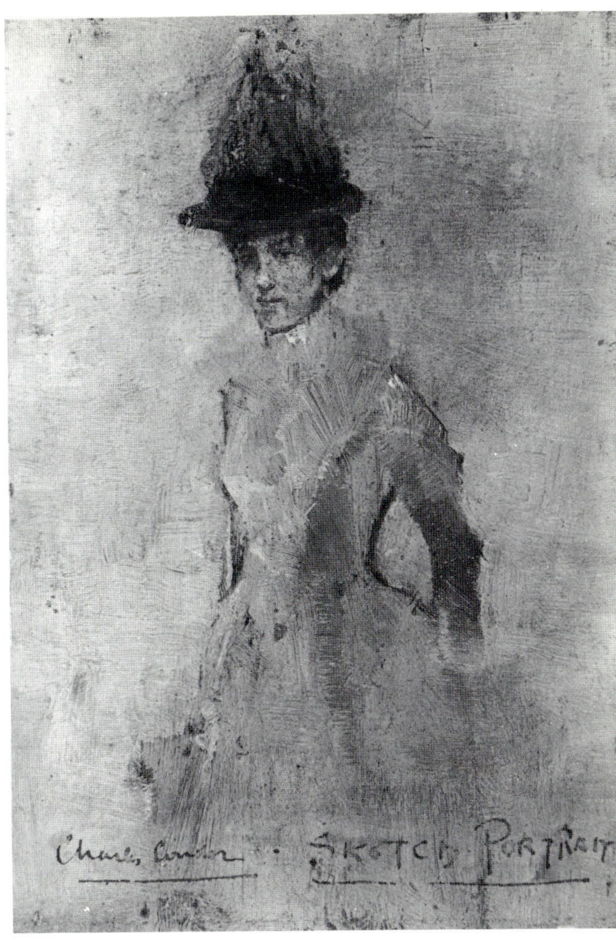

wood cut, as well as to Ashton. By putting down at first touch of the brush the form and tone of an object, Conder imparts a sense of spontaneity, of evanescence to his idyllic scenes. But this poetry of vision is always set in a decorative compositional scheme of great subtlety. This rare talent is best exemplified in the masterpiece of his Australian period, **Ricketts Point near Sandringham 1890 (Plate IX),** while the delicacy and sensitivity of his paint-handling is evident in the tiny **Sketch Portrait** 1889 **(18),** which was shown in the 9″ x 5″ Exhibition. Both Conder and Streeton gained something from the example of Girolamo Nerli (1863–1926), an Italian artist who came to Australia in 1886. Nerli's work caused much discussion when shown, and indeed the press referred to his street scenes as "impressions". His actual influence is a matter of debate, but it is known that his work was admired by Conder and Streeton. A consideration of Nerli's **Street Scene on a Rainy Night** c. 1888 **(20),** a typical example of his work with its broadly handled studies of watery reflections, reveals a strong kinship with Conder's **Departure of the Orient, Circular Quay** 1888 **(19)** and Streeton's **Redfern Station** 1893 **(21).**

As Roberts had made heroic the pastoral life of the outback, so Arthur Streeton made the landscape itself heroic. So much does his vision dominate landscape painting in Australia for the ensuing fifty years that for many people his pictures

18
Charles Conder
b. England, 1868–1909
Sketch Portrait 1889
Oil on board/panel
15.2 × 10.5 cm
Inscriptions. Recto: on lower margin "Charles Conder. Sketch Portrait".
Backed
Purchased 1970
A15/1970

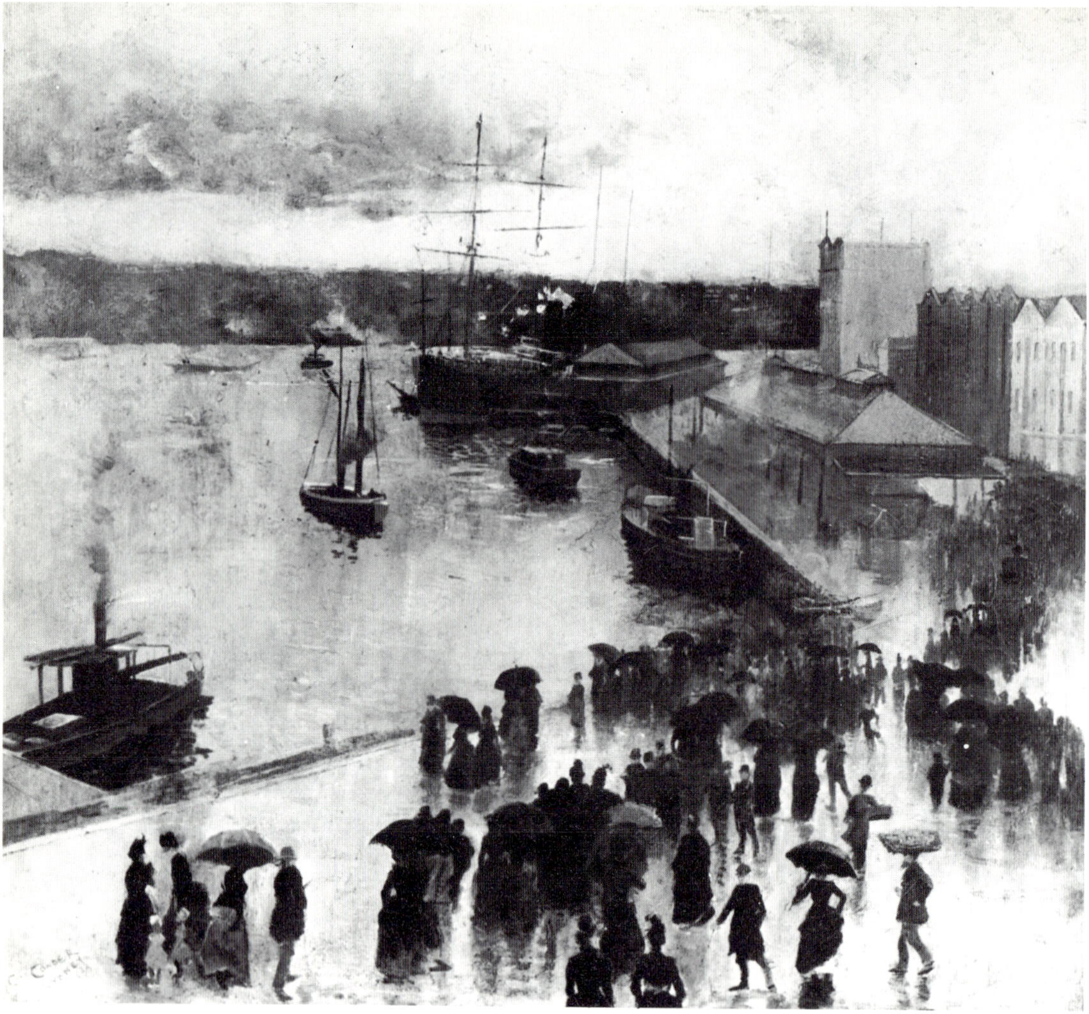

21
Sir Arthur Streeton
Australian, 1867–1943
**Railway Station,
Redfern** 1893
Oil on canvas
40.8 × 61.0 cm
Inscriptions. Recto: l.l.
"Arthur Streeton 1893"
Gift of Lady Denison,
1942
Art Gallery of New
South Wales, Sydney

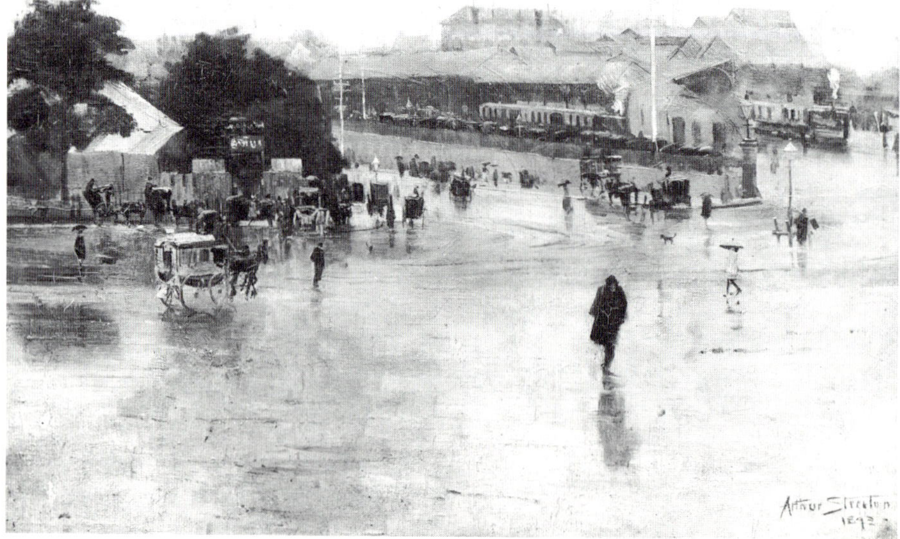

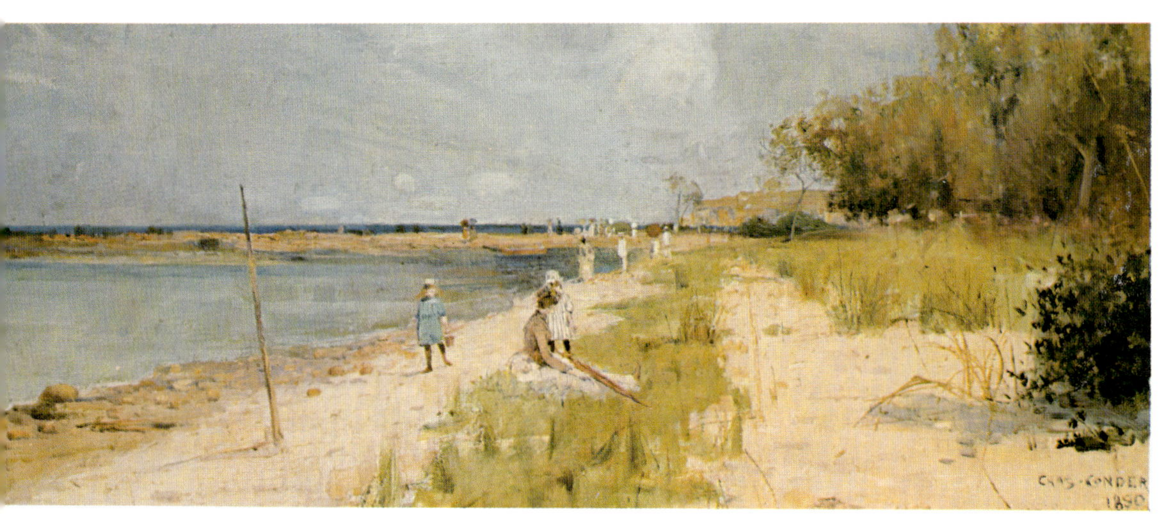

Plate **IX**
Charles Conder
b. England, 1868–1909
Ricketts Point near Sandringham 1890
Oil on canvas
31 × 76.7 cm
Inscriptions. Recto: l.r. "Chas. Conder, 1890"
Backed
Purchased 1951
2909.4

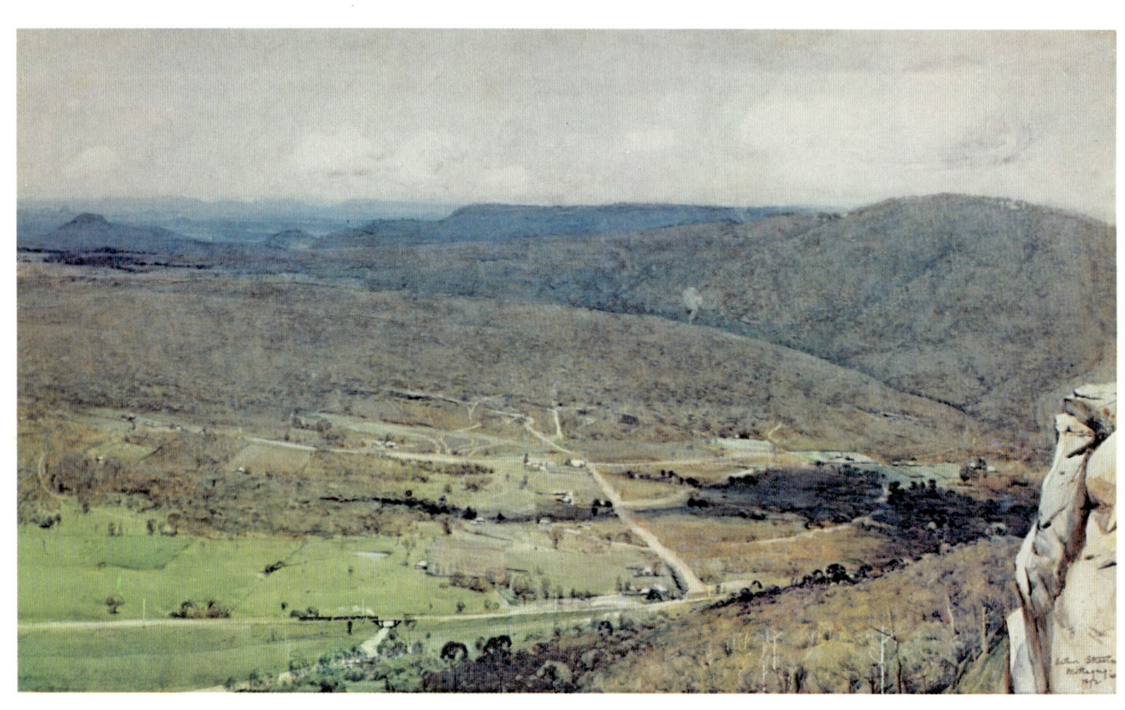

Plate **X**
Sir Arthur Streeton
Australian, 1867–1943
The Vale of Mittagong, N.S.W. 1892
Watercolour
56.5 × 97 cm
Inscriptions. Recto: l.r. ''Arthur Streeton Mittagong, N.S.W. 1892''
G. W. Booth Bequest 1961
913.5

19
Charles Conder
b. England, 1868–1909
Departure of the Orient—Circular Quay 1888
Oil on canvas
45.1 × 52.0 cm
Inscriptions. Recto: l.l. "Chas. Conder, Sydney, 1888"
Purchased 1888
Art Gallery of New South Wales, Sydney

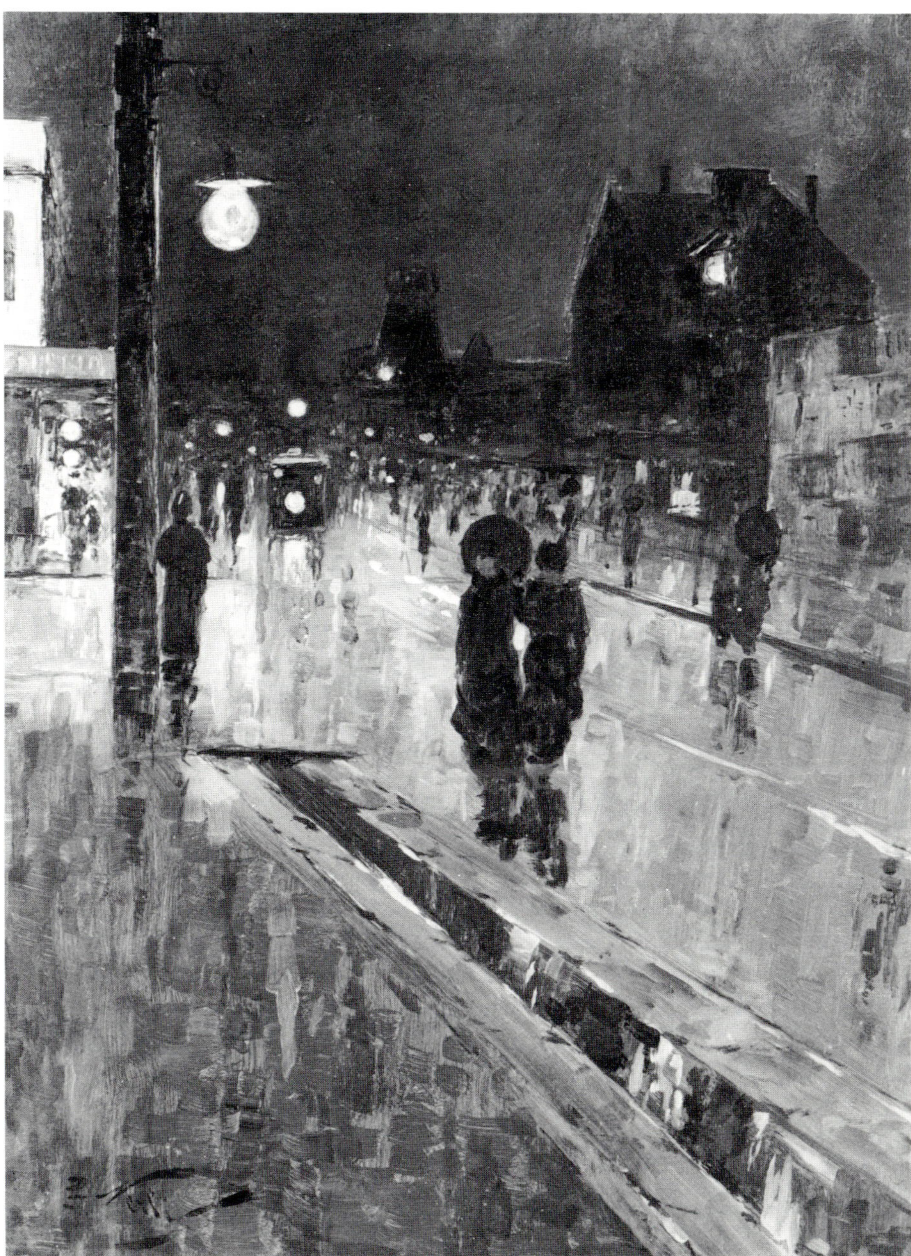

20
Girolamo B. Nerli
Australian, 1863–1926
Street Scene c. 1888
Oil on cardboard
31.1 × 23.2 cm
Inscriptions. Recto:
l.l. "G. Nerli"
Purchased 1951
2369.4

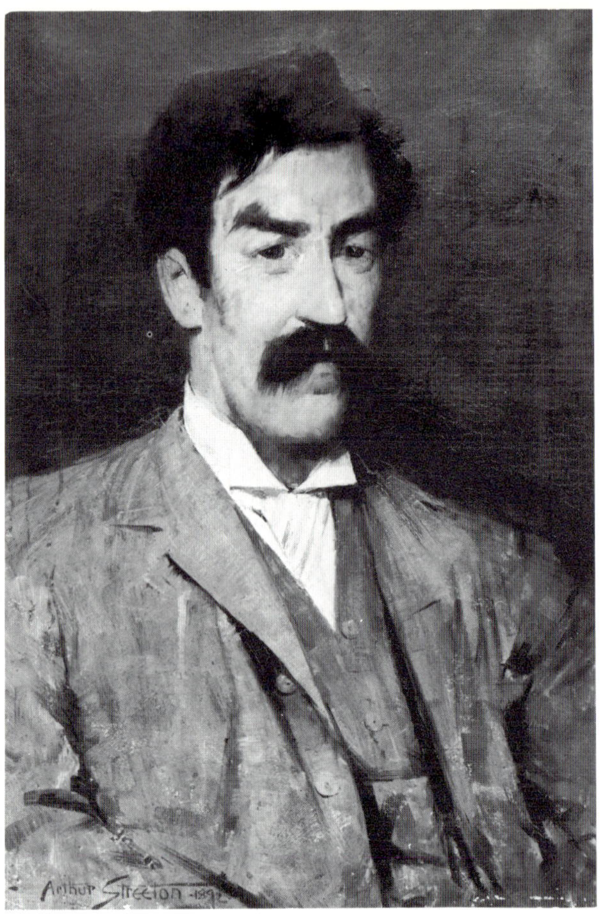

22
Sir Arthur Streeton
Australian, 1867–1943
**Portrait of G. W. L.
Marshall-Hall** 1892
Oil on canvas
76.2 × 51 cm
Inscriptions. Recto: l.l.
"Arthur Streeton 1892"
Bequeathed by Miss
Lorna Stirling through
the National Gallery
Society, 1956
1615.5

and the land are synonymous. It was not lack of ability that made him turn from figure painting or portraiture, as the immediacy of his portrait of G. W. L. Marshall-Hall 1892 **(22)** attests.

"This afternoon second sitting from G. W. L. Marshall-Hall. He's a fine chap and full of fun, gurgles away and the whole bally room shakes—splendid, very easy to stir him up. Remind him of some good joke or tell a story and the blankety roof nearly comes off."

Certainly Streeton captured something of that remarkable personality. But Streeton turned deliberately to the landscape. The early sensitive sketches like **The Clearing Gembrook** 1888 **(23)** inspired by Roberts's impressionism are followed by the great paintings of the 1890s in New South Wales. The fine series of Sydney Harbour painted after he settled with Roberts at Curlew Camp in 1891 are climaxed by three masterpieces painted on the Hawkesbury River 1895–6, the most famous of which is **The Purple Noon's Transparent Might** in the National Gallery of Victoria. The painting here illustrated, **Grey Day on the Hawkesbury River** 1896 **(24),** is the most subtly poetic in its restrained use of closely related tones and colours. There is even a hint of Whistlerian

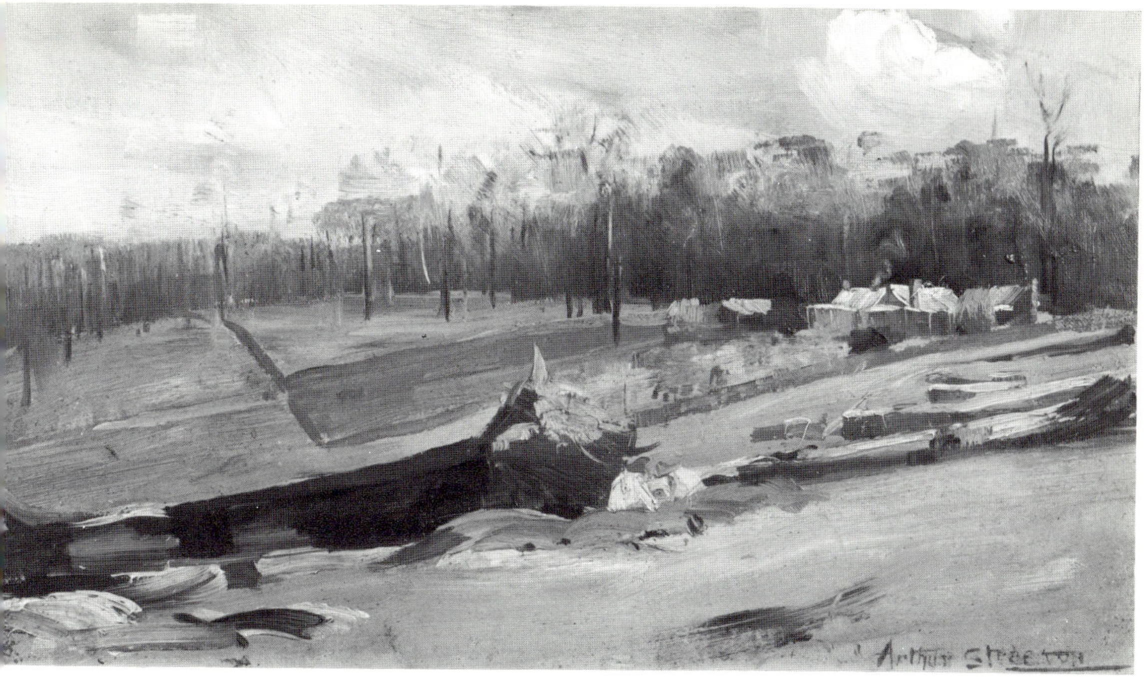

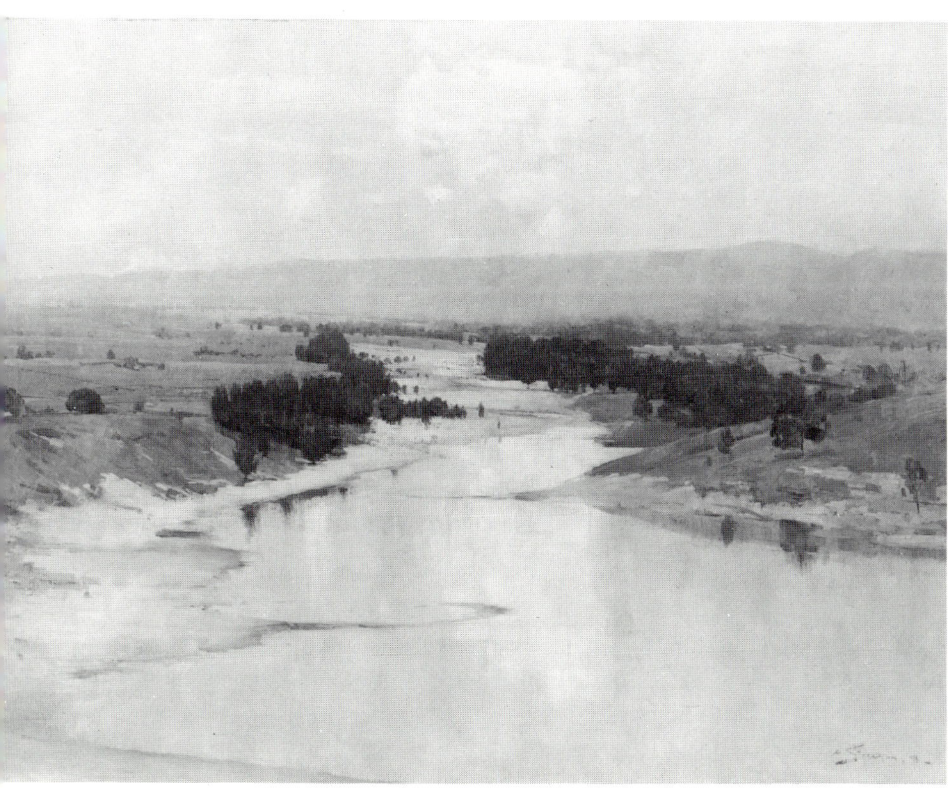

23
Sir Arthur Streeton
Australian, 1867–1943
**The Clearing,
Gembrook** 1888
Oil on canvas
25.4 × 45.7 cm
Inscriptions. Recto:
l.l. "1888"
u.c. Incised words
(indistinct)
l.r. "Arthur Streeton"
Backed
Felton Bequest 1952
1132.4

24
Sir Arthur Streeton
Australian, 1867–1943
**Grey Day on the
Hawkesbury River**
1896
Oil on canvas
61.5 × 181.5 cm
Inscriptions. Recto: l.r.
"A. Streeton, '96"
The Jack Manton
Collection on loan

aestheticism in its simplicity. Nevertheless, painted out of doors, in accord with impressionist dogma, using a square headed brush to avoid distracting detail, it shows Streeton's remarkable powers of acute observation and painterly expression fully extended. Perhaps the vivid small studies with their suggestions of sunlight, heat, air, winds, moving shadows all in flux have more immediate appeal. But it is in these great full scale paintings that Streeton expressed his original heroic vision of the Australian landscape as pure and paradisial. No Australian has yet equalled Streeton in his mastery of vast panoramic distances in aerial perspective, seen from a bird's eye view gained from the vantage point of a mountain overlooking a valley. Witness this same ability in the remarkable watercolour of 1892, **Vale of Mittagong (Plate X).**

"Have been 4 or 5 days on a picture from the summit of a huge precipice called the 'Gib' (Gibraltar). This picture I wish to make chiefly remarkable for its delicate colouring, and to that end have climbed the aforesaid rock (400 or 500 feetage) 5 times and down again, after a walk of $1\frac{3}{4}$ miles from the township. However, have done my best, and have, I think already made the picture. Much my best commencement for a picture in water colour paints. Mittagong is beautifully surrounded by high and rocky hills."

Thus wrote Streeton to "Dear Bulldog" from the Commercial Hotel, Mittagong, Wednesday, 1892. Only in an age of optimism, in a period of expansion, when the world seemed good and fair to look upon, would a man conceive such paintings. Only in youth would he have the physical stamina and boundless confidence to undertake their portrayal out of doors directly from nature, their source. In a letter to Roberts, Streeton admirably described the ambition which he turned into art of a high and valid order.

"I picture in my head the Murray and all the wonder and glory at its source up towards Kosciusko and the great gold plains; and all the beautiful inland Australia, and I love the thought of walking into all this and trying to expand and express it in my way. I fancy large canvases all glowing and moving in the happy light, and others bright, decorative and chalky and expressive of the hot trying winds and the slow immense summer!"

These paintings are representational but not photographic in any derogatory sense. They are based on a keen eyed romantic observation of the real world and display an intense visual acuity, sustained at this period by the poetry and enthusiasm which had blossomed at the never to be forgotten camp at **Eaglemont near Heidelberg (10).**

"I sit on our hill of gold on the north side; the wind seems sunburnt and fiery as it runs through my beard. Yes rather, see, look here; northeast the very long divide is beautiful, warm blue, far, far away, all dreaming and remote . . . Yes, I sit here in the upper circle surrounded by copper and gold and smile joy under my fly net as all the light, glory and quivering brightness passes slowly and freely before my eyes . . . Oh that I could roll some up—as a present. Oh, I'll try."

In the years between 1885 and 1900, Streeton tried and succeeded and these "presents" which he and his colleagues painted are now our heritage.

In this period of artistic awakening, many gifted painters became associated with these four key artists, and shared their impressionist aims and attitudes. Clara Southern, Tom Humphrey, Jane Price, John Ford Paterson, Jane Sutherland, E. Phillips Fox and others produced fine works. Two outstanding contemporaries were David Davies 1862–1930 and Walter Withers 1854–1914.

Walter Withers, an English-born painter who had trained before arriving in Australia in 1882, though not an initial and central member of the Heidelberg School, was very close to the movement, having spent much of 1889 with Roberts, Streeton and Conder at the Eaglemont camp. In 1890 he set up a second painting camp at the old house, "Charterisville", not far from Eaglemont camp, and it was from these two centres that impressionist practice was widely and rapidly disseminated into the Australian artistic community. His **Bright Winter's Morn** 1894 **(Plate XI)** is extremely impressionist. Its high-keyed colour, its avoidance of linear definition in its attempt to capture the general impression of the country-side caught in a net of sunlight modified by the misty atmosphere, had its counterparts in the French impressionists. However, the choice of subject is reminiscent still of Louis Buvelot who was an early influence on Withers, and that inspiration is even more closely recalled in his painting **Tranquil Winter** 1895 **(25).** This was painted at Heidelberg and reveals an inclination more towards tonal painting quite avoiding the trembling divisionist suggestions of pure colour that are approached in **Bright Winter's Morn.** However, both are works of the highest calibre which represent Withers at the height of his power. Though Withers painted many pictures of felicity and charm, it is in a few such pictures that he approached the force, inventiveness, and sustained creative vision of Roberts and Streeton, his Heidelberg colleagues.

David Davies was born at Ballarat and studied at the National Gallery School, Melbourne. Therefore it is surprising that he has been somewhat overlooked. This is probably due to the fact that he departed for Europe in 1897, not returning to this country or painting Australian subjects from that time. However, between 1893 and 1896 he lived at Templestowe where he painted the wonderful

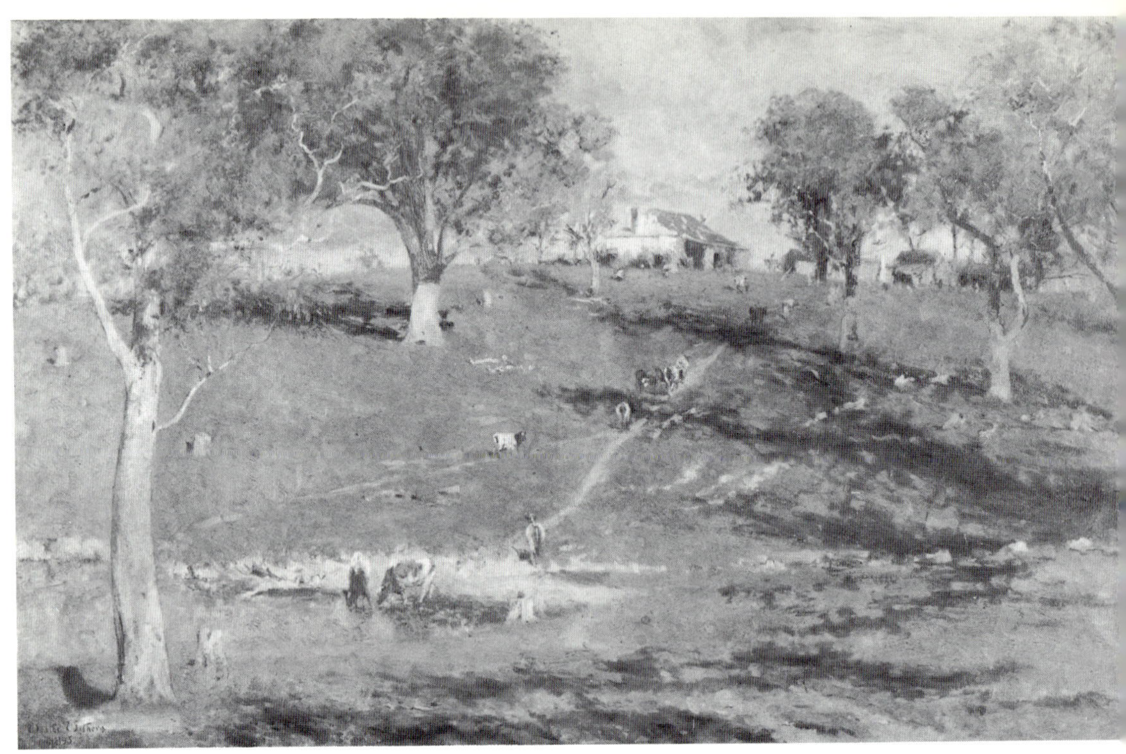

atmospheric **Moonrise** 1894 (**Plate XII**) with its most subtle gradations of gold greys, warm mauves and pink dusted skies. It is a most evocative and poetic rendering of the land caught between waking and sleeping, bewitched by the rising moon. This masterwork of Davies ranks with any produced by the Australian impressionists, and indeed it can be exhibited without apology among works of the French school. As in the work of Withers, it may be noted that **Golden Summer** of 1888 (**26**) is more a tonal study close to his training under Folingsby at the National Gallery School. It is a picture of monumental stillness, and the broad treatment of the foliage of the gums and of the distant hills is based on a true awareness of the modification of local colour in strong sunlight. The choice of subject with the bullock wagon and driver moving slowly towards the horizon under the fierce heat of the directly overhead sun puts one in mind of the Roberts's and McCubbin's history pictures of the pioneer outback. Walter Withers and David Davies shared an essentially romantic conception of nature and often chose the symbolic evocative hours of dawn and dusk to paint their soft-hued pictures which are a special delight within the oeuvre of the Australian Impressionists.

To understand the growth of Australian Impressionism it must be remembered that it is essentially a nineteenth century movement. That period is characterized by an emphasis on experiment in the naturalistic portrayal of landscape. These artists shared with their French counterparts the choice of a high key, of subjects from everyday life, and an ambition to capture on canvas the fleeting beauty of the visible world. They preferred the subject found to be invented. Nevertheless their larger works are not entirely spontaneous, but based on careful compositional studies. What offended the accepted taste of the time was the "lack of finish"

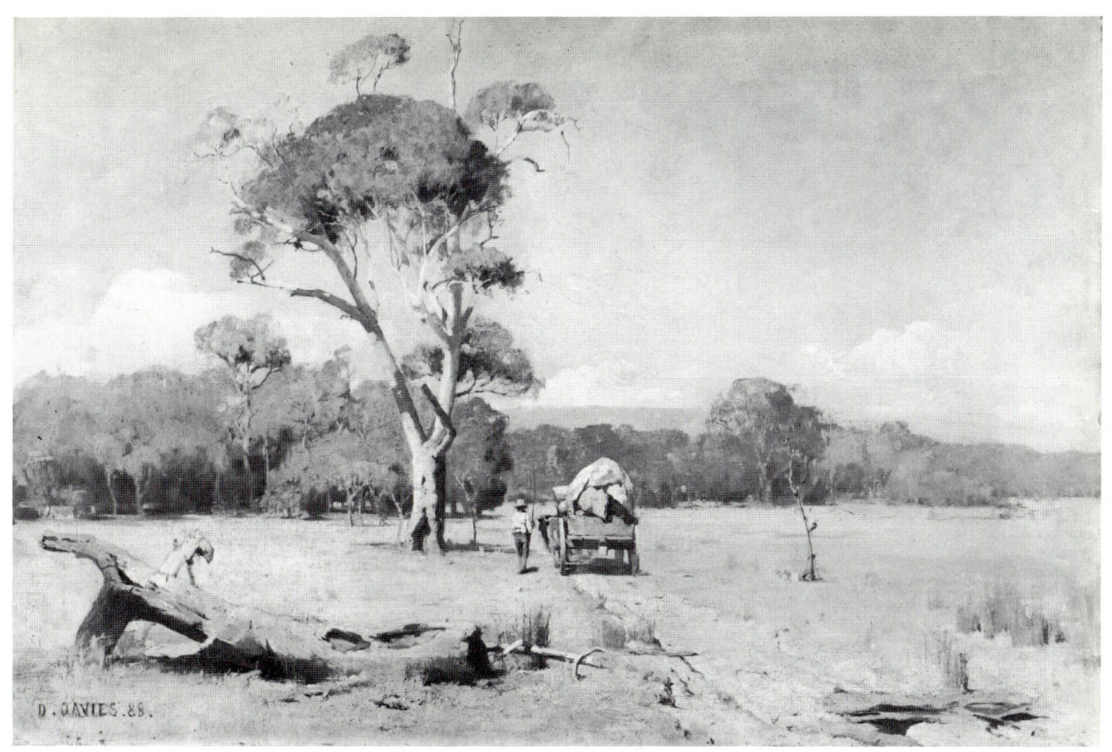

the "sketchy" nature of their work. The most admired painting at the Melbourne Great Exhibition of 1880 was Jules Lefebvre's **Chloe** which now resides at Young and Jackson's Hotel. The admiration for linear naturalism and explicit statement exemplified in that work was the norm of official taste. Despite their neglect and poverty in their youth, the impressionists were probably the last happy school of painters—only McCubbin portraying some melancholy aspects of the bush. Their impressionism took fire in a nationalistic desire to create a distinctively Australian art. Yet their achievement must be judged within the framework of a tradition and an era. Impressionism is a late but integral segment of the development of the atmospheric realism of the French school of naturalism. In the use of this idiom the Australian artists shared with their French and British counterparts philosophical and social attitudes of the second half of the nineteenth century. They paint a picture of the bourgeois good life, of a stable society in a perfectible world, wherein the middle classes enjoy their leisure. Witness the series of paintings of the beach where well dressed folk disport themselves at picnic. It may be thought that the long summers of Australia, the accessibility of its innumerable fine beaches alone prompted these pictures. But the steam railway had introduced European city dwellers to the delights of the seashore, and artists painted its pleasures, rather than the grandeur and peril of the sea, or the labours of humble fisherfolk and mariners. One need only recall the paintings of the Frenchman Boudin (1824–98), the Englishman William Dyce (1806–64), the Scotsman McTaggart (1835–1910) to perceive the shared appeal of this subject to artists of the time.

Artists of the later nineteenth century had a compulsion to record the life of their times, more often its pleasing aspects, though Degas (1834–1917) and

26
David Davies
Australian, 1862–1939
Golden Summer 1888
Oil on canvas
60.6 × 91.3 cm
Inscriptions. Recto: l.l.
"D. Davies '88"
Backed
Ex. Annual Exhibition
of National Gallery
of Victoria Art
School, 1888
Felton Bequest 1937
414.4

Courbet (1819–77) could be scarifying. Compare the paintings of Renoir (1841–1919), Tissot (1836–1902), Bertha Morisot (1841–95), Pissarro (1831–1903) with Roberts's **Coming South** and **Bourke Street;** Conder's **Ricketts Point near Sandringham** and **Departure of the Orient, Circular Quay.** These pictures of everyday life are a late inheritance from the tradition of Dutch genre pictures of the seventeenth century. The universality of this subject matter's interest is clearly revealed in the comparison just made. Tom Roberts persisted in recording the mundane life of his times on an historic scale, **Shearing the Rams, The Breakaway, Bailed Up,** despite the admonitions of the critics to seek nobler subjects, as did his contemporary, the American Thomas Eakins (1844–1916).

In the landscape painting of the Australian Impressionists their attitude to nature has a Wordsworthian pantheistic sentiment. Perhaps the decay of religious dogmatism underlies the acceptance of a mystique of nature as the new eternal verity, the fount and origin of truth and beauty. Theirs is a sentimental and literary society rather than intellectual. In their converse and their correspondence they quote tags from Shelley and Keats. They give their paintings romantic titles: Streeton, **The Purple Noon's Transparent Might;** Roberts, **Evening When the Quiet East Flushes Faintly at the Sun's Last Look.** It is an art of realism and idealism. It rests poised on acute visual observation of the tangible world portrayed with increasing exactness of tone and colour and a vision of romanticized ideal nature. The style of portrayal also is dual, drawing its naturalistic quality from impressionism, and its decorative quality from the Orient and the aestheticism of Whistler, Conder alone enlivened this mode with wit and natural sophistication. Though their art is not unique, drawing its origins from sources of European tradition, their achievement in founding a distinctively Australian school cannot be minimized. Native born, or in this country from youth, they forged a new visual convention capable of interpreting in artistic terms the original qualities of this country.

Like the flowering summer landscapes they painted, the Heidelberg School came quickly to bloom, and then faded. By 1909 Conder was dead, having won a permanent niche in European art as a symbolist. McCubbin died in 1916; the late years of his life glowing with the most luminous pictures he painted. Roberts and Streeton lived to earn public fame and honour. But after their sojourn in Europe, neither recaptured the vivid directness of their early Australian work. The efflorescence of the Heidelberg School was in the 1880s and '90s, the time to which they all looked back in nostalgia, as the years drew them apart.

In 1890, Conder just arrived in Paris wrote to Roberts:

"Nothing can exceed the pleasures of that last summer, when I fancy all of us lost the 'Ego' somewhat of our natures in looking at what was Nature's best art and ideality, give me one summer again with yourself and Streeton—the same long evenings, songs, dirty plates, and last, pink skies. But these things don't happen, do they? And what's gone is over."

While Streeton, lonely in London in 1902, recalled the days of their youth when the Heidelberg School was born.

"I never forget . . . our happy summer evenings at Mentone and Box Hill. Lord, how far back it all seems, yet how clear—every detail and trifle ingrained in my brain for life—the Houstens, the creek, the horehound patch, the black wattle, the messmate, the long open space up to the road, the hurrying up the hill on Sunday evenings with Proff. well to the fore; Heidelberg, the she-oak and sienna dust over all; the straw-brown hills; pale Dandenongs; the Old England; College tennis pines and coppery light; hazels, japonica; Impressionist Exhibition; gorse up the drive; girls; the picnics in the twilight and all the loveliness—all a dream!"

(1968)

1851	Gold Rush Begins
1855	Fred McCubbin (1855–1917), born Victoria
1856	Tom Roberts (1856–1931), born England
1860	Burke and Wills Expedition leaves Melbourne
1865	Louis Buvelot (1814–88), arrives Melbourne
1867	Arthur Streeton (1867–1943), born Victoria
1868	Charles Conder (1868–1909), born England
1869	Roberts arrives Melbourne
1871	**Coleraine and a Waterpool,** by Buvelot
1872	Transcontinental Telegraph to Europe Opens
1874	Monet, Renoir, Sisley, Pissarro, Degas, etc. hold first Impressionist Exhibition, Paris
1875	Roberts joins National Gallery School, Melbourne
1878	Conrad Martens (1801–78), dies Sydney Julian Ashton (1851–1942) arrives Melbourne
1880	Exhibition Building, Melbourne opens Ned Kelly sentenced to death S. T. Gill (1818–80), dies Melbourne
1881	Roberts leaves to study in England
1882	Walter Withers (1854–1914) arrives Melbourne
1883	Roberts meets artists Barrau and Casas in Spain
1884	Conder arrives Sydney
1885	Roberts returns to Melbourne Painting camp set up at Housten's Farm, Box Hill **Bourke Street** by Roberts
1886	Painting camp set up at Mentone Streeton meets Roberts Girolamo Nerli (1863–1926), arrives Melbourne **Coming South** by Roberts **The Artists Camp** by Roberts **The Lost Child** by McCubbin
1887	Queen Victoria's Jubilee **The Sunny South** by Roberts Conder meets Roberts

1888 Australia 1788–1888, Centennial Celebrations
     Buvelot dies, Melbourne
     Street Scene on a Rainy Night by Nerli
     North Head, Sydney Harbour by Ashton
     Cove on the Hawkesbury by Conder
     Departure of the Orient by Conder
     The Clearing, Gembrook by Streeton
     Golden Summer by Davies
     Painting camp set up at Eaglemont
1889 The 9″ x 5″ Exhibition of Impressions opens, at Melbourne
     Sketch Portrait by Conder
1890 **Eaglemont near Heidelberg** by Streeton
     Ricketts Point near Sandringham by Conder
     Shearing the Rams by Roberts
     Conder leaves for Europe, April 26
     Withers founds the "Charterisville" painting camp
1891 Collapse of the "Boom". Industrial Unrest
     The Curlew Camp set up at Sirius Cove, Mosman
     The Breakaway by Roberts
1892 Discovery of Gold at Coolgardie
     Vale of Mittagong by Streeton
     G. W. L. Marshall-Hall by Streeton
1893 **Redfern Station** by Streeton
1894 **Moonrise, Templestowe** by Davies
     A Bright Winter's Morn by Withers
1895 **Tranquil Winter** by Withers
     Bailed Up by Roberts
1896 **Grey Day on the Hawkesbury River** by Streeton
1897 Davies leaves for Europe
     A Winter Evening by McCubbin
1898 Streeton leaves for Europe
1901 Foundation of the Commonwealth of Australia
     Roberts goes to London
1904 **The Pioneer** by McCubbin
1909 Conder dies, London
1914 World War I
     Withers dies, Melbourne
1916 **Autumn Morning, South Yarra** by McCubbin
1917 McCubbin dies, Melbourne
1918 Armistice   43

27
Fred. McCubbin
Australian, 1855–1917
The Lost Child 1886
Oil on canvas
114.3 × 72.4 cm
Inscriptions. Recto: l.l. "F. McCubbin 1886"
Ex. no. 30 "Lost" V.A.S. Summer Ex., 1887
Felton Bequest 1940
1077.4

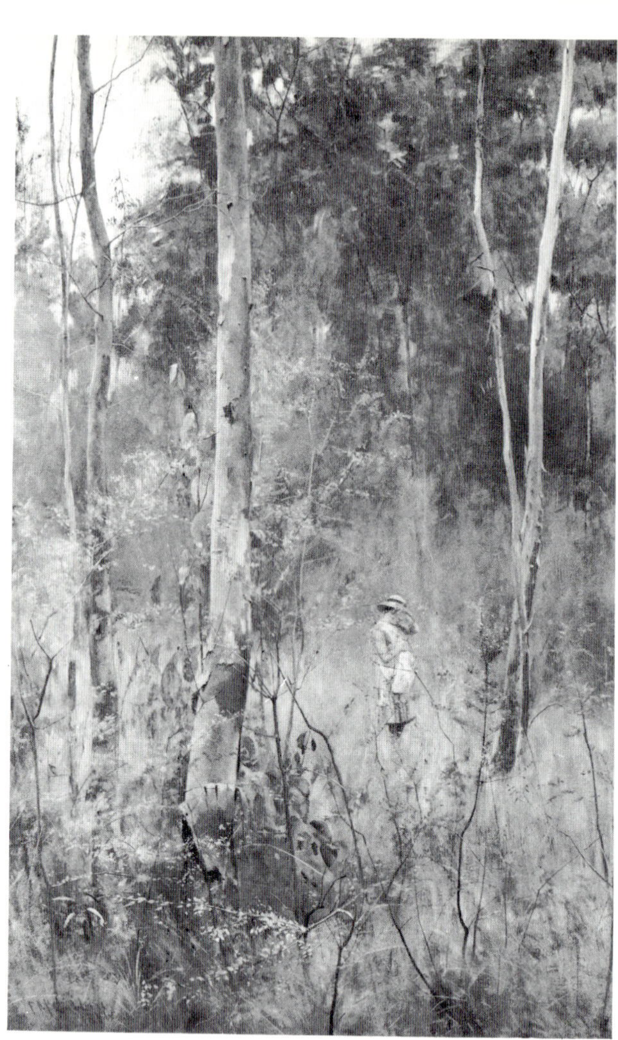

28—refers **Plate XIII**
(photograph)
Family Party at Fern Tree Gully
In the back of her Mercedes, driven by
chauffeur Theophile Paris, sits Mrs Louis
Abrahams beside her brother-in-law Henry.
Her daughter, Ruby, is sitting on the
running board and her niece, Alice,
daughter of Lawrence Abrahams, is beside
the chauffeur.

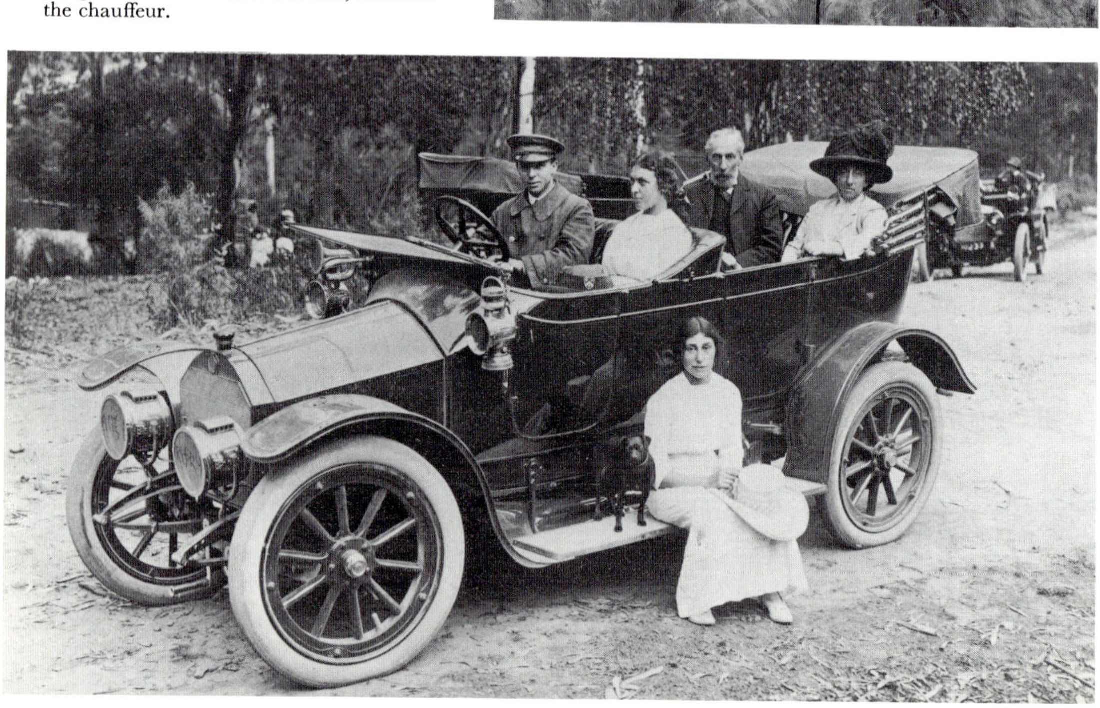

27
Fred McCubbin, Australian, 1855–1917
The Lost Child. 1886
Fred McCubbin was one of the earliest students of the Melbourne National
Gallery School. He became a major figure in the emerging school of Australian
landscape painters, and was the first native born artist to discover the lyrical
quality of the wooded foothills. He never ceased to extend his art, which ranges
from low-keyed narrative compositions in a realist manner to landscapes of
sparkling texture and romantic colour.

The Lost Child belongs to the earlier phase of his work. It was painted at
Box Hill where McCubbin and Roberts founded the first painting camp for
Victorian artists. The delicate blue-grey of the scrub is sensitively portrayed,
and the peeling bark of the foreground gum is enhanced by elegant drawing.
McCubbin chose to paint the bush close up, as though he were enveloped by it,
rather than at a distance. In this natural setting he posed the figure of the lost
child, a literary motif symbolizing the quiet and loneliness of the bush.

A.P.
(1961)

Plate XIII
28
Tom Roberts, b. England, 1856–1931
Portrait of Mrs Louis Abrahams in a Black Dress. 1888
Portrait of Mrs Louis Abrahams in a Black Dress (Plate XIII) shows Tom
Roberts's understanding of the Aesthetic Movement and Japonisme. These art
styles were inspired by oriental works of art and curios which were widely admired
and collected in the second half of the nineteenth century. Following Commodore
Perry's visit to Japan in the 1850s, Japanese works of art were exported to Europe
and gained wide popularity through the Great Exhibitions in London and Paris.
They were studied and collected by artists like James McNeil Whistler and
James Tissot, who both influenced Tom Roberts.

Painted in silvery grey tones, the black dress and subdued colours of this
portrait are relieved by touches of red and yellow in furniture and flowers.
These colours, and the attitude of the sitter, placed to one side of the closed
composition, are close to Whistler's portrait compositions which Roberts would
have seen when in England and France, (1881–5), and later, as illustrations
in Australia.

The subject of this intimate portrait is Golda Brasch about the time of her
marriage to Louis Abrahams. Surrounded by fashionable oriental objects, she

is seated in an Eastern bamboo chair, in a room draped in grey muslin with a fur rug—an exotic aesthetic interior of the 1880s.

Louis Abrahams was Tom Roberts's friend and one of the artists at the Box Hill camp set up in 1885. He married Golda Figa Brasch in Sydney on 21 March, 1888. It is likely Tom Roberts painted this portrait as a wedding present, for the marriage certificate shows he was a witness to the ceremony. Louis Abrahams is listed on the certificate as a cigar manufacturer of Carlton. He abandoned his artistic career to manage his family business. In this he was successful, but he died in 1903. This painting is probably the **Portrait of Mrs. L. A. Abrahams,** no. 31 in the November exhibition of the Victorian Artists' Society, 1888, and also the picture **Interior with Figure** by Tom Roberts, sold in the 1918 auction of the paintings from the estate of Louis Abrahams.

On the same visit to Sydney when he witnessed Louis Abrahams's and Golda Brasch's marriage, Tom Roberts was painting with Charles Conder. Conder was to become devoted to aesthetic and symbolist art, and in the work of both artists at this time, apart from the depiction of oriental objects, can be seen elements of Chinese and Japanese art. In the portrait of Golda Abrahams, the light falling on separate objects is of the kind seen in European academic painting but the flat areas of colour with solid outline, the vertical composition with the figure placed high within it against a flat background, and the fine sketchy brush strokes on reeds and grasses all owe their origin to the arts of China and Japan.

B.F. and J.P.
(1975)

Footnote: photograph (**28**) shows Mrs Louis Abrahams, seated in the back of her Mercedes, which establishes the identity of the portrait by Tom Roberts.

29
Sir William Rothenstein, English, 1872–1945
Portrait of Charles Conder.
The National Gallery of Victoria has the most important public collection of Charles Conder's Australian pictures, together with a painting from his visit to Spain in 1905, the superb **Blue Waters of Algeciras (30).** The Gallery also possesses extremely fine works by the English artist William Rothenstein: **Aliens at Prayer** 1905 and the self portrait **An Artist in France** 1917–18. Rothenstein and Conder were firm friends. Rothenstein met Conder in Paris and had his first exhibition with him at the Galerie Thomas, Paris, 1891. Henri de Vallombreuse from whose collection this work comes, was a friend of them both. When

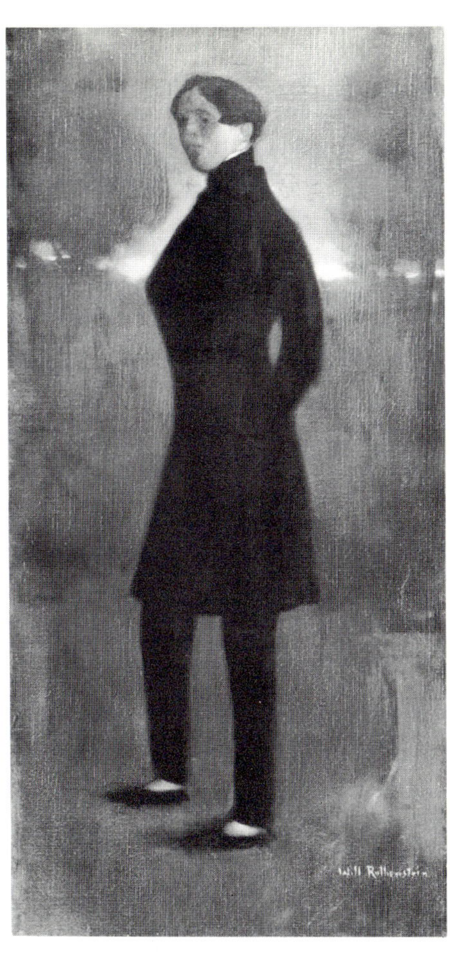

29
Sir William Rothenstein
English, 1872–1945
**Portrait of Charles
Conder**
Oil on canvas
64.9 × 31.9 cm
Inscriptions. Recto: l.r.
"Will Rothenstein"
Purchased 1966
1579.5

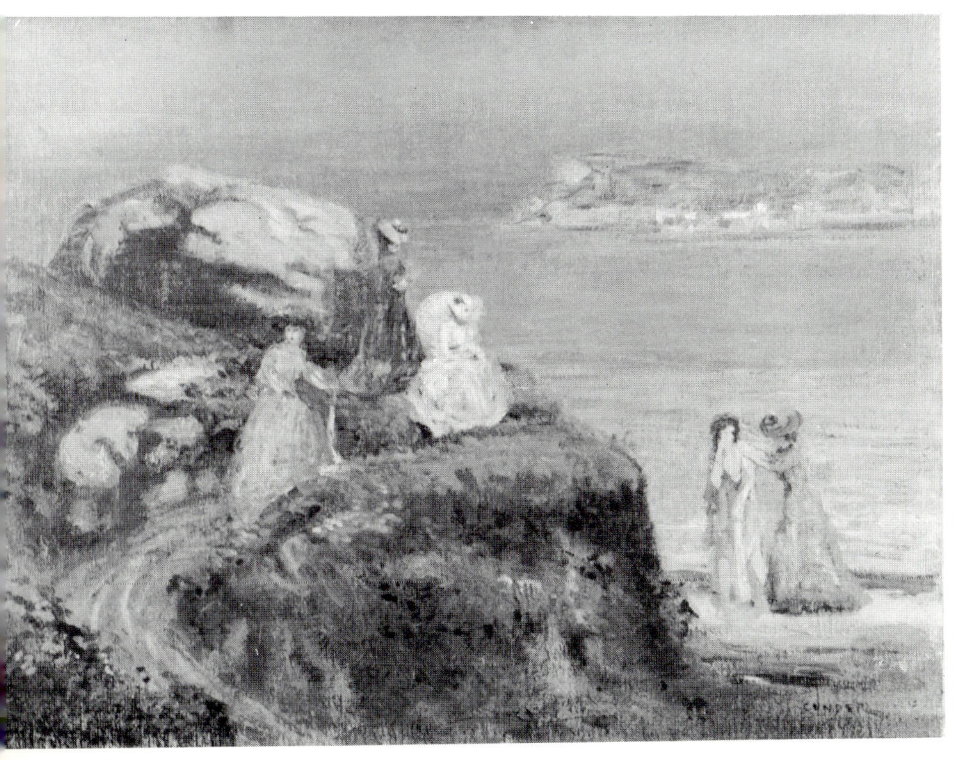

30
Charles Conder
b. England, 1868–1909
**Blue Waters of
Algeciras**
Oil on canvas
66.2 × 91.5 cm
Inscriptions. Recto:
l.r. "Conder"
Backed
Felton Bequest 1932
4669.3

Conder fell ill in Paris at the end of 1891 it was Vallombreuse who invited him to spend a few months on his estate near Mustapha, Algiers. Many letters to Rothenstein survive from that visit, some being quoted in John Rothenstein's book *The Life and Death of Conder*. In the catalogue of that volume is recorded a painting in the collection of Sir Charles Biron **White Cliffs of Dieppe** with an inscription "Souvenir from Charles Conder September 1891 to H. de Vallombreuse". Again in the collection of Sir Edmund Davis is recorded a painting **Composition** inscribed "A Mon ami de Vallombreuse—Souvenir de Chas. Conder Mars '92". Innumerable drawings, sketches, and a self portrait were inscribed by Conder to Will Rothenstein "Souvenir de notre longue amitie".

The personal associations of this portrait, the relationship of sitter, artist and owner make the inclusion of the painting in the Gallery's collection extremely interesting. A collection cannot be judged only by its masterworks. This painting is somewhat outside Rothenstein's typical manner. The compositional debt to "Japonisme" is a tribute to Conder's later decorative style and the evocative misty landscape setting to the romanticism of his work. Superb examples of this early flowering of Conder's European style were painted during his stay with Henri de Vallombreuse. Another portrait of Conder, by William Rothenstein in 1896, reflecting similar interest in its vertical form and composition, is in the Musée du Jeu de Paume, Paris. It is reproduced in John Rothenstein's book, *Life and Death of Conder*.

(1966)

31

Aby Altson, b. England, 1867–c. 1930

Contemplation. 1896

Although the collection of the National Gallery of Victoria holds a number of works by the artist Aby Altson, very little reliable information about his life is available. Born in Middlesborough, England, in 1867, he arrived and settled in Melbourne in the early 1880s. He was followed a few years later by his brother, Meyer Daniel Altson, who established himself as a portraitist and etcher before returning to Europe. Living with relatives at St Kilda and working in a tannery, Aby maintained an active interest in drawing and sketching. He showed his work to George Folingsby, painting master at the Melbourne National Gallery School (1882–91), and commenced taking lessons at the Gallery School for two nights a week with his uncle's approval. He later started painting full-time and attended the painting classes from 1887–90. Recognition came as early as 1886 when the Melbourne *Argus* on 11 March, reported that he had been awarded an honourable mention for still life composition in the art students' annual

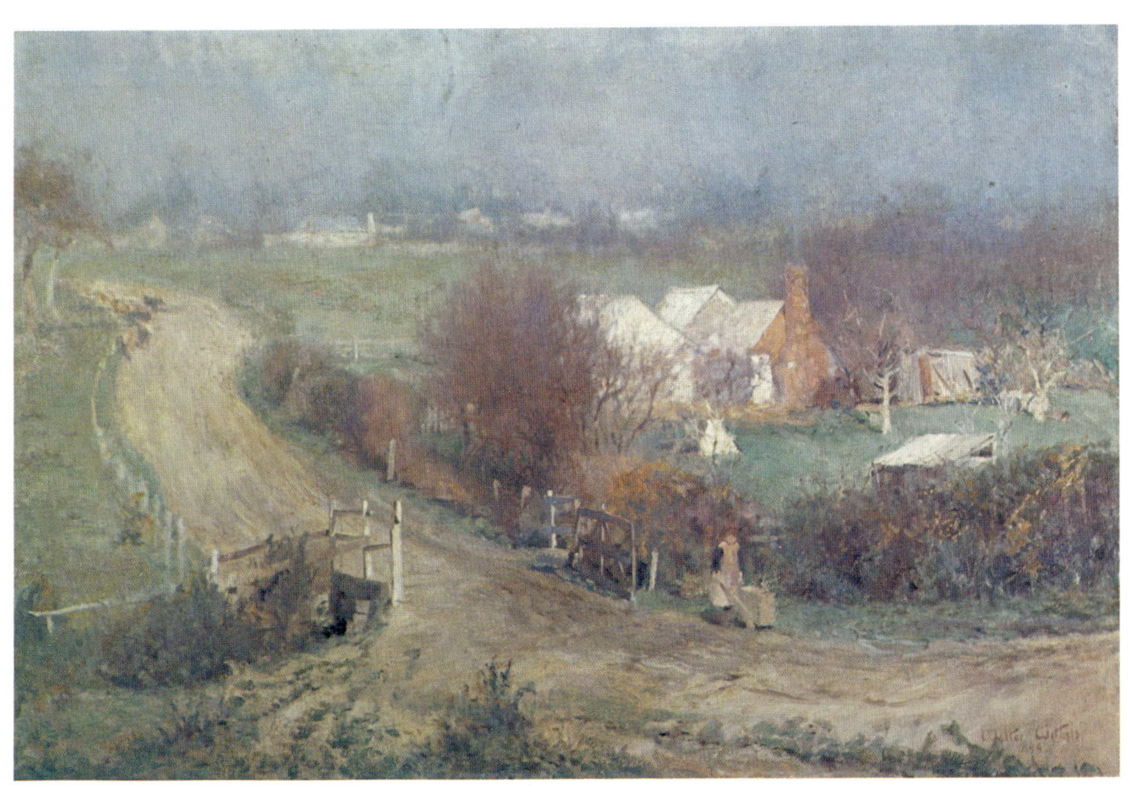

Plate **XI**
Walter Withers
b. England, 1854–1914
A Bright Winter's Morn 1894
Oil on canvas
60.5 × 91.2 cm
Inscriptions. Recto: l.r. "Walter Withers 1894"
Bequest of Mrs Nina Sheppard 1956
3389.4

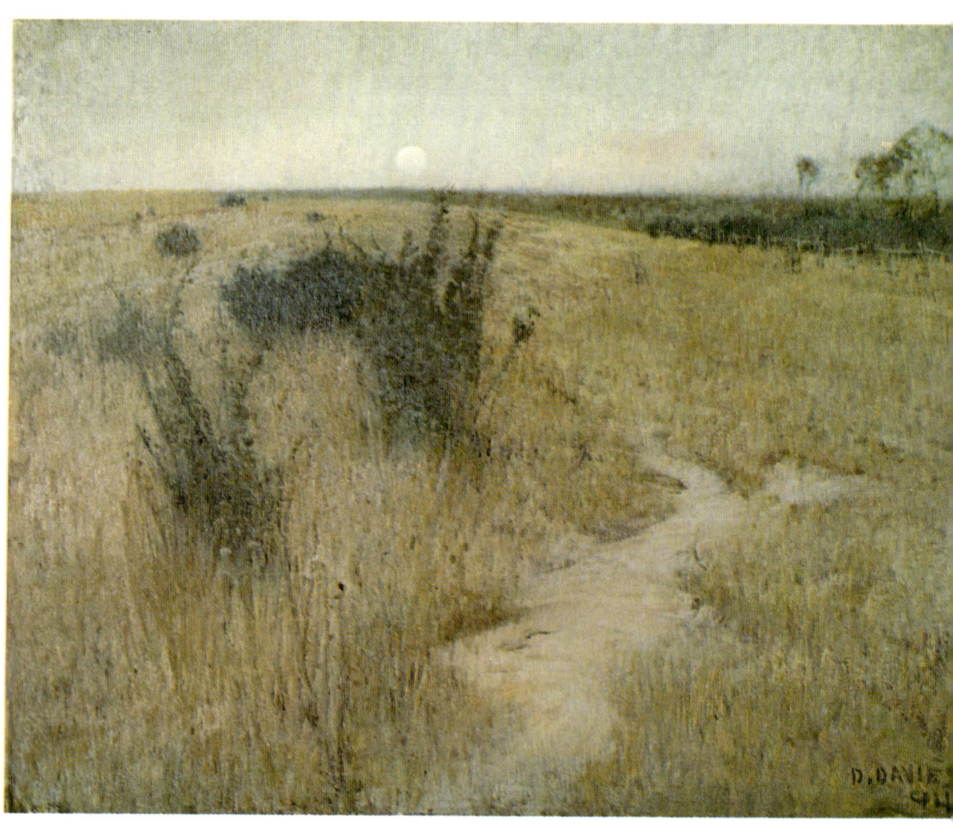

Plate **XII**
David Davies
Australian, 1862–1935
Moonrise, Templestowe 1894
Oil on canvas
118.1 × 148.2 cm
Inscriptions. Recto: l.r. ''D. Davies '94''
First exhibited Victorian Artists' Society Annual Exhibition, 1894
Purchased 1895
p.402.1

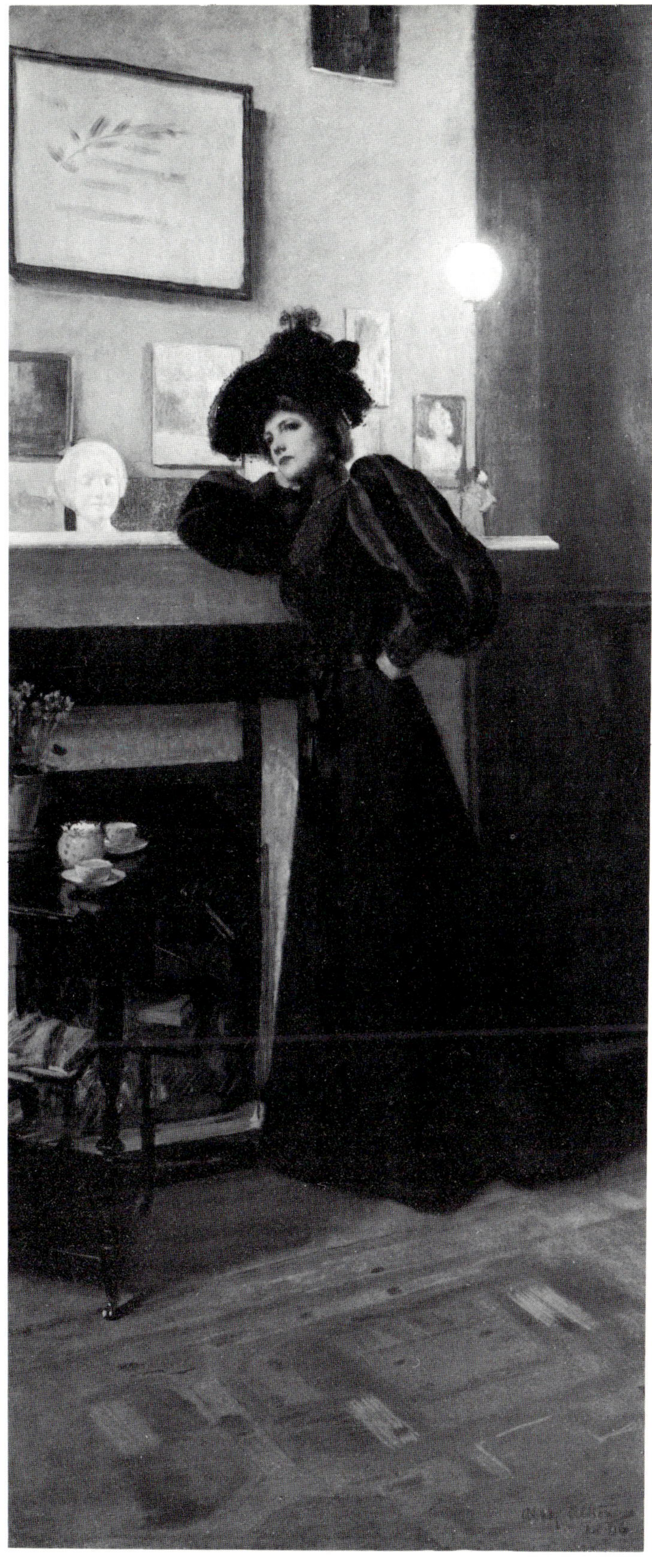

31
Aby Altson
b. England, 1864–??
Contemplation 1896
Oil on canvas
99.5 × 44.7 cm
Inscriptions. Recto: l.r.
"Abbey Altson, 1896"
Purchased 1971
A16/1971

49

exhibition at the National Gallery of Victoria. He was also awarded student prizes in 1887, 1888, 1889 and 1890. In 1890 he was later awarded the Travelling Scholarship and left Melbourne on 4 March 1891 on the steamer *Damascus* going directly to Paris. In Paris he worked at Julian's studio under Courtois, Blanc and Dagnan-Bouveret and exhibited at the Salon in 1892. He married an Englishwoman who was the model in **The Golden Age** (1893) a work which gained him a "Mention Honorable" at the Salon, Paris, and which was accepted by the Royal Academy, London in 1894. By 1894 his address was at Bedford Gardens, London, and in 1895 the Royal Academy accepted another painting by him, **Portrait of a Lady.** In 1895, the Trustees of the National Gallery of Victoria received and accepted **The Golden Age** as the third picture under the terms of the Travelling Scholarship and he also began exhibiting as a member of the Royal Society of British Artists in both the regular and the Winter Exhibitions. While in London he made contact with the Indian Prince Ranjitsinjji of Nawanagar who offered him the position of court painter. The advent of the Great War put an end to these plans and not until 1924 was the contact renewed. His wife died before he was finally able to leave for India in September 1924. He worked on portraits of a number of the ruling princes of the feudatory States and members of the royal family, as well as executing murals throughout the palace. In 1927 he returned to London where he painted the portraits of his uncle and aunt with whom he had lived at St Kilda. From England he emigrated to the United States of America and established himself with the dealers on 5th Avenue, New York. Information concerning the later years of Aby Altson's life is difficult to obtain and it is thought he died in the United States in his sixties or seventies. This *fin de siecle* portrait study **Contemplation** 1896, added to the collection in 1971, reveals the symbolist and intimist influences and trends that had so fascinated the times.

The pale-faced young lady in the black skirt, striped blue/black blouse and heavy black hat rests lost in thought against the mantel of the fireplace in the deep maroon-pink shadows of the plaster and panelled interior. The walls and mantel reveal the fashions and dreams of the time. On the wall a glowing pink gas light illuminates small oil sketches carefully arranged with oriental souvenirs. On the mantel rests more oil sketches, a small red Japanese doll figure and a bust of **L'inconnue de la Seine,** taken from the death mask of a young girl found drowned in the Seine. Completely unknown, she is said to have looked like Da Vinci's **Mona Lisa** with the same enigmatic smile. The bust was found in fashionable salons, residences and studios of the time. Red and green books, mauve cyclamen in a terracotta pot and blue and white china are carefully arranged on the dark wood trolley. The painterly not-quite-filled-in-quality, particularly of this area of the canvas, adds subtlety to the dream-like quality while at the same time strengthening the apparent firmness and reality of the rest of the composition/interior through the contrast of brushwork. A deep cherry parquetry floor is used to create a hard contrast with strong abstract pattern, that again subtly heightens the soft quality of reverie that seems to fill the interior and occupy the figure.

G.B. in N.G.S.B.
(March, 1974)

32
Amy May Vale, Australian, c. 1860–1940
Spring at Mayfield. 1890s
A relatively unknown Australian artist, May Vale was born in Ballarat, daughter of the Hon. W. M. K. Vale. As a girl she attended the South Kensington School in London. In Melbourne, she studied at the Gallery School from 1879 to 1889, and then in London where she enrolled at the Linton School under Sir James Linton P.R.I. and Henry J. Stock R.I. She also studied at Julian's in Paris for six months, under Lefebvre and Robert Fleury. Arriving back in Melbourne she began exhibiting at the Victorian Artists Society from 1892—her address in the 1890s was "Mayfield", Church Street, Abbotsford—and began to teach art. She moved to Sydney in 1899, and exhibited with the Royal Art Society of New South Wales. By 1906 she had returned to London to study enamelling at the Chelsea Polytechnic, and while there she married Alex Gilfillan on 20 August, 1908. From this study at the Chelsea Polytechnic, she combined her talents in the production of hand-painted enamelled brooches, some of which were exhibited in Sydney in 1919 at the Society of Artists' Exhibition.

Spring at Mayfield is certainly May Vale's finest work discovered to date, and in quality places her among the ranks of female artists such as Jane Sutherland, Clara Southern and Jane Price, who early this century were working in a similar intimate style.

This orchard scene of cascading white blossoms displays a delicate and skilful handling of the Heidelberg School impressionist techniques as interpreted by May Vale. According to a note on the original frame **Spring at Mayfield** was exhibited at the Australian Exhibition of Women's Work in Melbourne held at the Exhibition Building during October 1907. "Mayfield" was the name given to the old premises owned by Sir Francis Murphy on the Yarra, near Hoddle Street, Abbotsford.

F. McC in N.G.V.S.B.
(Jan/Feb 1972)

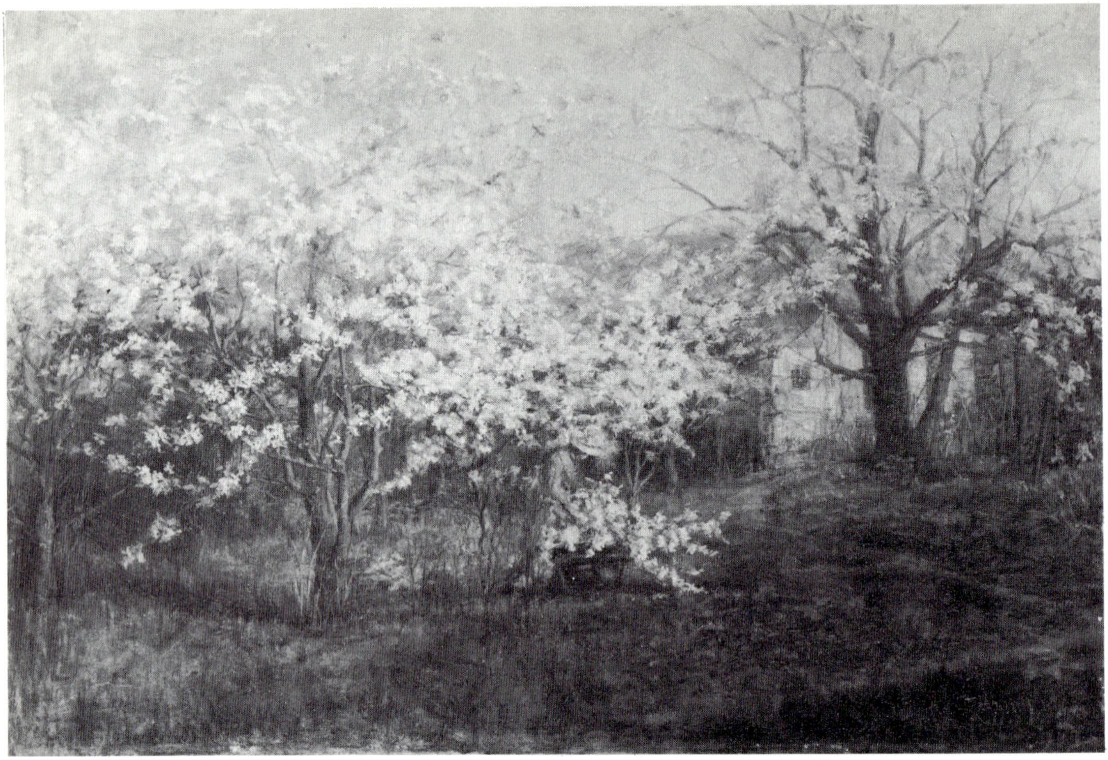

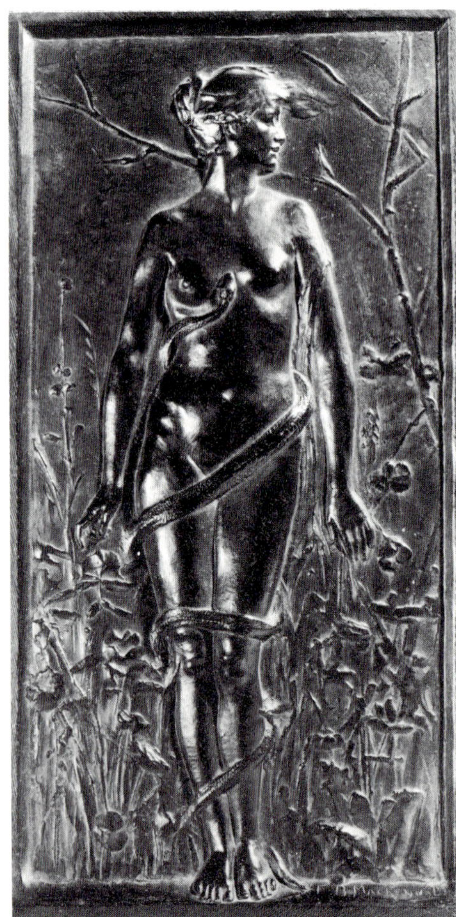

32
Amy May Vale
Australian, c. 1860–
1940
Spring at Mayfield
Oil on canvas
50.5 × 76 cm
Inscriptions. Recto:
l.r. "Vale" (?)
Verso: Label of
Australian Exhibition
of Women's Work in
Melbourne, October,
1907. Note on frame
in artist's hand reads
"Mayfield. The old
premises owned by
Sir Francis Murphy.
Reached by going
along Hoddle Street,
Abbotsford. It lies
across the River Yarra.
The old house has
since been pulled
down, the land sold
and three villas
erected on the site".
Purchased 1971
A5/1971

33
Sir Bertram Mackennal
Australian, 1863–1931
Eve
Bronze plaque
47 × 24.7 cm
Inscriptions. Recto: l.r.
"E. B. Mackennal"
Verso: foundry mark—
"E. Gruet jeune.
Fondeur 44 Avenue
de Chatillon—Paris"
Presented by Mrs D.
A. Chartres, 1969
127.6

33

Sir Bertram Mackennal, A.R.A., Australian, 1863–1931
Eve.
Sir Bertram Mackennal was the most distinguished Australian sculptor of the
Edwardian era. We own his famous marble bust of **Madame Melba,** 1899 and
Circe, 1893. This smaller work **Eve** is most helpful in showing his art nouveau—
and academic classicism—on a smaller scale.

(1969)

Footnote: Born in Melbourne in 1863, Mackennal studied sculpture under his
father, J. S. Mackennal, at the Gallery School in Melbourne, and in London in
1883, and met in Paris the French sculptor, Auguste Rodin, who instructed and
advised him. From 1888 to 1891, Mackennal was in Melbourne sculpting mainly
commissioned works.

Returning to Paris, his work was accepted for the French Salon, and in 1893
he received a "Mention Honorable". On the advice of the English sculptor
Alfred Gilbert, Mackennal moved to London. His successes at the Royal Academy
exhibitions, with art nouveau and symbolist works like **Circe,** established his
reputation, and sculptures executed by him were bought by the Tate Gallery,
London, in 1907 and 1908. He executed many public commissions, including a
memorial to Edward VII and the Eton War Memorial; he was elected to the
Royal Academy in 1909. He was acclaimed when he visited Australia in the
period 1926–7, and he died in Devon in 1931.

J.P.
(1976)

34

Sir John Longstaff, Australian, 1864–1941
**Arrival of Burke, Wills and King at the deserted camp at Cooper's
Creek, Sunday evening, April 21, 1861.** 1902–7
John Longstaff, the first Australian painter to receive the honour of a knighthood,
was born at Clunes, Victoria. Winning the first travelling scholarship from the
Melbourne Gallery School in 1887, he continued his studies in Paris. He won
fame as a painter of landscape, figure composition and particularly of portraits,
winning the Archibald prize on five occasions.

In the Commissioners' choice of subject matter, and its handling by Longstaff
on such an heroic scale, we see reflected the myth-making, the creation of national
heroes, which was a marked feature of Australia's growing self-awareness at the
time of Federation.

53

34
Sir John Longstaff
Australian, 1862–1941
**Arrival of Burke, Wills and King at the Deserted Camp
at Cooper's Creek, Sunday Evening, 21st April 1861,** 1902–7
Oil on canvas
282 × 429.2 cm
Inscriptions. Recto: 1.1. "J. Longstaff 1907" Commissioned by the Trustees
of the Public Library and National Gallery of Victora through
Gilbee Bequest. Gilbee Bequest
343.2

The Burke and Wills' exploring party left Melbourne on 20 August, 1860,
intending to cross the continent of Australia from south to north. The party
arrived at Cooper's Creek, in south-west Queensland, in December. Here Burke
instructed the main body of the expedition, under the leadership of Brahe, to
wait for three months, while he and three companions pushed forward to accom-
plish their tasks.

Burke, Wills, King and Gray reached the estuary of the Flinders River, in the
Gulf of Carpentaria, on 4 February, 1861. On the return journey Gray died.
After suffering incredible hardships, and in the last stage of exhaustion, Burke,
Wills and King returned to the camp at Cooper's Creek on the evening of Sunday,
21 April, to find that on the same morning the main body of the party, after
waiting eighteen weeks, had left the camp to return south.

The unfortunate explorers are depicted at the deserted camp. A small supply
of provisions and a letter had been left for them in a cache, and instructions for
finding these had been cut on the bark of a tree. Too prostrated to follow, Burke
and Wills died of starvation within a few weeks. King alone survived and lived
with some Aboriginals until rescued in September by a relief party.

C.C.
(September, 1959)

35
Max Meldrum, b. Scotland, 1875–1955
Picherit's Farm. 1910
36
Max Meldrum, b. Scotland, 1875–1955
Portrait of the Artist's Mother. 1913

Max Meldrum was born in Scotland in 1875 and came to Melbourne with his
parents at the age of fourteen. He studied at the National Gallery School under
Bernard Hall (1859–1935) who talked much of Velasquez and of tonal values.
Winning the Travelling Scholarship in 1899, Meldrum left for Paris, where,
independently, he studied the masterpieces in the Louvre. By concentrating on
the realist tradition of European art, he developed a theory of objective vision
and the paramount importance of tonal analysis. Returning to Australia in 1913,
he vigorously preached and practised his doctrines, which he outlined in a book
The Invariable Truths of Depictive Art (1917). The intense feeling aroused for and
against Meldrum the propagandist must not blind us to his work as an artist.

Picherit's Farm is an essay in tone. Briefly, tone is the range from light to
dark observable in any solid body irrespective of its colour. Here Meldrum aims
at scientific observation of the impersonal contrasts of light and dark. Nevertheless,

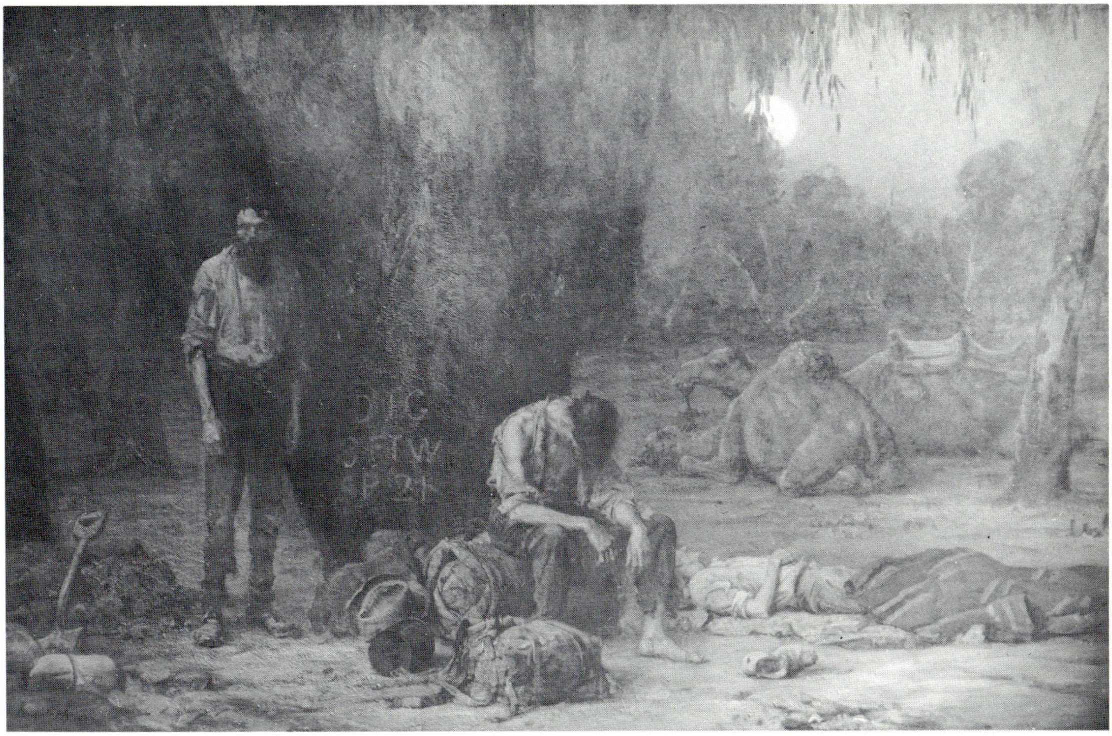

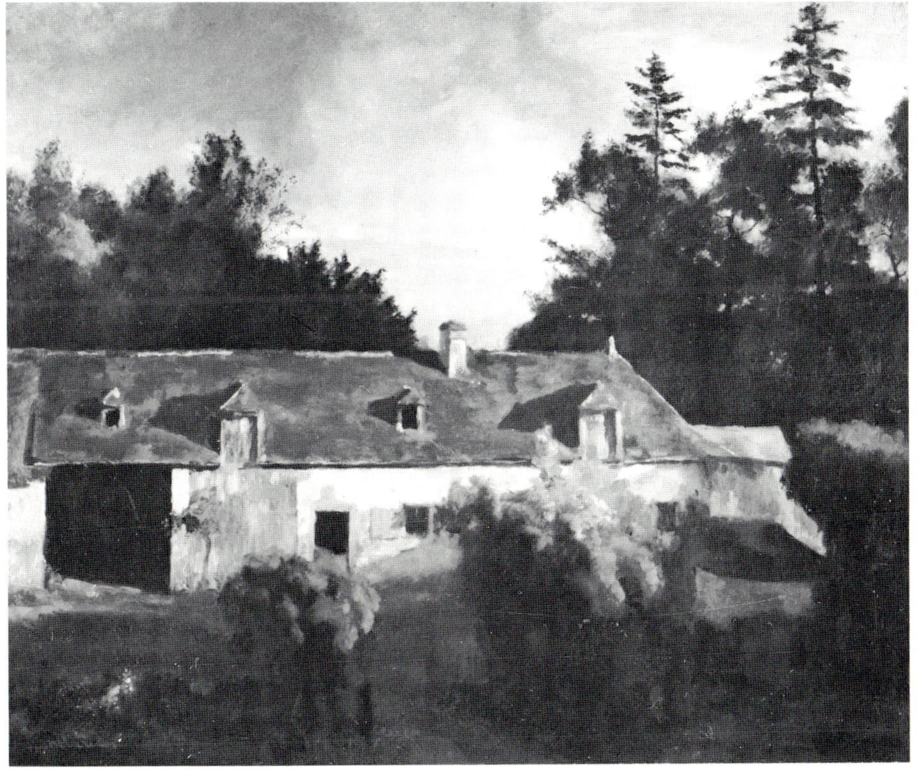

35
Max Meldrum
b. Scotland, 1875–1955
Picherit's Farm 1910
Oil on canvas
86.4 × 104.8 cm
Inscription. Recto:
l.l. "M. Meldrum"
Backed
Felton Bequest 1951
2908.4

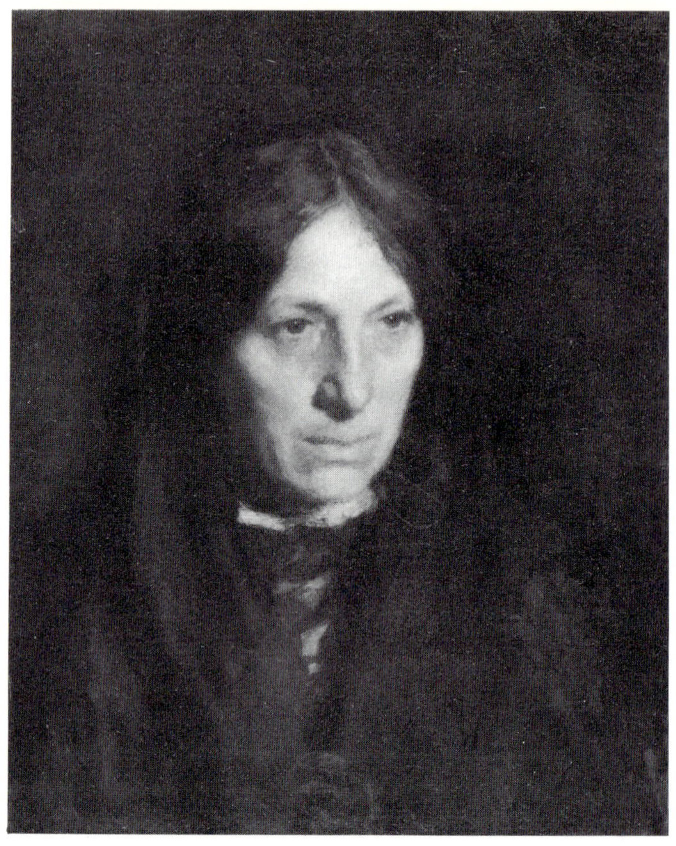

36
Max Meldrum
b. Scotland, 1875–1955
Portrait of the Artist's Mother 1913
Oil on canvas
61 × 49.5 cm
Inscriptions. Recto: l.r. "Meldrum"
Verso: on stretcher " 'Portrait of my Mother'
Max Meldrum"
Felton Bequest 1913
570.2

37
Rupert Bunny
Australian, 1864–1947
Endormies c. 1904
Oil on canvas
128.3 × 198.1 cm
Inscriptions. Verso: l.r. "Rupert C. W. Bunny"
Backed
Ex. no. 20, Athenaeum Hall, Melbourne, 1911
Felton Bequest 1911
549.2

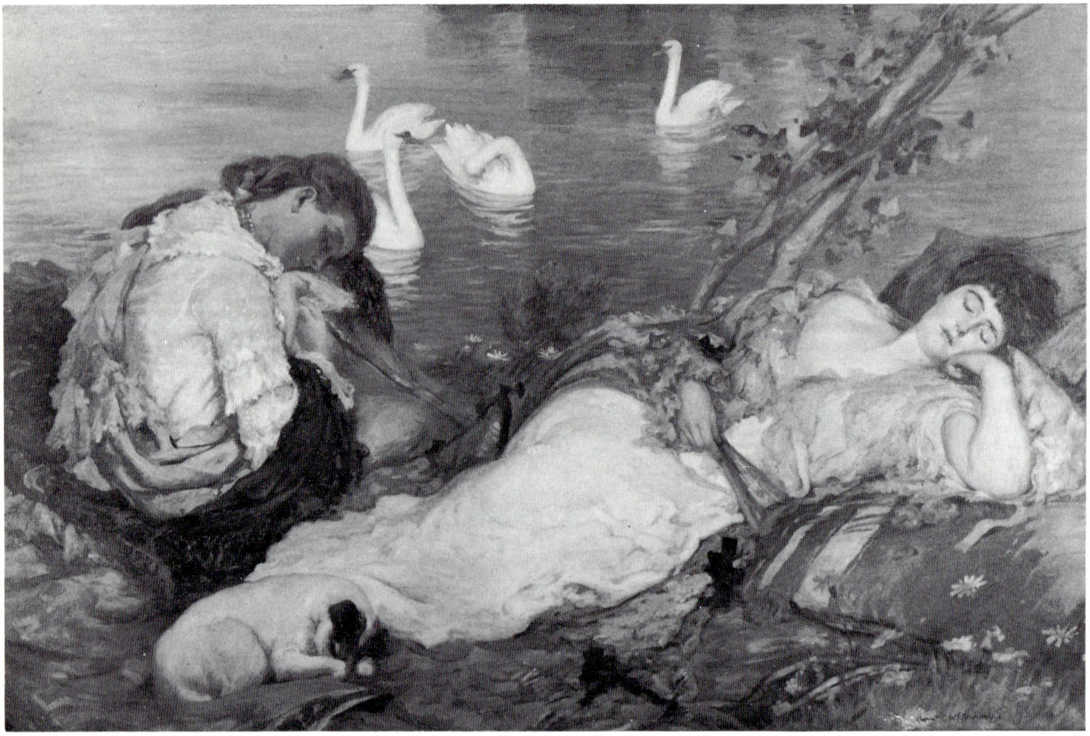

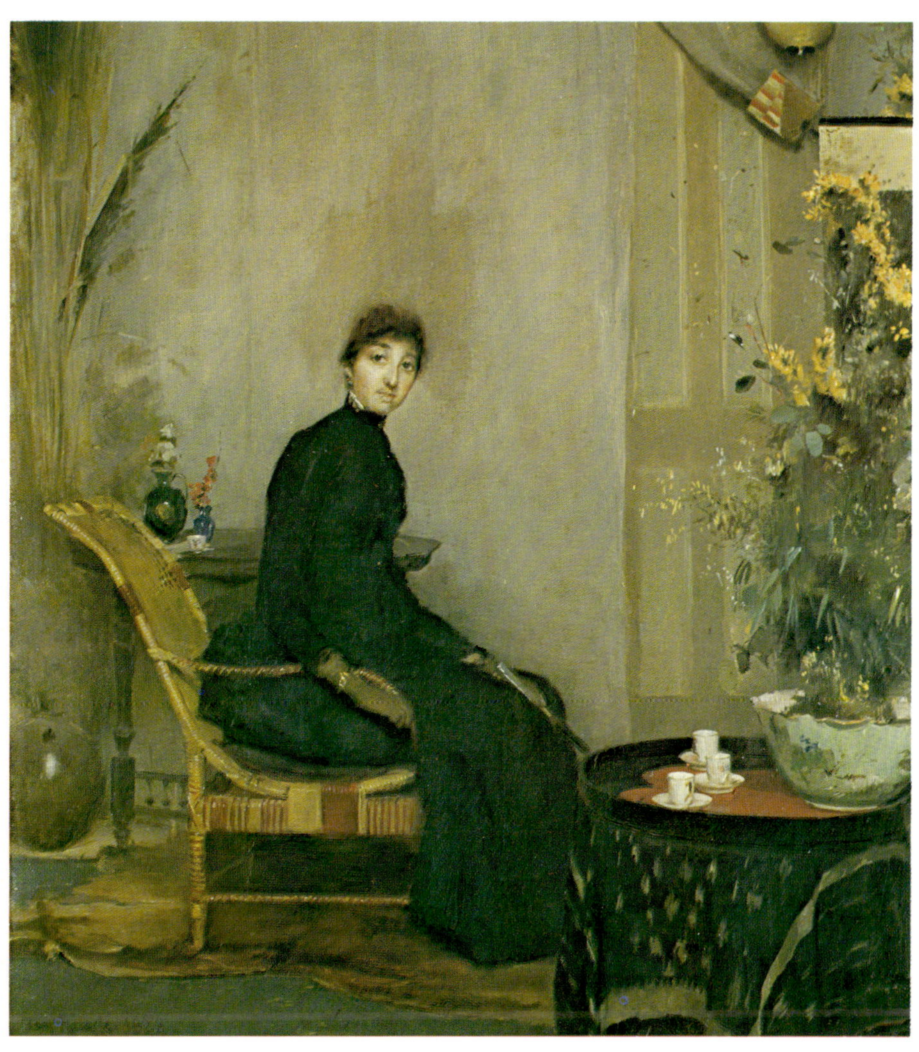

Plate **XIII**
Tom Roberts
b. England, 1856–1931
Portrait of Mrs Louis Abrahams in a Black Dress 1888
Oil on canvas
40.6 × 35.6 cm
Inscriptions. Recto: l.l. "Tom Roberts 1888"
Backed
Ex. no. 31 Victorian Artists' Society, Spring, 1888
Purchased 1946
1650.4

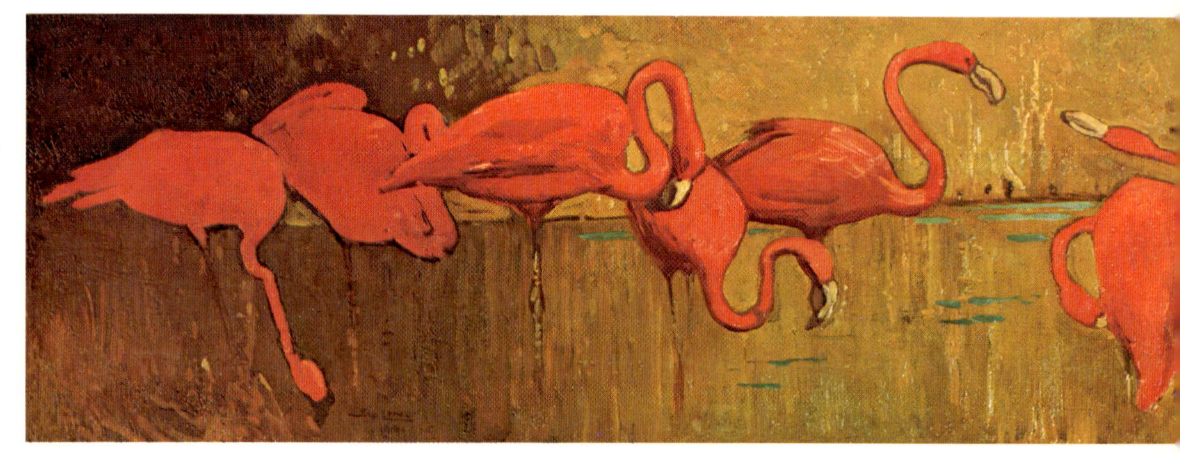

Plate **XIV**
Sydney Long
Australian, 1878–1955
Flamingoes 1916
Oil on panel
27.9 × 54.6 cm
Inscriptions. Recto: l.l. "Sid. Long 1916"
Presented by the National Gallery Women's Association 1972
A6/1972

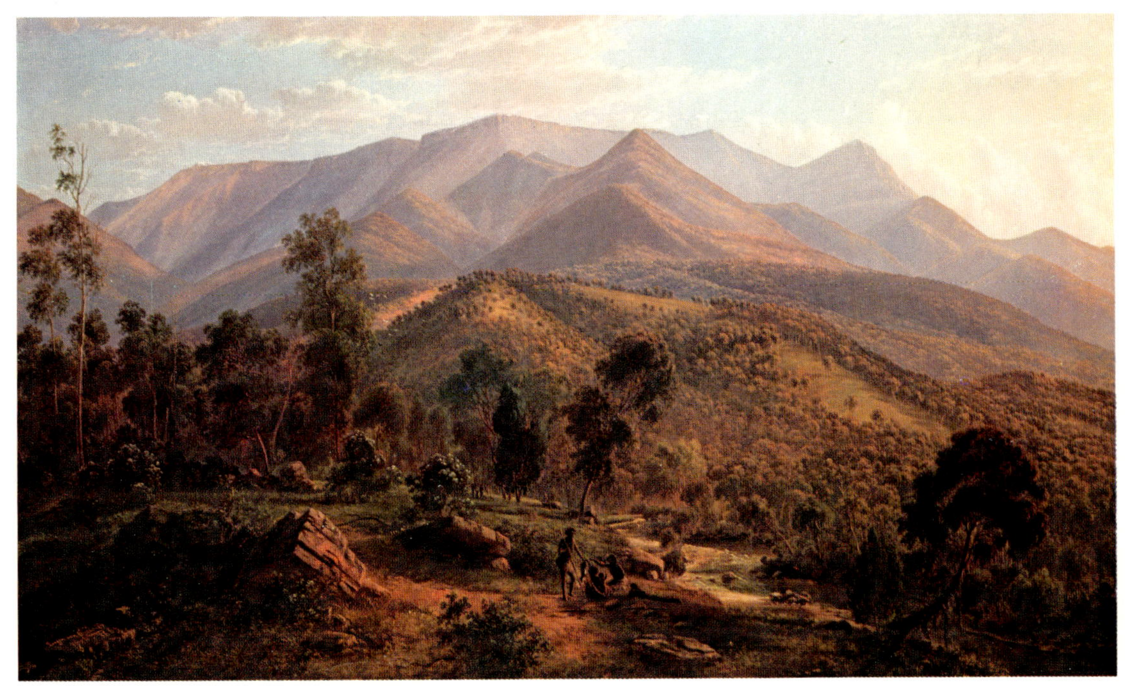

Plate **XV**
Eugen Von Guerard
b. Austria, 1811–1901
A View of the Snowy Bluff on the Wannangatta River 1864
Oil on canvas
25.2 × 152.4 cm
Inscriptions. Recto: l.l. "Eugen Von Guerard pinxit 1864"
Verso: label "View of the Snowy Bluff on the Wannangatta River in the Gippsland Alps, Victoria,
Australia. The Small Creek seen in the painting descends from the Valley between mount Kent
(to the left of the picture) and the Snowy Bluff. It had no name at the time of the first exploration
of this part of Gippsland, By Eugen Von Guerard . . . "
Purchased 1965
1524.5

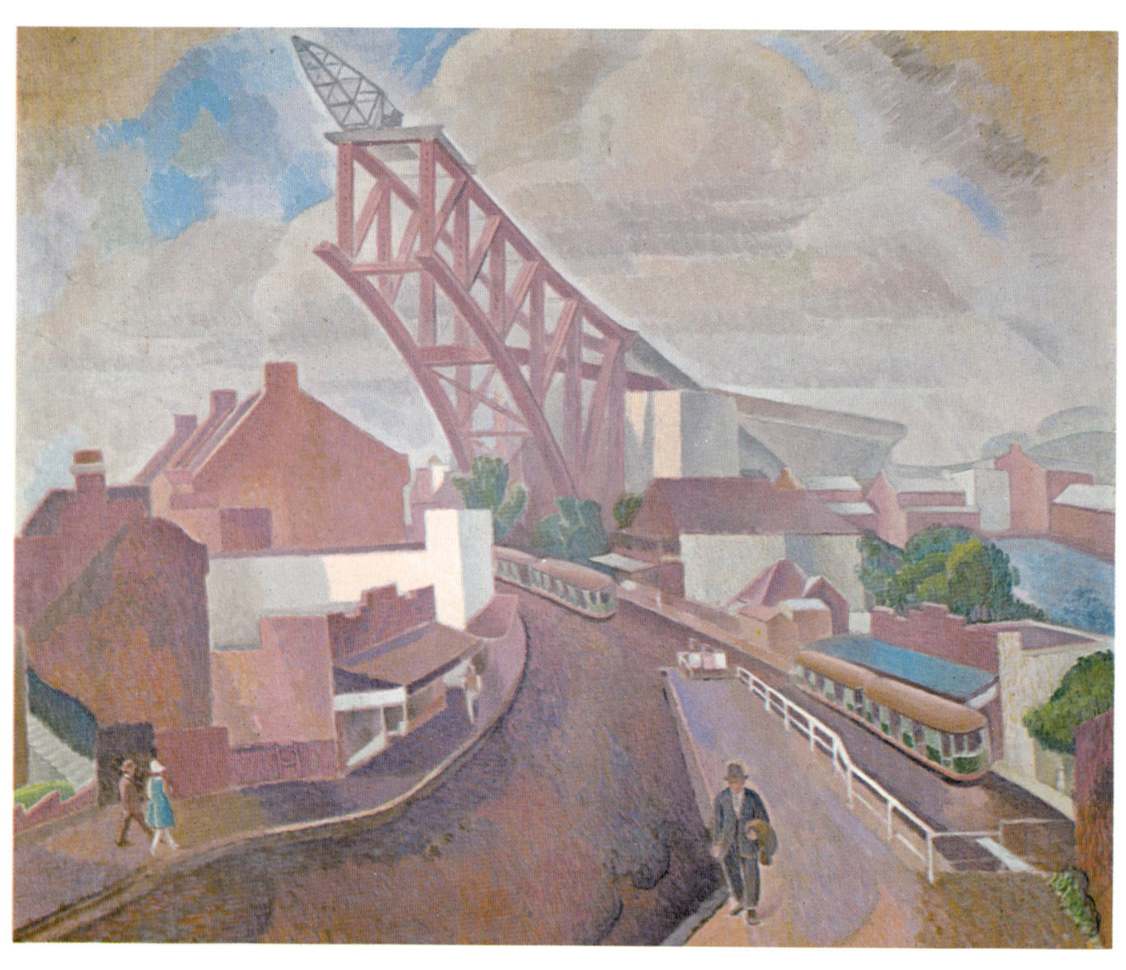

Plate **XVI**
Roland Wakelin
b. New Zealand, 1887–1971
The Bridge under Construction c. 1928–9
Oil on canvas on board
101.2 × 121.6 cm
Purchased 1967
1758.5

this is a most sensitive work, full of subtlety in exploring the range of its colours. Meldrum painted landscape, portraits and still life with equal distinction.

A.P.
(1961)

Portrait of the Artist's Mother particularly reflects Rembrandt. Conceived as a study of tone, the picture is painted in a low key with a limited palette of warm browns.

But although Meldrum preached a doctrine of the scientific impersonality of the art of painting, this picture reveals a warm human respect and affection. It is an outstanding piece of painting and also an outstanding document among those many pictures which artists in all ages have painted—"The portrait of the Artist's mother".

Extract from *C.C.*
(May, 1961)

37
Rupert Bunny, Australian, 1864–1947
Endormies. c. 1904
The warm tones of this picture speak to us of the slumbrous languor of a summer's afternoon in terms of Edwardian elegance.

Rupert Bunny, the Australian artist who spent the greater part of his life in France, painted this picture at that time in his career when he was described by the historian William Moore as "an Australian painter of beautiful women". The soft muted colours of pinks, blues and golds, the rounded forms and tranquil rhythms of the composition all reinforce the quietude of the sleepers. The little terrier curled at the feet of Rupert Bunny's wife, the French girl Jeanne Morel, asserts the unaffected charm of the familiar which is such a strong feature of this painting.

The simple, the unheroic, the innocent idleness of the afternoon has been made into a great decorative picture.

It is a sorry thought that Bunny spent his long life without any commission to paint a series of mural decorations. It was always his ambition, alas unfulfilled, to paint great pictures for a great room, to emulate the integral decorative schemes of the chateaux of France. We must remember that decorative is not a word of abuse, only one of description and limitation. To enrich great halls with graceful composition praising the beauties of life is out of favour. The lovely woman is supplanted by the bedraggled hoyden. No doubt the modes of the world before the horror of 1914 are gone for ever, but we need not spurn the reminder of their more pleasing aspects in the work of our francophile civilized Australian, Rupert Bunny.

C.C.
(January, 1960)

38
Sir Hans Heysen, b. Germany, 1877–1968
A Summer's Day. 1912
Hans Heysen came to Australia from Germany at the age of six. After studying in Adelaide and Melbourne, he was assisted to return to Europe by four Adelaide businessmen, who were impressed by his talent. His landscapes always have something of the definition and solidity of the paintings of the Dutch landscapists like Ruisdael (1628–82) and Hobbema (1638–1709).

Melbourne in the Edwardian era was the centre of the patronage of art in Australia. There, in 1908, Heysen held his first exhibition. Its great success enabled him to settle at Hahndorf, South Australia, where he has practised as a professional artist ever since. He has won the Wynne prize nine times, holds the O.B.E. and was knighted in 1959. His vision of the landscape has joined that of Arthur Streeton as a symbol in the nation's consciousness.

Two subjects dominate his work: the ragged anatomy of the eucalypt, both giant gum and sapling, and the harsh colours and eroded shapes of Central Australia's mountains. This watercolour perfectly displays his habit of painting "contre-jour", that is, into the light. Often the oblique beams of dawn or dusk silhouette the various fantastic patterns of his beloved gum trees. His art is an impressionist one, strengthened by an emphasis on defined contours and precise draughtmanship.

A.P.
(1961)

   Footnote: Sir Hans Heysen died in 1968.

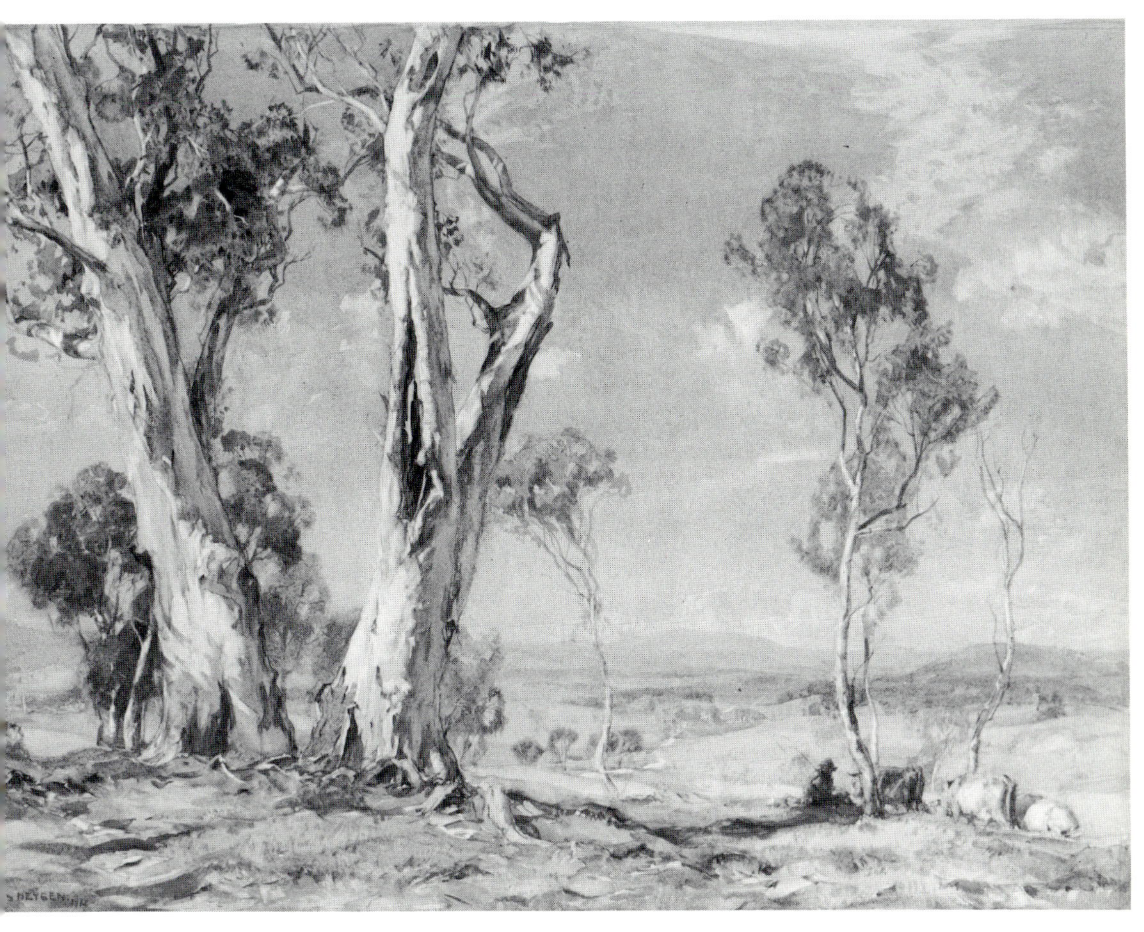

38
Sir Hans Heysen
b. Germany, 1877–1968
A Summer's Day 1912
Watercolour
Inscriptions. Recto: l.l. "Hans Heysen 1912"
Ex. no. 61, Athenaeum Gallery, Melb. 1912
Purchased 1914
661.2

Plate XIV
Sydney Long, Australian, 1878–1955
Flamingoes. 1916
Sydney Long's most significant works are those in which he incorporated the style and spirit of the art-nouveau movement into the Australian landscape. This means that instead of a naturalistic portrayal of nature, great emphasis is placed on decorative curvilinear patterning. By the turn of the century the imagination of many Australian artists, including Sydney Long, had been captured by a romantic poetic approach to the landscape. Nymphs and wood sprites now appeared in bushland settings infused with a degree of symbolism.

Painted in 1916, **Flamingoes** is a striking example of Sydney Long's decorative style. It relates to a larger painting of the same title, but painted in 1902, which belongs to the Art Gallery of New South Wales. Watercolours of the same subject also exist.

Flamingoes belongs to the same period as Long's much acclaimed art-nouveau fantasy painting **Spirit of the Plains,** of which an etching was acquired for the Print Collection in 1971.

Long's preoccupation with painting flamingoes obviously stems from their innate decorative qualities and from their exotic and erotic connotations.

In **Flamingoes** Sydney Long has silhouetted the blazing red birds against a green background. Surface flatness is emphasized by the horizontal shape and by the long necks of the birds which twist with serpentine grace across this frieze-like composition.

It is an extremely elegant and decorative painting.

Sydney Long was born at Goulburn, New South Wales, in 1878. He studied with Julian Ashton in Sydney and later taught at his school. He went to London in 1910 where he exhibited at the Royal Academy, and in 1920 was elected an Associate of the Royal Society of Painter-Etchers. He returned to Australia in 1925. He was director of the Royal Art School, Sydney, and from 1933 to 1949, a Trustee of the Art Gallery of New South Wales. He died in 1955.

F. McC. in *N.G.S.B.*
(April, 1972)

Landscape as a means of pictorial expression has characterised the development of Australia's art. During the period of the European settlement of Australia in the nineteenth century, landscape as an independent art form became the dominant mode of expression. Thus the natural impetus created by the novelty of the countryside was reinforced by the prevailing tide of European art. It is little wonder, therefore, that Australian painters have long sought their artistic expression in landscape, and continue to do so. The paintings by Von Guerard and Fred Williams exemplify the National Gallery of Victoria's continuing interest in this sphere.

Eugen Von Guerard came to Victoria in 1853. He must have been a man of great physical energy for he travelled widely, to the most remote and inaccessible parts of the colony, in search of picturesque subjects for his topographical painting. He was an artist of considerable quality in a field of meticulous linear naturalism. His calibre has been somewhat undervalued through a popular enthusiasm for the impressionistic landscape achievements of the ensuing Heidelberg School. This typical painting of 1864 is of an almost gaudy beauty, in its depiction of the Aboriginal group in the foreground, over-shadowed by the theatrical backdrop of sunset-stained mauve mountains and pink sky **(Plate XV)**. In 1870, Von Guerard was appointed the first "Master of the Painting School and Curator of the National Gallery of Victoria" which post he retained until 1881, when he returned to Europe. So it is particularly appropriate that Melbourne should represent him by first rate works.

By way of contrast, Fred Williams is regarded as one of the most important of the modern landscapists. His original interpretation of the ragged spontaneous unpredictable appearance of eucalyptus scrub country has won him wide acclaim. In this **Upwey Landscape (39)** the growth crawls up the hillside in warm patches of blue and pink, while on the horizon against a white sky, the trees explode like fireworks in fan tracery.

The two portraits of young women painted respectively by George Walton in 1886 and George Bell in 1934 are both aesthetically satisfying and historically illuminating **(40)** and **(41)**. Each artist was involved with progressive movements of their time. Walton was an English painter who had been a fellow student of Tom Roberts at the Academy School, London. In 1884 he was in Paris with John Russell, the impressionist and Bertram Mackennal the sculptor. Through these Australian friends, he came to this country shortly afterwards in search of a climate beneficial to his health. In Melbourne he took a studio in Grosvenor Chambers, Collins Street, where Roberts also had his studio. Through him he became friendly with Conder and Streeton who both admired his work. In 1890 he returned to Europe, at the same time as Conder, the two artists being given a farewell dinner at Legals by the Victorian Artists' Society. When he died two

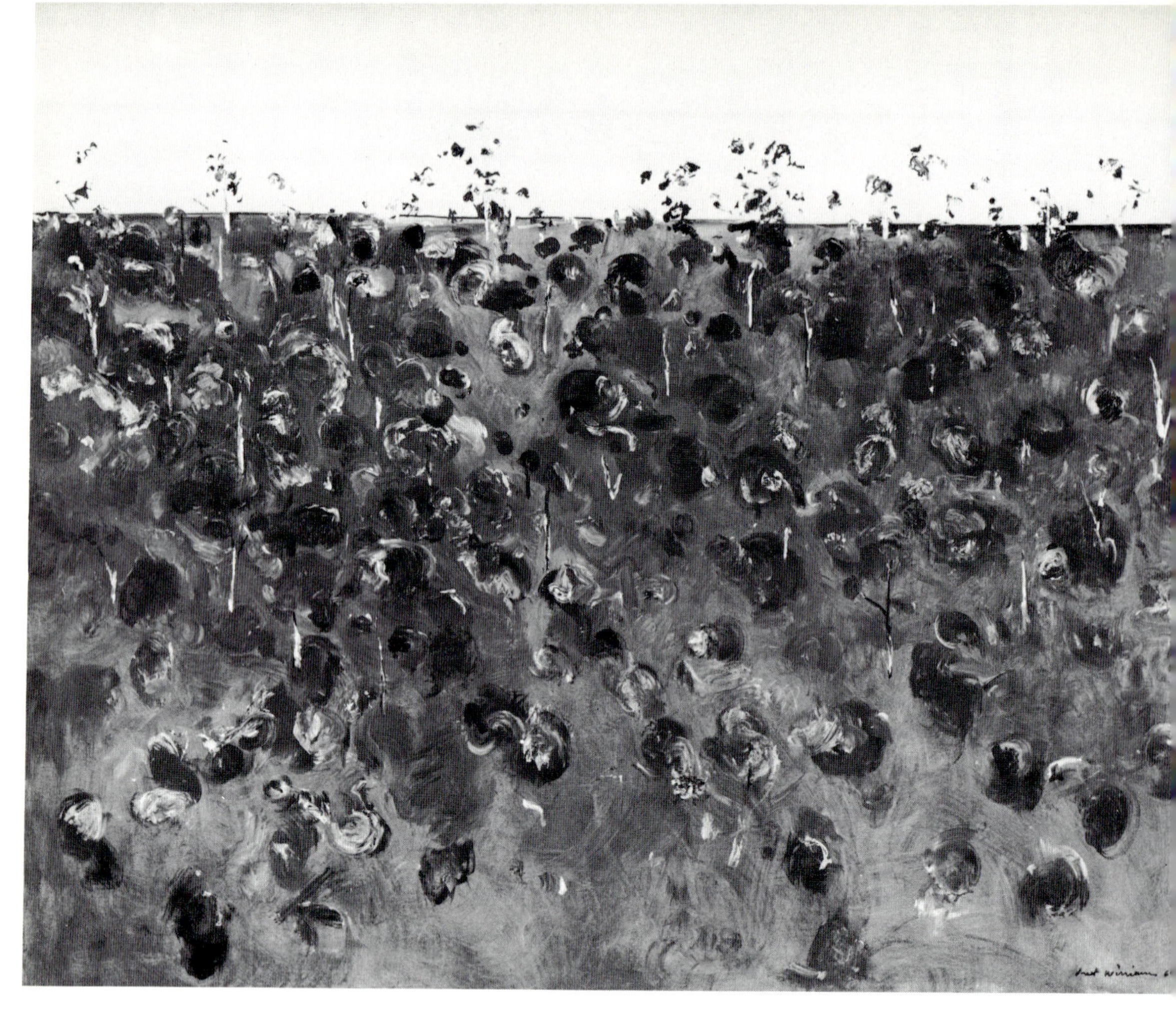

39
Fred. Williams
Australian, 1927–
Upwey Landscape 1965
Oil on canvas
143.3 × 182.9 cm
Inscriptions. Recto: l.r. "Fred Williams '65"
Felton Bequest 1965
1553.5

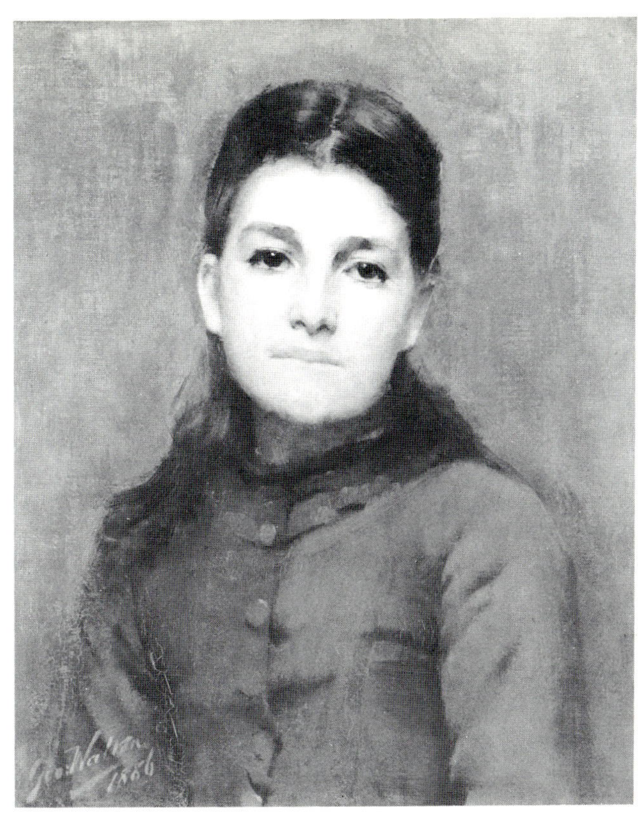

40
George Walton
b. England, ?–1904
Priscilla 1886
Oil on canvas
48 × 40.3 cm
Inscriptions. Recto: l.l. "Geo. Walton 1886"
Verso: label, (torn) "Priscilla"
"St John's Wood N.W. . . . "
Purchased 1966
1673.5

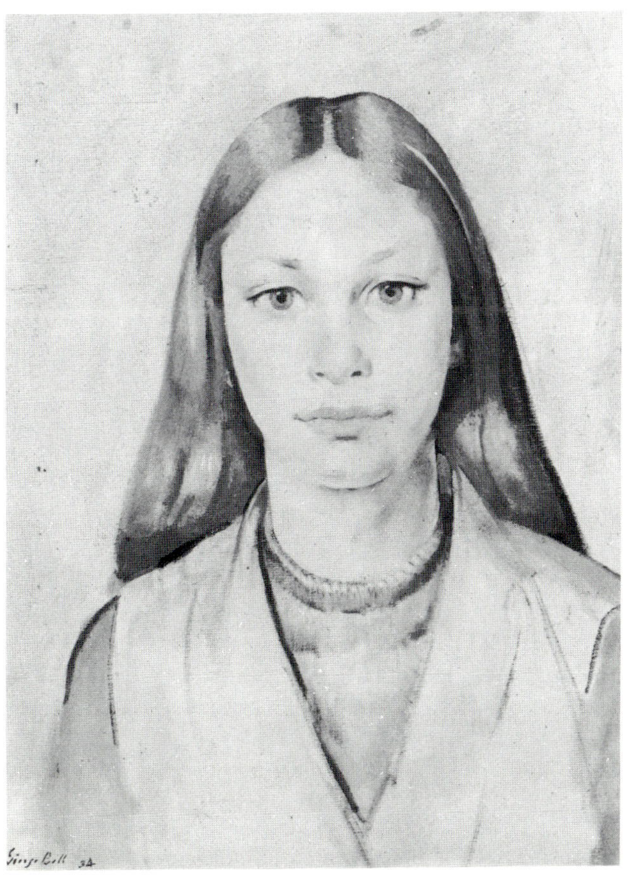

41
George Bell
Australian, 1878–1966
Portrait of Toinette 1934
Oil on canvas on board
50.8 × 39.7 cm
Inscriptions. Recto: l.l. "George Bell '34"
Backed
Purchased 1966
1672.5

years later, Roberts said of him "He was the finest painter of the head when I was at the Academy Schools".

This painting has a strong affinity to Roberts's portraiture. It shows a knowledge of, and sympathy with, contemporary French painting, noticeably Manet, while its soft-hued, understated palette of mauve-greys and olive-browns is of Whistlerian tranquillity.

George Bell's portrait of his daughter Toinette has a classical simplicity in its controlled form, and limited palette in high tonality. It well displays the interest in post-impressionist principles which he championed in Melbourne in the 1930s. It is difficult now to recapture the intensity of the controversy which enveloped the emergence of "modern art" in Victoria. The school which George Bell and Arnold Shore founded in 1932, and which Bell continued alone from 1937, had a profound influence. Bell was an inspiring teacher and painters who worked with him have contributed greatly to contemporary Australian art. This splendid example of his mature manner hangs very happily with the later work of his students in this Collection especially the masterly **Two Children** by Russell Drysdale.

"Modernism" of a post-impressionist nature reached Sydney about a decade earlier than Melbourne. The acknowledged leaders of the first wave of revolt against the entrenched but waning forces of impressionism were Roy de Maistre, Grace Cossington Smith and Roland Wakelin. Its starting point was the Saturday classes of the Royal Art Society under Dattilo Rubbo and his encouragement of experiments prompted by the theories and photographic examples of post-impressionism brought back to Australia by Norah Simpson in 1913. Two works by Wakelin and three by Cossington Smith have been acquired recently, greatly enhancing the collection and making possible an intelligent consideration of the period.

The Bridge under Construction c. 1928–9 **(Plate XVI)** exemplifies Wakelin's mature manner inspired by an admiration for the art of Cezanne. It is an exercise in disciplined composition, with a strong simplified design executed in a range of dry subdued greyish pinks and blues. It is difficult to recapture the historical atmosphere in which the works of these artists, with their structural and colouristic vigour and genuine search for a revitalized idiom, provoked such virulent criticism.

The second wave of the modern movement in New South Wales was championed by Grace Crowley and Rah Fizelle in the 1930s. From 1932 to 1937 they conducted Sydney's only school of modern painting. This may be regarded as being parallel to the Bell-Shore school in Melbourne in its influence, though its principles and sources were different. From 1927 till 1930 Grace Crowley was in Europe, chiefly in Paris where she studied with André Lhote, and later with Albert Gleizes. **Girl with Goats** 1928 **(49),** was painted while in France. Miss Crowley is a

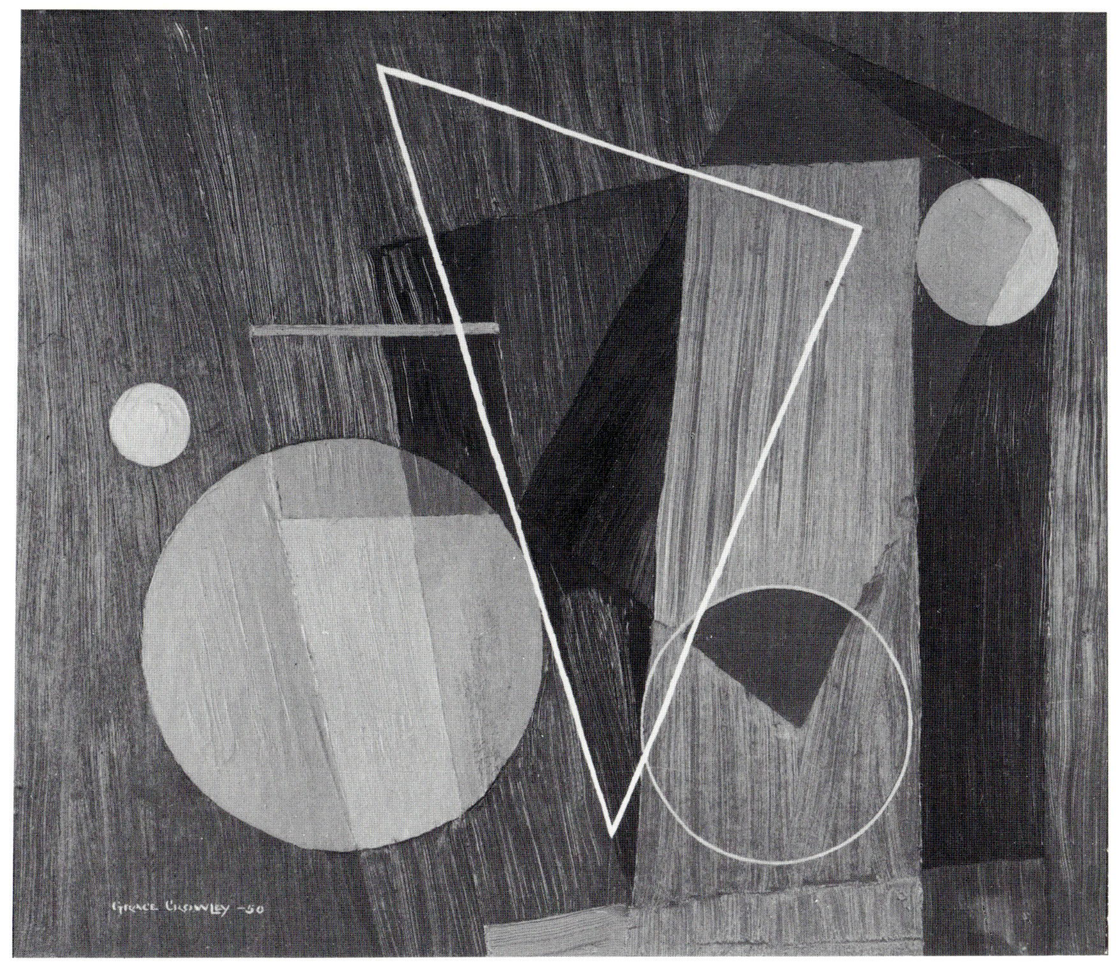

highly conscious artist, and most selective in her output. Her interest in formal values increased gradually and from 1940 her work has been purely abstract in geometric forms. One of these works, **Painting** 1950 **(42),** has also entered the collection, together with a typical work of about 1936 **Portrait of Betty Collings (43),** by her friend and colleague Rah Fizelle.

Currently, artists of equal integrity and ability are working in the disparate fields of figurative and abstract painting. Examples of these diverse trends in the work of senior artists which have been added to the Collection are **Harbourside** by John Passmore and **Configuration** by Roger Kemp, **(44)** and **(45)**; while amongst the work of artists in their early maturity are **Window Shadow Large Reflection (46)** by Charles Blackman and **Canto No. 21 (47)** by Sydney Ball.

John Passmore spent from 1933 to 1950 studying and working in Europe, after his initial studies at the Julian Ashton School, Sydney. Since his return he has had wide influence as artist and teacher. **Harbourside** shows one aspect of his work, and is part of a series of paintings of fishermen and bathers around the beaches of Sydney. It is indebted to his admiration of Cezanne. His later manner, and his influence upon his students, has been towards more informal abstraction, which led to the development of abstract expressionism in Sydney about 1956.

42
Grace Crowley
Australian, 1890–
Painting 1950
Oil on hardboard
63 × 76.2 cm
Inscriptions. Recto: l.l.
"Grace Crowley –50"
Purchased from the
artist, 1967
1760.5

65

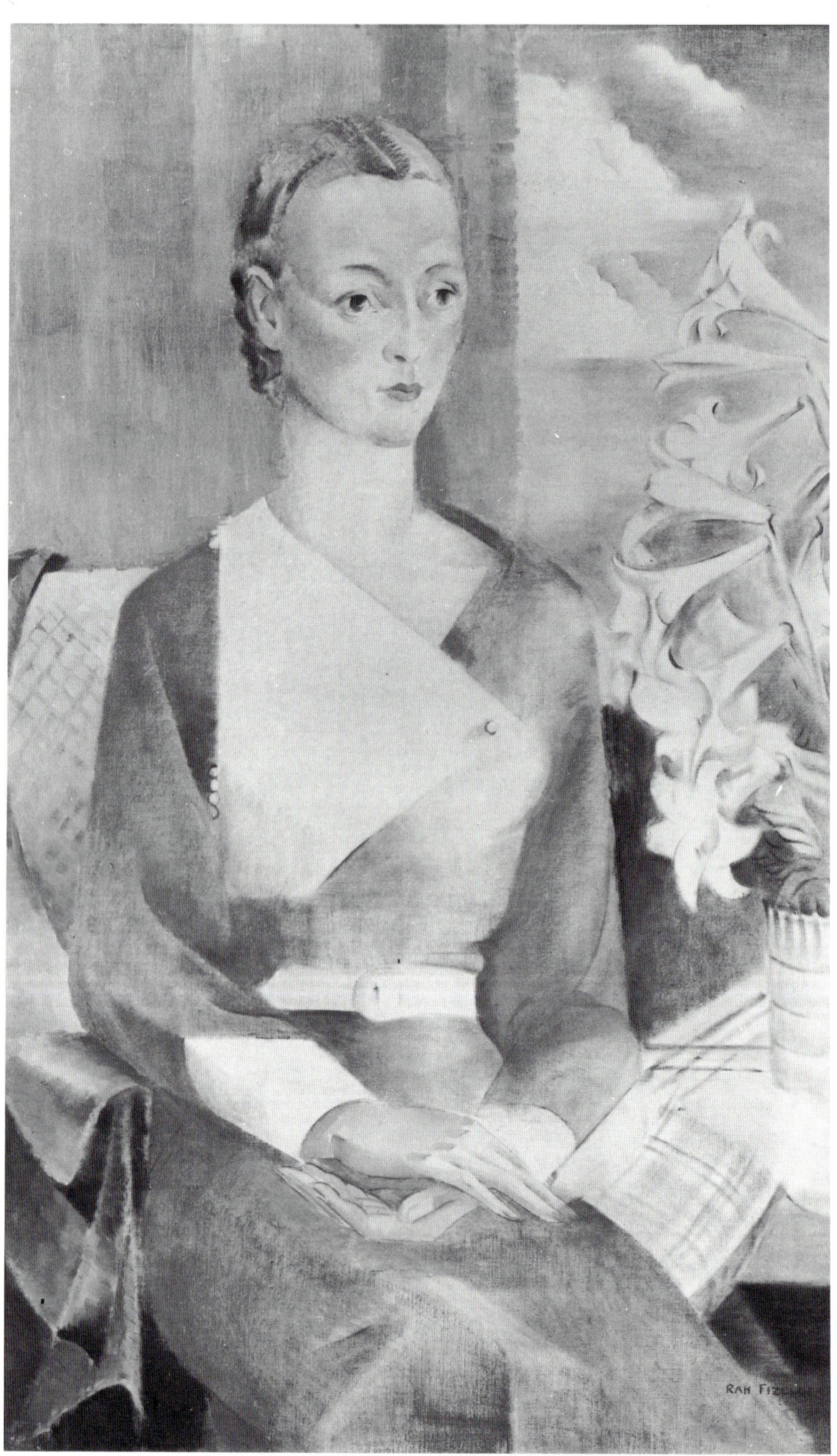

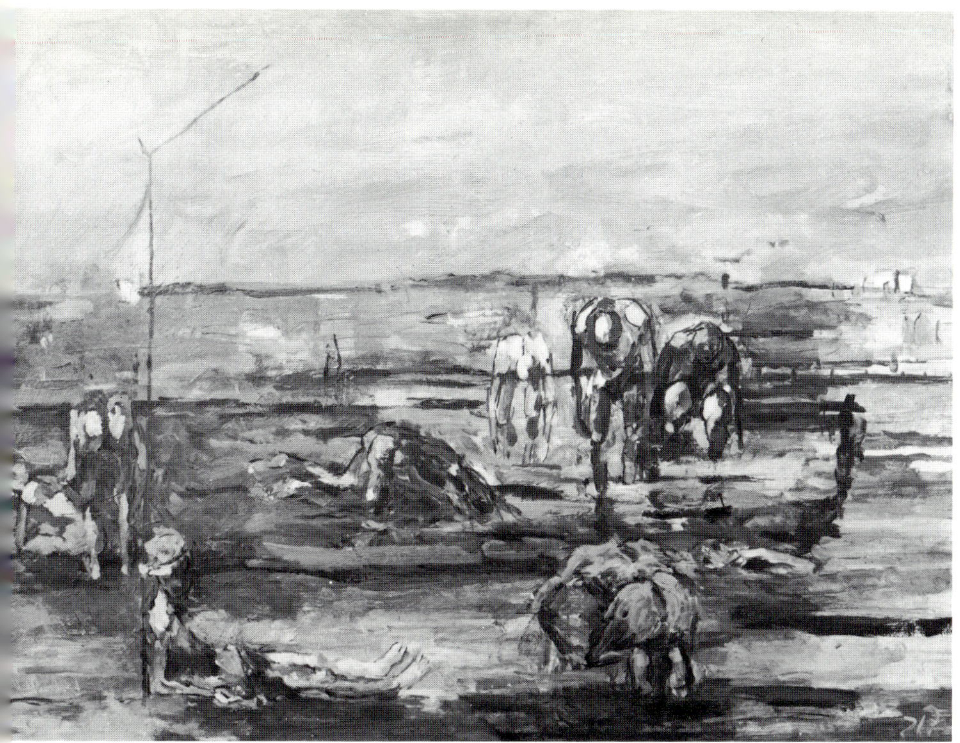

44
John Passmore
Australian, 1904
Harbourside 1955–60
Oil on hardboard
61 × 85.1 cm
Inscriptions. l.r. "J.P."
Purchased 1966
1576.5

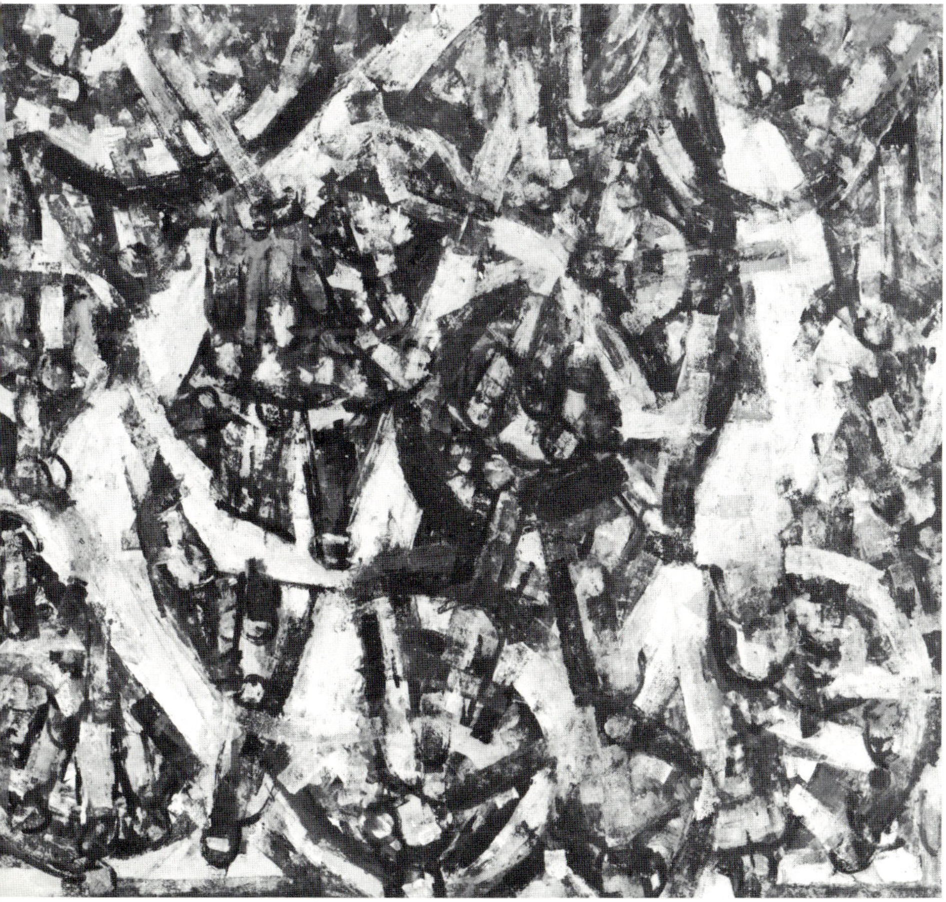

45
Roger Kemp
Australian, 1908–
Configuration 1964
Oil on hardboard
137 × 152 cm
Inscriptions. Verso:
"Configuration 64"
"Roger Kemp"
Purchased 1965
1550.5

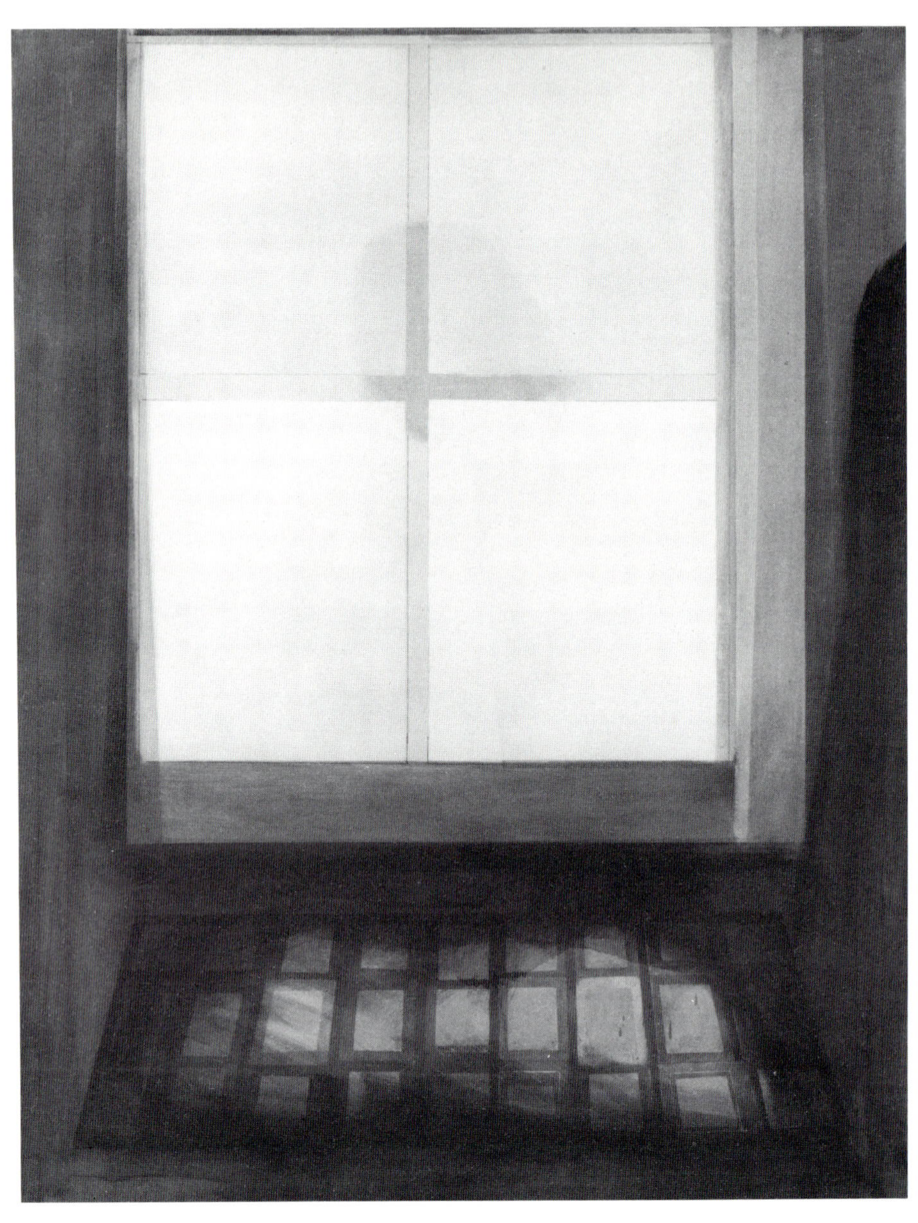

46
Charles Blackman
Australian, b. 1928
Window Shadow—Large Reflection 1965
Oil on canvas
182.9 × 142.2 cm
Inscriptions. Recto: l.l. "Charles Blackman 1965"
Purchased 1966
1580.5

Roger Kemp is a painter of symbolical abstraction whose slow developing devotion to his art has been an inspiration to a number of painters in Melbourne. His art is austere and uncompromising in its intent, but richly emotional in its colour and handling. Only recently has he been honoured by critics and favoured by prizes. **Configuration** is a very freely painted work, in an almost monochromatic range of blue and white, revealing a more spontaneous and expressionist form than his earlier more cerebral paintings in the Melbourne collection.

Charles Blackman and Sydney Ball may seem oddly juxtaposed in the Collection, their respective idioms of humanist representation and geometric abstraction being so different. However, the artists are but a few years apart in age and their art has certain affinities. Each artist is absorbed in conveying a sensation of glowing light and a simplification of form, though their objectives vary. **Window Shadow Large Reflection** shows Blackman at the height of his evocative powers. The general cool tonality of the painting in related blues is emphasized and challenged by the vivid reds of the light-drenched rug beneath the window. A moment of solitary hushed privacy is revealed in a pattern of strength and simplicity derived from a union of abstraction and tonal painting. Sydney Ball, to the contrary, seeks to impart a mystical awareness of colour, light and archetypal form without reference to personal experience. His art is difficult to define, lying somewhere between hard-edge and op-painting. His pictures do not confuse the retinal impressions of the viewer, but their colour relationships are deliberately chosen to create an impression of confined power which commands the eye. Charles Blackman is building on a long tradition of figurative, humanist painting while Sydney Ball is finding his own voice in the language of contemporary painting in New York, a city where he studied under Theodore Stamos from 1963 to 1965. Yet each artist plays a valid role in the contemporary art of Australia.

Contrary to a wide spread myth of romantic origin, knowledge does not stifle appreciation of the visual arts. Therefore, while the Department of Australian Art continues its basic curatorial role in the creation and maintenance of a repository for the fine art of the community, it is hoped that by a catholicity of taste, it will act also as a prophylactic against prejudice. To this end the Gallery not only collects, but organises temporary loan exhibitions, both "Retrospectives" of an historical nature and "Surveys" of the recent work of Australian artists. From the permanent collection and from such exhibitions, the public may inform themselves of the growth of the art of the past, and of the condition of the present. A true appreciation of the nature of the emergent arts in this country can do no other than assist the judgment and guide the direction thereof.

Extract from *A. B.* article
(1967–8)

47
Sydney Ball
Australian, b. 1933
Canto No. 21 1966
Oil on canvas
182.9 × 152.4 cm
Inscriptions. Recto: ''Sydney Ball
Canto No. 21 February 1966''
Purchased 1966
1648.5

48
George Lambert, A.R.A., b. Russia, 1873–1930
A Sergeant of the Light Horse. 1920
One of the most striking portrait studies in the collection of Australian paintings
in the National Gallery of Victoria is **A Sergeant of the Light Horse.** In this
portrait, George Lambert revealed not only an individual but a type: the
essential countryman born in the saddle whose heroism during the First World
War is a proud part of our history.

George Lambert was the outstanding Australian portraitist of his time. An
insistence on draughtmanship was reinforced by his study of the Italian Renaissance and Mannerist masters. Here the cockaded hat held in the strongly modelled
hands makes a forceful balance to the sitter's head. The soldier sensitively looks
downward, his thoughts withdrawn from war and the rocky desert of Palestine.

George Lambert was born in Russia, the son of an American father who died
before his birth, and an English mother who brought him to New South Wales
at the age of fourteen. Julian Ashton trained his great natural gifts to such an
effect that he won a Travelling Scholarship in 1900, and settled in London,
exhibiting regularly at the Royal Academy. During the First World War he was
an official artist with the A.I.F. in Palestine. His return to Australia in 1921 was
of great significance to the artistic life of Sydney. His work is well represented in
Melbourne, but the Art Gallery of New South Wales has the most comprehensive
collection of his work.

C. C.
(October, 1961)

Footnote: The subject of the painting is thought to be Thomas Henry Ivers, an artist who
served in the Australian Light Horse in Palestine. He worked with Captain Lambert in London
in 1919, helping him make "sketches and painting of pictures relating to the Light Horse in
Palestine". (Australian Army Records.) Ivers returned to Australia in 1920.

J. P.
(1976)

Plate XVII
M. Napier Waller, C.M.G., O.B.E., Australian, 1893–1972
Virgil. c. 1922
Within the shadow of his death I recall many aspects of Napier Waller, a fine
man and a fine artist, to whom history will allow his just position.

I was in my youth when first I went to his home in Ivanhoe, and there met
Napier Waller: a whole man, an artist craftsman of a proud tradition; a truly

48
George Lambert
b. Russia, 1873–1930
A Sergeant of the Light Horse 1920
Oil on canvas
77.1 × 61.2 cm
Inscriptions. Recto: l.r. "G. W. Lambert 1920"
Backed
Ex. no. 3, Fine Arts Soc. Gallery, Melb., 1921
Felton Bequest 1921
1182.3

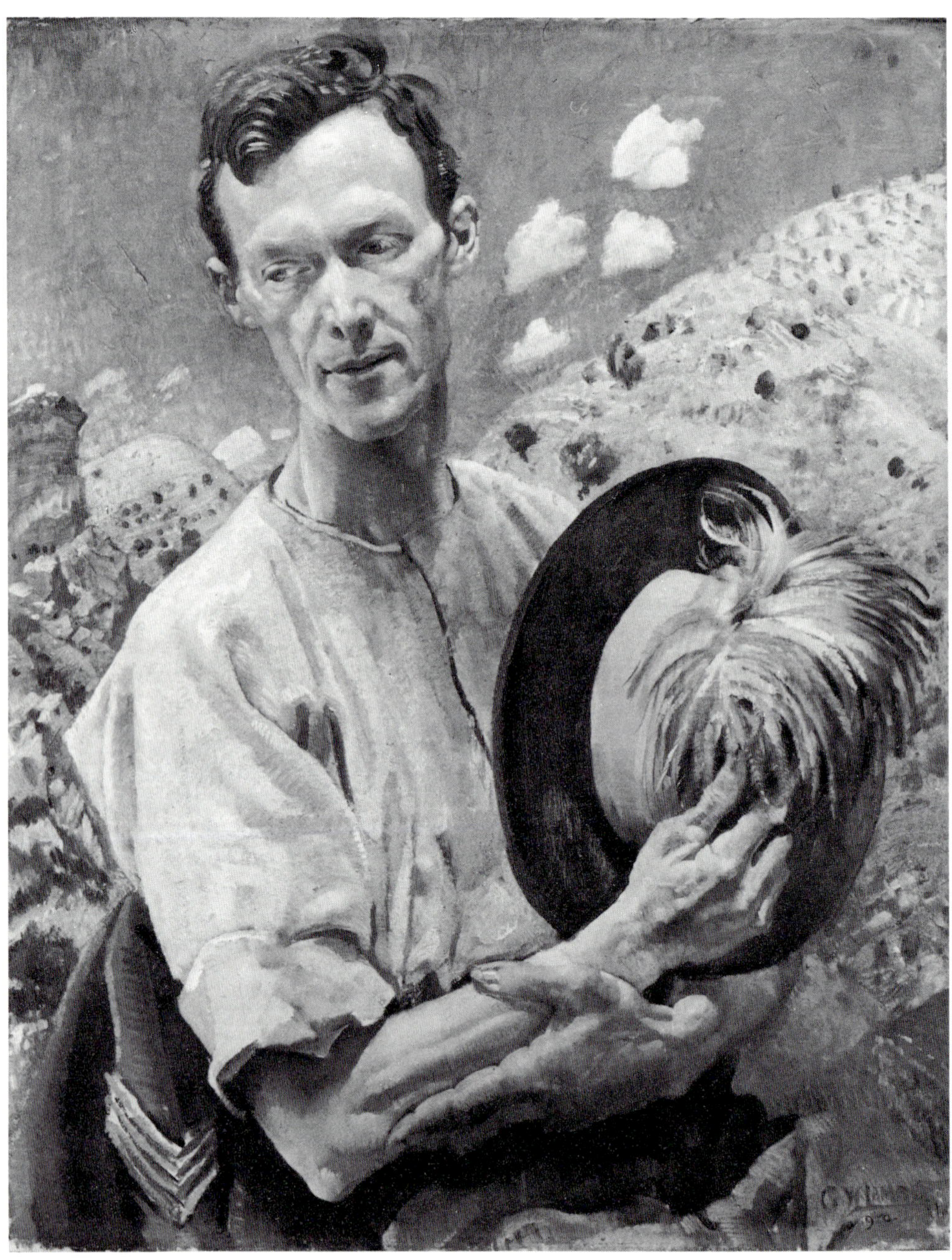

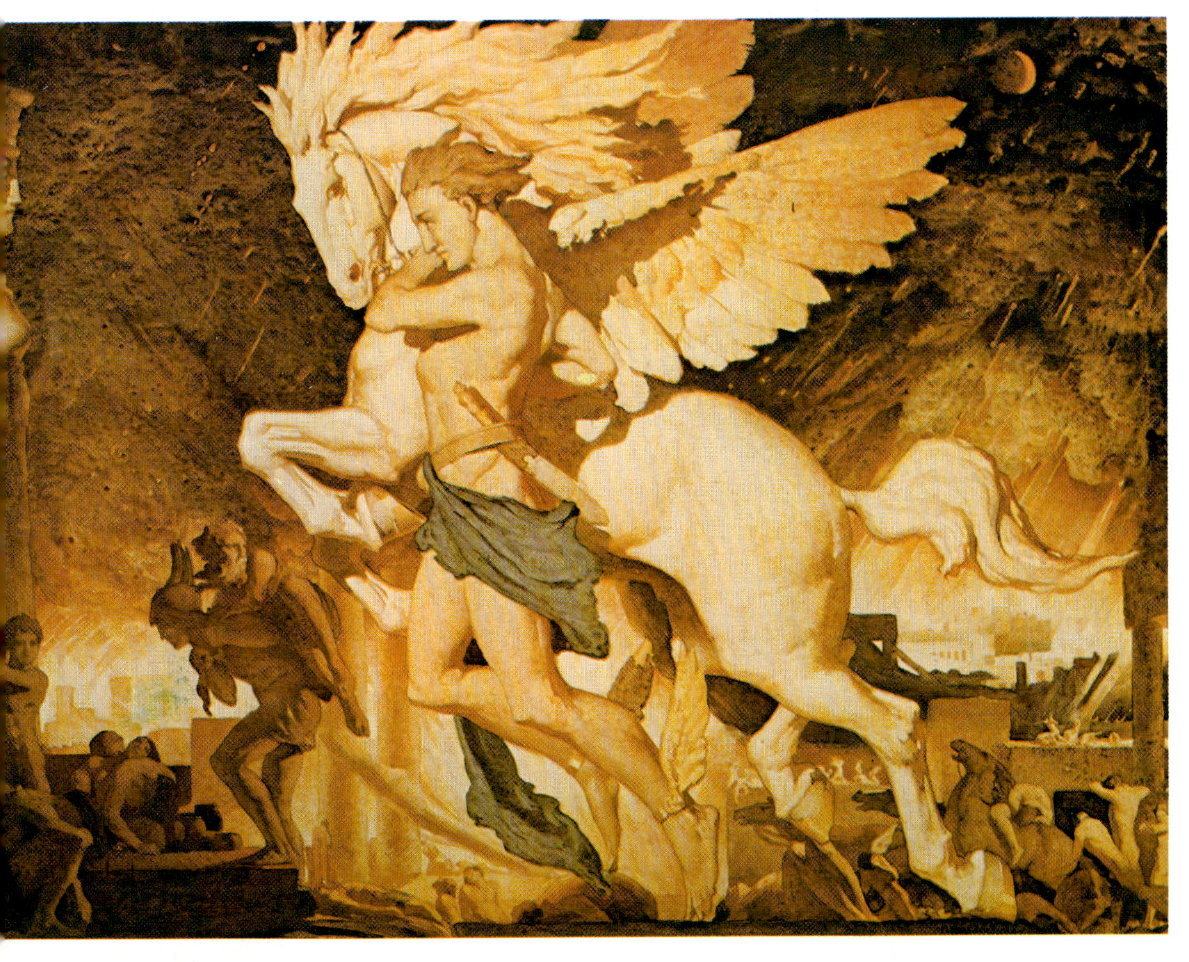

Plate **XVII**
Mervyn Napier Waller
Australian, 1893–1972
Virgil c. 1922
Watercolour
53.4 × 72 cm
Inscriptions. Recto: l.r. "M. Napier Waller"
Verso: charcoal sketch of horsemen and soldiers
Ex. Austn Art Association, Melbourne, 1922
Felton Bequest 1922
1257.3

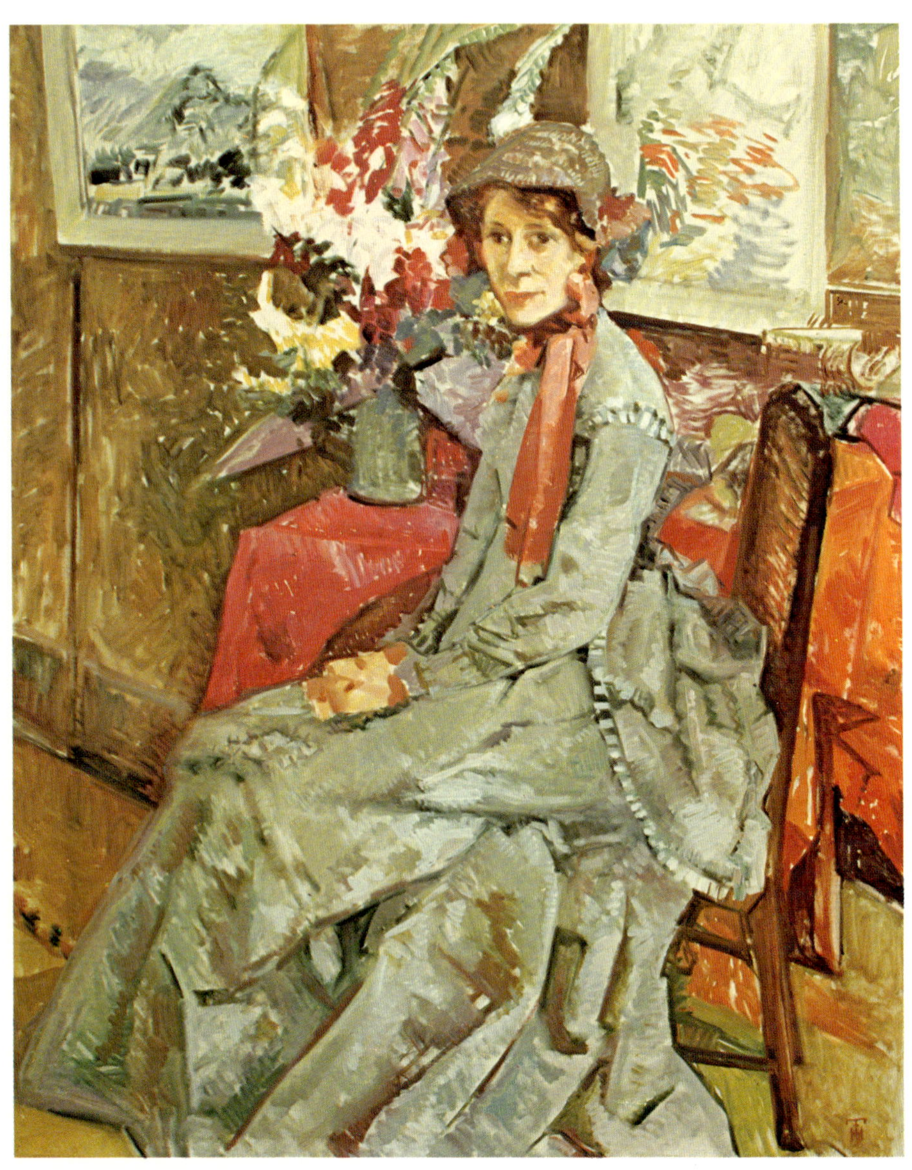

Plate **XVIII**
Isobel Hunter Tweddle
Australian, 1877–1945
Portrait of Ivy Ball in Fancy Dress
Oil on canvas
128.3 × 103.5 cm
Inscriptions. Recto: l.r. monogram "I.H.T."
Presented by Miss Ivy Ball 1963
1312.5

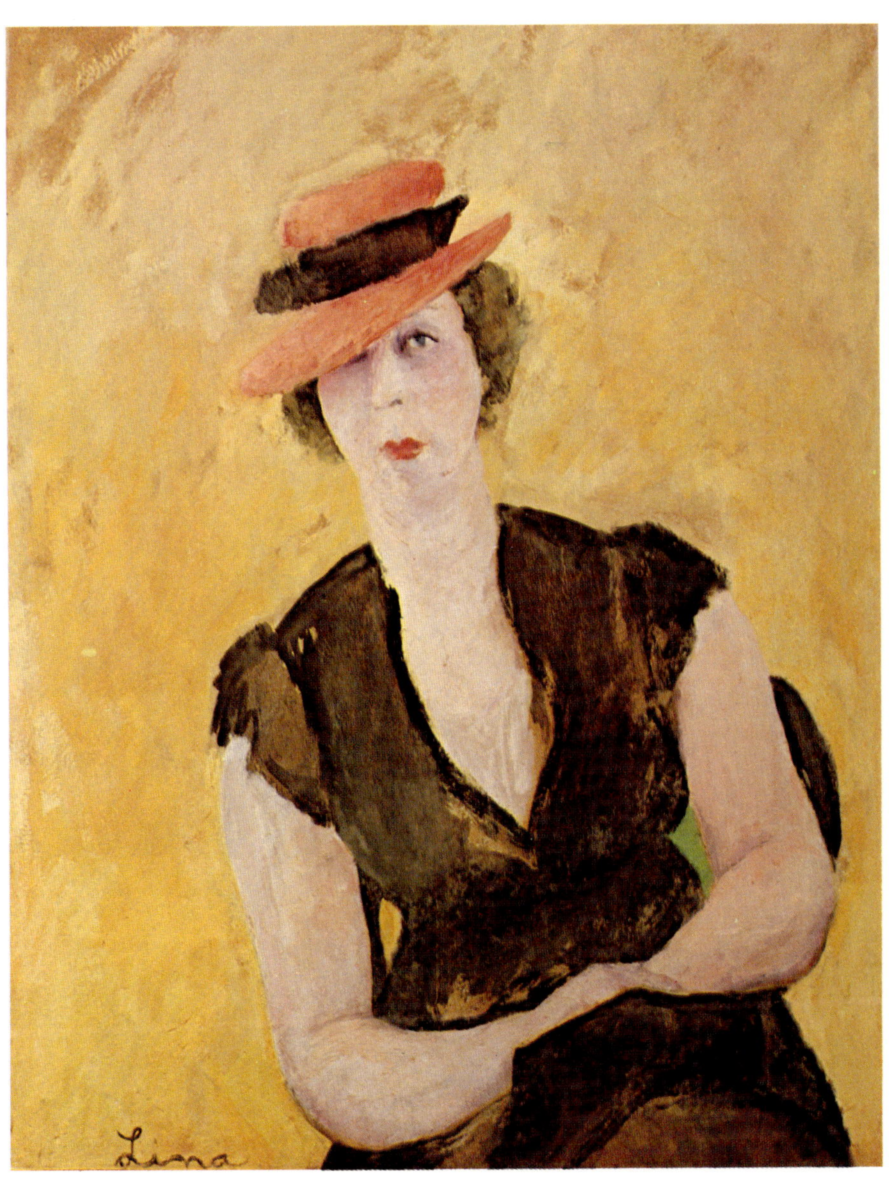

Plate **XIX**
Lina Bryans
b. Germany, 1909–
The Babe is Wise (Portrait of Jean Campbell) 1940
Oil on cardboard
94.1 × 73.2 cm
Inscriptions. Recto: l.l. "Lina"
Verso: "(The Babe is Wise) (Jean Campbell) 1940"
Ex. no. 274 Contemporary Art Society 6th Annual Exhibition, Sydney, 1944.
Presented by Miss Jean Campbell 1962
1063.5

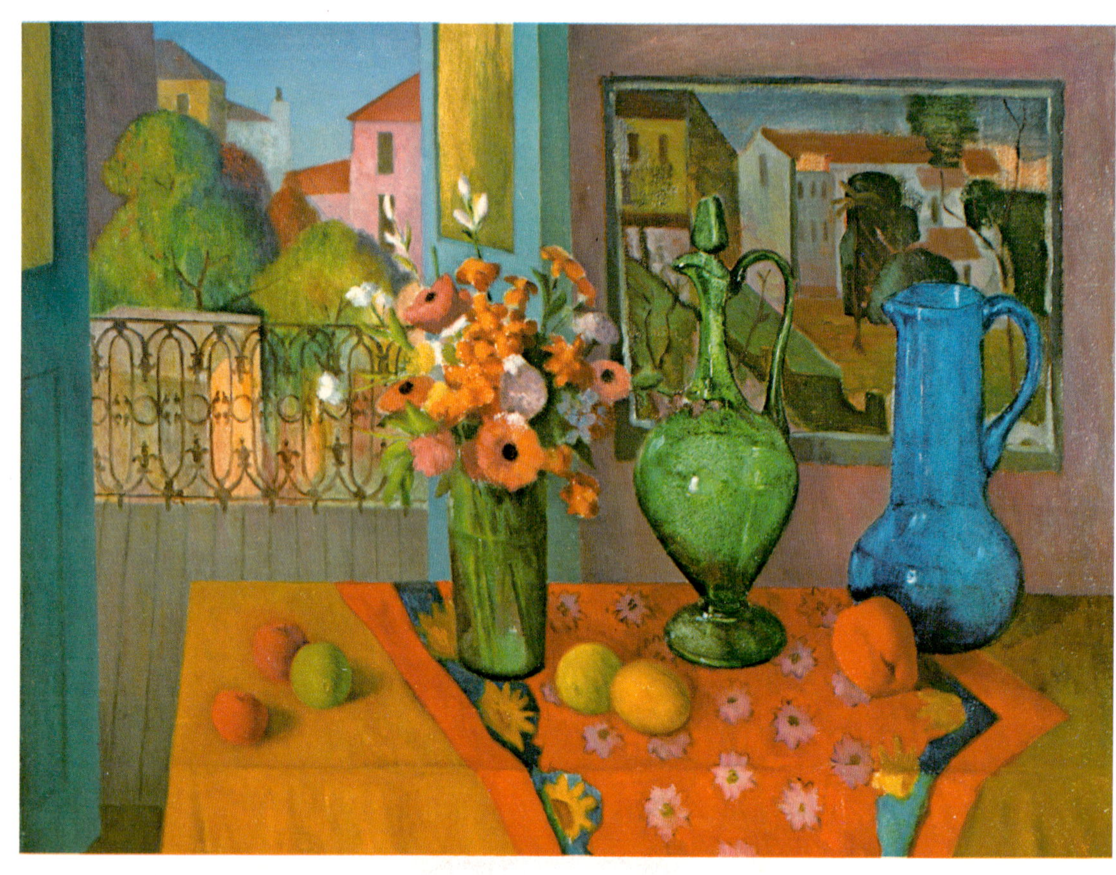

Plate **XX**
Justin O'Brien
Australian, 1917–
Still Life 1950–1
Oil on canvas
61 × 76.2 cm
Backed
Ex. no. 3 Macquarie Galleries, Sydney, 1950
Purchased 1952
2952.4

civilized man; versed in the classics, aware of the stylistic forms of mannerism, the power and beauty of Chaldean and Mesopotamian art. That was long before mere followers drew their superficial responses from the wisdom and achievement of those past civilizations.

Creator of murals, mosaics, stained glass, oil paintings, water colours and wood blocks, his protean output surrounds us. Daily, we pass and are enriched by his decorative achievements. The mosaic on Newspaper House in Collins Street **I'll Put a Girdle Round About the Earth** is splendid. Among many others there is a specially beautiful window in St Peters Church, Eastern Hill, Melbourne. The mosaics for the Australian War Museum in Canberra are known to all. The finest example of the art of the "Deco" period in Australia is the suite of paintings in the Myer Mural Hall, Bourke Street. It is the responsibility of our generation to preserve his decorative work; to save it when the developer comes with his attendant wreckers.

Virgil, a water-colour of about 1922, is a splendid example of his imaginative handling of a literary theme. It is designed in something like the frieze form of a carved sarcophagus, the vigorous central group commands by its position, scale and high key. With a dramatic drop in scale—a device of Italian mannerism— the figures silhouetted in flight and the toppling ruins of the burning city are deployed as in the low relief of a carved background. Colouristically the painting is almost monochromatic but it is enlivened by a richness of tonal contrast within the framework of its strongly disciplined design.

N. G. S. B.
(May, 1972)

49

Grace Crowley, Australian, 1890–

Girl with Goats. 1928

Grace Crowley was born at Cobbadah, New South Wales, in 1890, and since her youth has made a ceaseless, continuing contribution to direct and honest experiment in visual experience. From 1912–18 she studied under Julian Ashton at the Sydney Art School, and her abilities were so evident that she became head teacher there from 1918 till 1922. Her search for knowledge took her to Europe in 1927, where her interest was centred mainly in Paris. A woman of intellect and conviction, she freely acknowledged the help given her by André Lhote's understanding of the abstract principles in figurative painting. The painting **Girl with Goats** exquisitely combines representation and organization. I had the privilege of hearing Miss Crowley describe the unpredictability of goats as models when she described to me the painting of this picture in France. For all

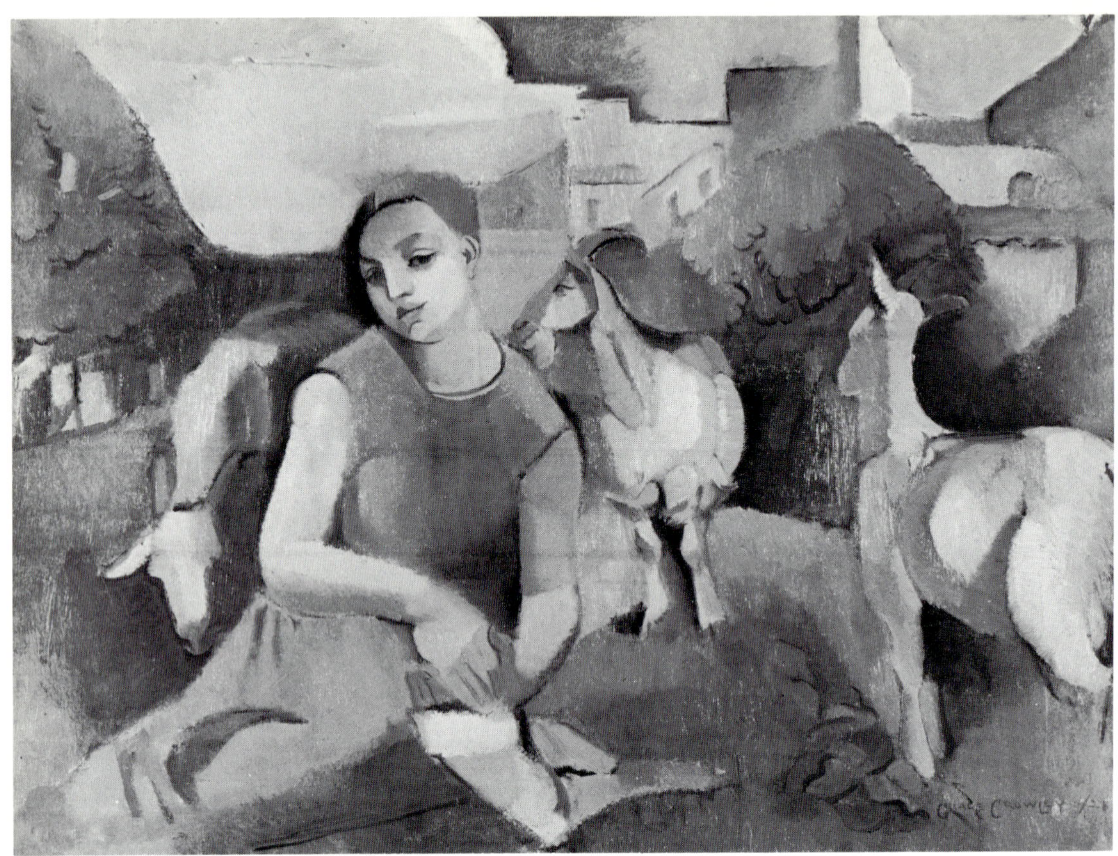

49
Grace Crowley
Australian, 1890–
Girl with Goats 1928
Oil on canvas
54 × 72.1 cm
Inscriptions. Recto: l.r.
"Grace Crowley/28"
Ex. Salon des
Independents francais,
1929
Presented by the
National Gallery
Society of Victoria,
1967
1759.5

its formal control and restrained colour, this picture was based on *plein air* experience. In it one can see the fine intellect which later led Miss Crowley to be a leader of the second wave of modernism in Sydney.

In the 1930s, together with Rah Fizelle, Miss Crowley founded Sydney's only contemporary art school. The association of Fizelle, Crowley, Balson and Hinder at that time is now history. But it would be a mistake to think of these artists as a narrow coterie working only one artistic vein. This elegant painting, for all its grace of colour and depiction, nevertheless presages the conceptual abstraction evidenced in her abstract picture **Painting 1950 (42)** also in the Melbourne Collection.

N. G. S. B.
(January, 1969)

74

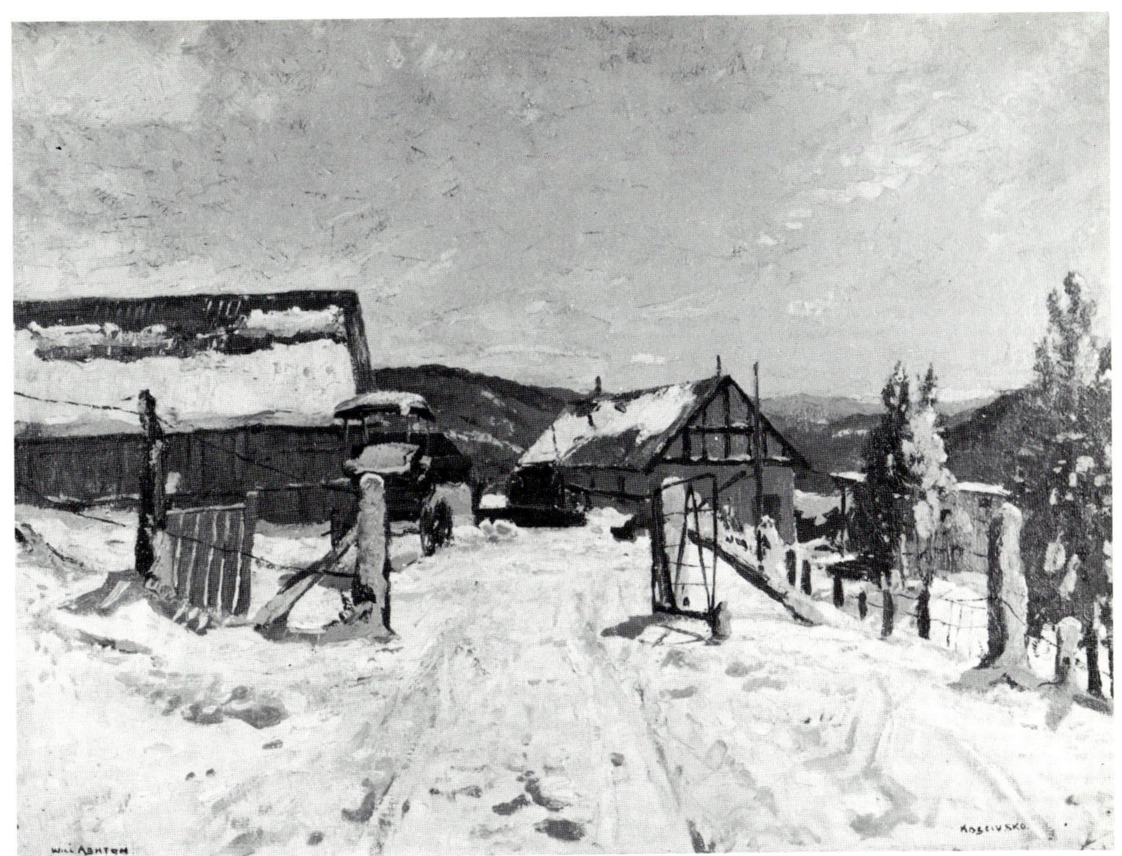

50

Will Ashton, b. England, 1881–1963

The Farm in Winter Kosciusco N.S.W. c. 1930

Sir John William Ashton was born at York, England, in 1881, son of James Ashton (1860–1935), who was a seascape painter and art teacher. He was brought to Adelaide, South Australia in 1884 and made his first art studies under the tuition of his father. In 1900 he studied in England at St Ives, Cornwall, with a group of *plein air* artists under the tutelage of Julius Ollson and Algernon Talmadge. Later he went to Julian's Academy in Paris. A modified impressionist technique used in obedience to *plein air* doctrines informs his many views of famous cities and places.

As an administrator he wielded a strong influence towards conservatism in the art establishment. He was adviser to the Trustees of the National Gallery of South Australia 1913–16, Director of the National Art Gallery of New South Wales 1937–44, appointed a member of the Commonwealth Art Advisory Board in 1918 and its chairman in 1953. He was awarded the Wynne Prize in 1908, 1930 and 1939, and in 1944 was presented with the New South Wales Society of Artists' medal for his services to Australian art. He was awarded the O.B.E. in 1941 and knighted in 1960. Sir John died in 1963.

50
Will Ashton
b. England, 1881–1963
The Farm in Winter, Kosciusco, N.S.W.
c. 1928
Oil on canvas
45.5 × 61 cm
Inscriptions. Recto:
l.l. "Will Ashton"
l.r. "Kosciusco"
Verso: "Exhibited on the Line"
"R.A. 1931." On Stretcher
Ex. no. 27, New Gallery, Melbourne, 1928
Felton Bequest 1944
1396.4

(1970)

Plate XVIII
Isabel Hunter Tweddle, Australian, 1877–1945
Portrait of Ivy Ball in Fancy Dress
Isabel Hunter Tweddle née Hunter was born in Deniliquin in 1877, and studied
at the National Gallery School under Fred McCubbin and L. Bernard Hall.
In the 1920s she moved from the realist tradition to a form of free and spontaneous
impressionism owing something to the late French tradition. She became associated
with William Frater and Arnold Shore and at the 1931 exhibition, "Twenty
Melbourne Painters", her works were hung with theirs and were singled out for
favourable comment by the critic Basil Burdett. A painter of still life, landscape
and portraits in oil, pastel and charcoal, her painting was executed rapidly and
is noted for an elegant use of pure high-keyed colour.

(1970)

Footnote: The subject of this portrait is Miss Ball whose family was connected with the recently
closed Melbourne department store, Ball and Welch.

J.P.
(1976)

51
Arnold Shore, Australian, 1897–1963
The Vegetable Garden. 1939
52
Arnold Shore, Australian, 1897–1963
Ideal Landscape. 1959
Stained glass artist, painter in oils, mainly of landscape and still life, some
portraits, lecturer, teacher and newspaper critic, Arnold Shore studied at the
National Gallery School Melbourne, 1911–16 while working as an apprentice
stained-glass craftsman at Brooks Robinson Studios. For a time he studied under
Max Meldrum and was influenced by his uncompromising theories of tonal
realism. From 1930 he worked as a professional artist supplementing his income
by teaching and writing, then as a newspaper critic for the *Argus* then *The Age*
while working as a guide lecturer (1950–60) at the National Gallery of Victoria.

In 1932 he founded a modern art school in Melbourne with George Bell.
During 1934–5 while Bell was absent abroad for some sixteen months, Shore
ran the school alone, deputising for Bell as art critic on the *Sun News Pictorial*.
The partnership was dissolved in 1937, Bell continuing the school alone. Shore
was a life-long friend of William Frater, but did not share Frater's devotion to
the example of Cezanne. Shore's art found its impetus more in admiration of the

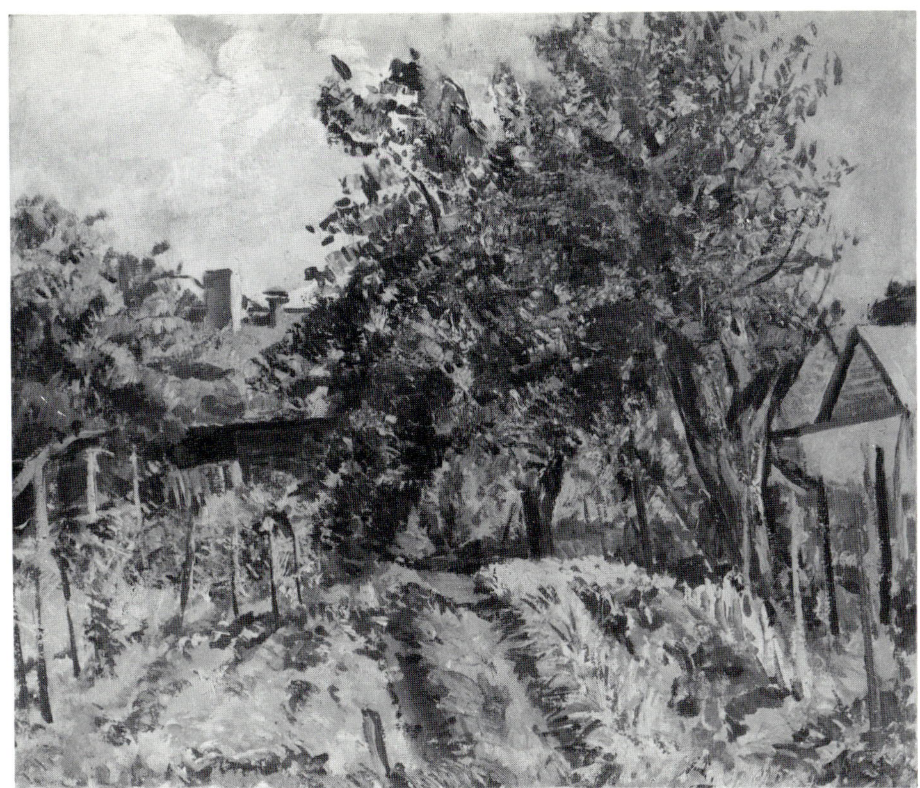

work of Vincent Van Gogh. The Shore/Bell art school was the first "modern art" school in Melbourne and its influence was germinal to many artists. However Shore's real importance lies in his painting. At his best his works have a spontaneity and vitality which emphasises the living quality of those things he most liked to paint: flowers, gardens, and the growing vigour of the enveloping bush.

(1970)

Expressionism makes of the object an emotionally charged symbol of the artist's subjective feelings. **The Vegetable Garden** is a tranquil domestic scene of surprising vivacity and power which well illustrates this principle.

A. P.
(1961)

Arnold Shore almost invariably portrayed his vivid awareness of wooded landscapes in fairly small canvases. The only exception to this is the cloth collage **Ideal Landscape** he made for Madame Vigano. It is unique. Its strong formal pattern shows the influence of stain-glass working which was the mainstay and support of many artists including William Frater and Alan Sumner.

(1971)

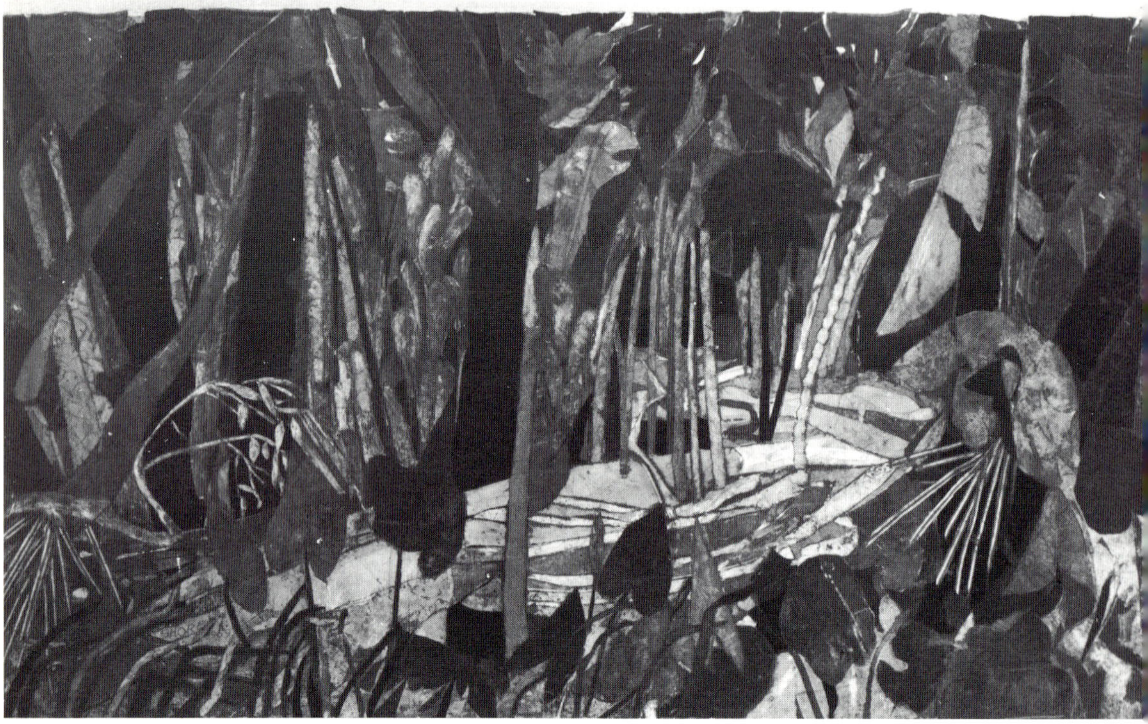

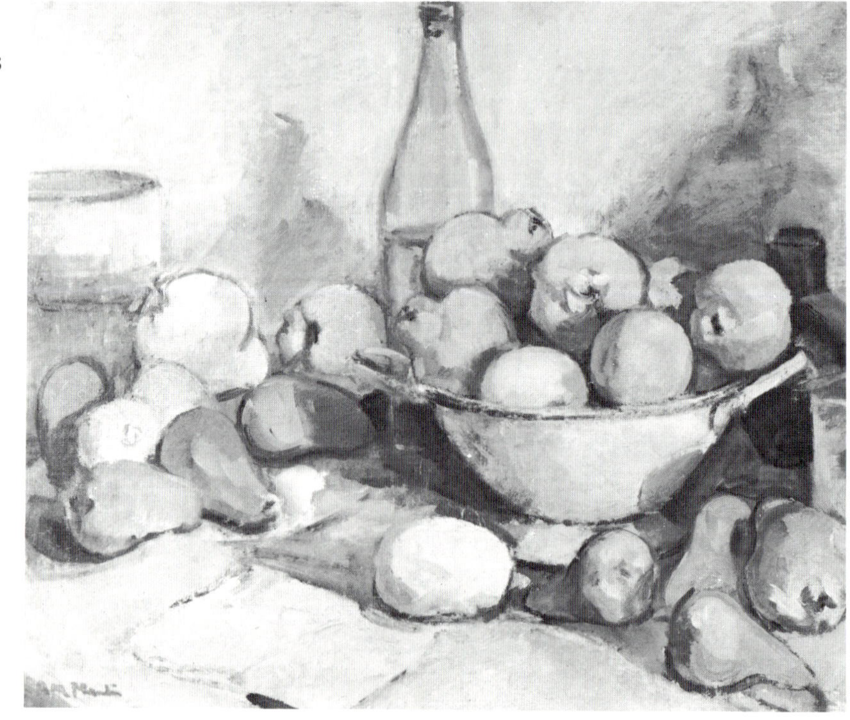

52
Arnold Shore
Australian, 1897–1963
Ideal Landscape
1959
Cloth collage
205 × 504 cm
Inscriptions. Recto:
l.l. "Shore 1959"
Commissioned by
Madame Vigano for
Mario's Restaurant,
Melbourne.
Purchased from the
estate of Maria
Teresa Vigano 1971
A1/1971

53
Ada May Plante
b. New Zealand,
1875–1950
"Quinces" c. 1940
Oil on canvas on
hardboard
50.5 × 60.5 cm
Inscriptions. Recto:
l.l. "A. M. Plante"
Purchased 1945
1487.4

53

Ada May Plante, b. New Zealand, 1875–1950

Quinces. c. 1940

Painter of landscape, still life and portraits in a post-impressionist manner, Ada May Plante was born in Temuka, New Zealand in 1875 and came to Melbourne in 1888. Her first art studies were made at the National Gallery School, Melbourne. About 1902 she proceeded to Europe for further study, as did most of her generation, first in London and then at Julian's Academy, Paris. Returning to Melbourne she shared a studio with Isabel Hunter Tweddle. In the later 1920s, prompted by William Frater, both artists became associated with the emergent post-impressionist school, then criticized as "modern". She exhibited with the inaugural exhibition of the "Contemporary Art Group Melbourne" in 1932. In the 1940s Plante had a studio at the Darebin home of Lina Bryans. She spent her last years at Research, then a rural outer suburb of Melbourne, there sharing a cottage with Miss Asquith Baker.

Miss Plante was an artist of selective output, her virtues of restrained colour and closely considered composition are seen to best advantage in her still life.

(1970)

54

James Gleeson, Australian, 1915–

We Inhabit the Corrosive Littoral of Habit. 1940

James Gleeson was born in Sydney where he is now well known both as artist and as art critic. His initial training was pursued mainly at East Sydney Technical College. From there he entered the Education Department as lecturer on art but continued to paint, making his effective artistic debut in 1939, at the inaugural exhibition of the Contemporary Art Society in Melbourne. There he appeared as one of the first Australian artists to be influenced by the European surrealist movement.

There is always a time-lag in the transfer of styles from great centres of artistic activity to outlying places. The surrealist creed, whose first modern appearance dates from the "Dada" movement of 1915–22, did not reach Australia till its time of revitalized activity about 1936. Surrealism is influenced by psychoanalysis. By associating unexpected objects literally portrayed, the painter seeks super-real images of the subconscious mind or the poetic intimations of dreams. No surrealist has worked for long according to its rigid doctrine of unconscious images uncontrolled by reason. Least so Gleeson, who is an intellectual artist. His imagination uses the literary symbols of the cycle of life and death, spring and winter, decay and regeneration. This painting displays the important role

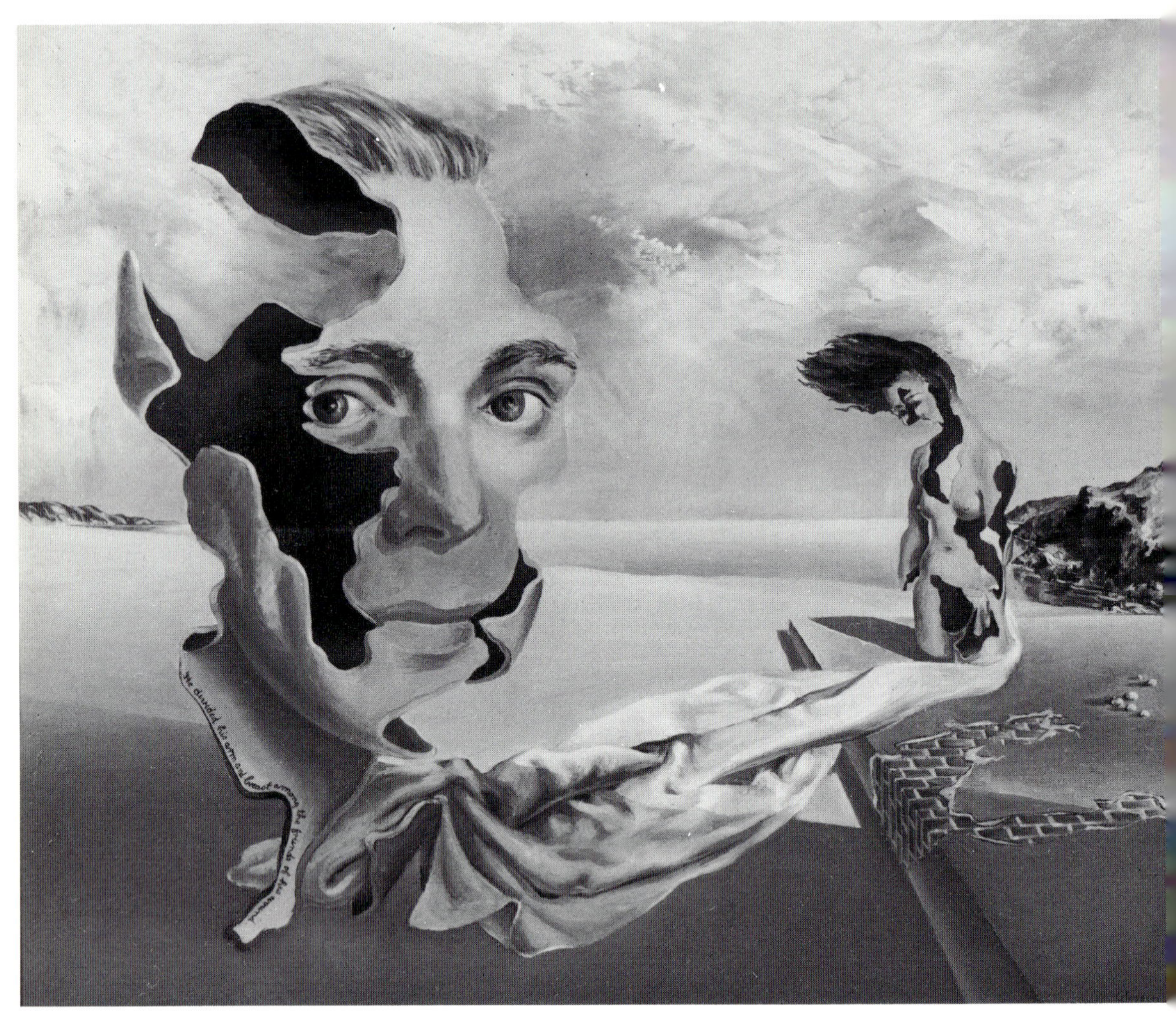

54
James Gleeson
Australian, 1915–
We Inhabit the Corrosive Littoral of Habit 1940
Oil on canvas
40.7 × 51.1 cm
Inscriptions. Recto: l.r. "Gleeson 1940"
Backed
Ex. no. 68, Contemporary Art Society Annual Ex., 1940
Presented anonymously through the Contemporary Art Society 1941
1096.4

of the title as integral part of surrealist pictures. Gleeson now works in a much more vivid technique but, more than any other Australian painter, he remains within the orbit of surrealism.

A. P.
(1961)

Plate XIX
Lina Bryans, b. Hamburg, 1909–
The Babe is Wise. (Portrait of Jean Campbell) 1940

Lina Bryans is a painter in oil of landscapes, city scapes and portraits, and she also paints portrait studies in pastel. Lina Bryans, nee Hollenstein was born in Hamburg of Australian parents. It is nevertheless in Melbourne that her artistic life was formed. About 1937 she made her first essay in painting with William Frater, and for the next decade the two artists painted together. During this period Lina Bryans was closely associated with the champions of intellectual and artistic liberalism in Victoria, notably Vance and Nettie Palmer, Clem Christesen, Danila Vassilieff, Adrian Lawlor, A. M. Plante, Arnold Shore and Norman Macgeorge. For two years from 1945 Ian Fairweather worked in a studio at her home at Darebin. However Lina Bryans's art developed in a personal somewhat expressional fashion allowing free rein to her gifts as an emotional colourist. In recent years her work has shown an increasing freedom of idiom in the use of abstract forms which are nevertheless closely related to realist observation.

(1970)

The painting illustrated introduces one to the work of two artists, Lina Bryans, the painter, and Jean Campbell, the novelist, who is the sitter.

This portrait shows the vigorous, personal originality which enabled Lina to break free of the almost ubiquitous traditions of Art Deco before the Second World War. Her paintings demand of the beholder an immediacy of response akin to that which prompted the artist herself. Her abilities as a superb colourist are deployed in a sensitive understanding of the psychology of the sitter.

Miss Jean Campbell is a woman who contributed considerably to the emergence of the Australian novel.

The title of the painting is the title of one of Miss Campbell's novels, published in 1939. The insouciant chic of the hat reflects the sophistication of Miss Campbell's writing and her awareness and involvement in all aspects of its fashion and art. The colour scheme and freedom of brush work emphasizes the aware and probing eye of the novelist's somewhat sardonic philosophy in regard to the life of metropolitan cities.

This painting which was presented to the collection most generously by Miss Campbell adds important dimensions of both sociological and artistic acuity.

N. G. S. B.
(August, 1970)

55

Eric Wilson, Australian, 1911–46
Design for a Mural. 1941
Before his untimely death in 1946, Eric Wilson advanced further towards a form of intellectual abstraction than any other Australian painter. He was born in Sydney, trained first under Julian Ashton, and won a travelling scholarship in 1937. In London he studied under Amedee Ozenfant, a French artist who introduced him to the art of moving from real objects towards abstractions. This manner is well displayed in this formal design, where the starting point for the abstract shapes is still visible. A comparable picture is **Stove Theme** in the Art Gallery of N.S.W.

Wilson returned to Australia in 1939, where as teacher of abstract design at East Sydney Technical College he had much influence. A man of refined sensibility, he always sought formal rhythms, even in those paintings of Paris and Glasgow which are basically realistic views of city architecture. Wilson was an artist of classical bent seeking the eternal forms beneath the fleeting impressions of nature. The style of abstract art he ably represents has not been pursued greatly in Australia. Contemporary painters seek rather the emotional power of expressionist art or the symbolic content of narrative painting.

A. P.
(1961)

56

Sir Russell Drysdale, b. England, 1912–
Moody's Pub. 1941

Russell Drysdale was born in England, but came to Australia as a child. Upon leaving school he intended to follow his family's pastoral interests, but an inclination towards art was stimulated by travels in Europe. In 1935 he became a full-time student at George Bell's studio in Melbourne.

During his several visits to Europe, it was the rich colour of the Venetian

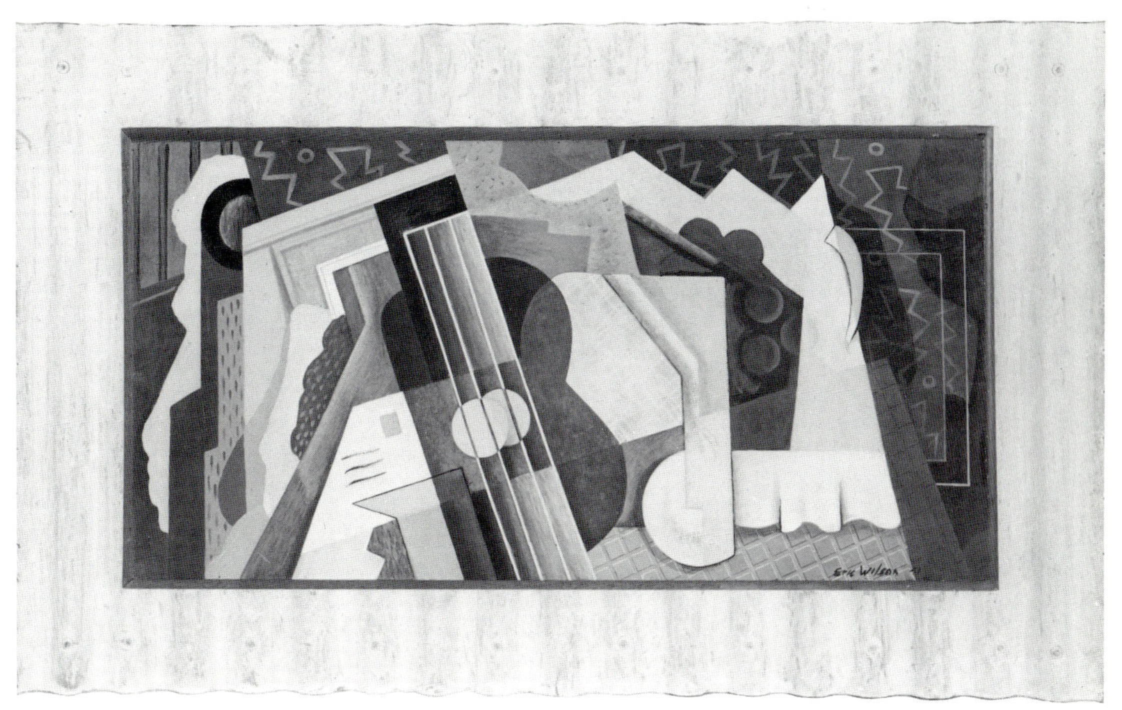

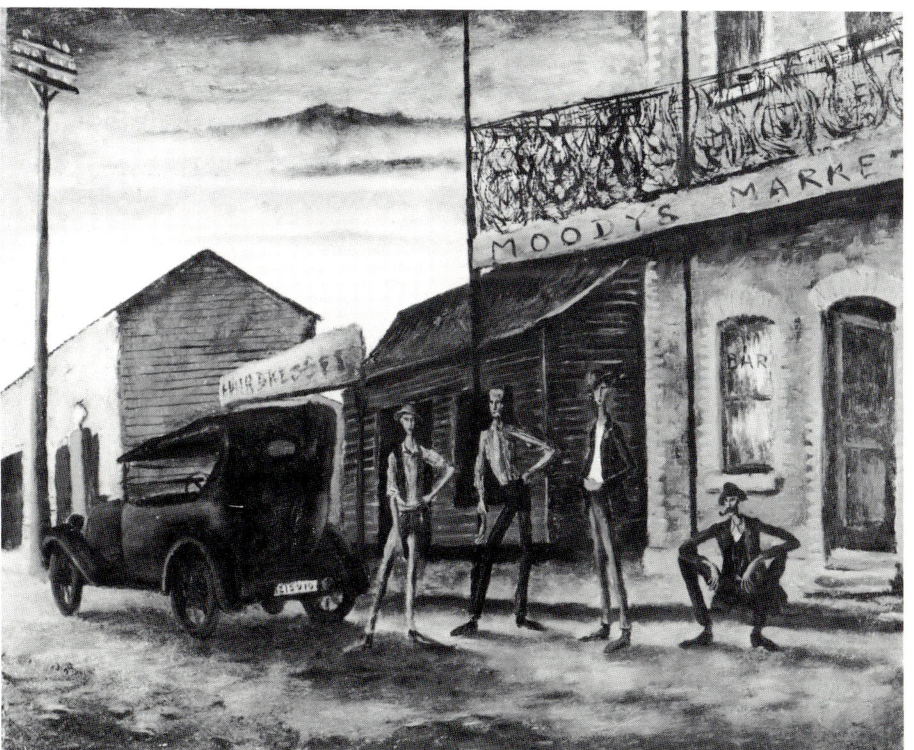

55
Eric Wilson
Australian, 1911–46
Design for a Mural
1941
Oil on plywood
53.3 × 106.2 cm
Inscriptions. Recto: l.r.
"Eric Wilson '41"
Ex. no. 252 "Design
for a Mural",
Contemporary
Art Soc. Annual Ex.,
Melb. 1941
Purchased 1958
54.5

56
Sir Russell Drysdale
b. England, 1912–
Moody's Pub 1941
Oil on panel
50.8 × 61.6 cm
Inscriptions. Recto:
l.r. "Russell Drysdale"
Backed
Ex. no. 4, Macquarie
Galleries, 1942
Purchased 1942
1147.4

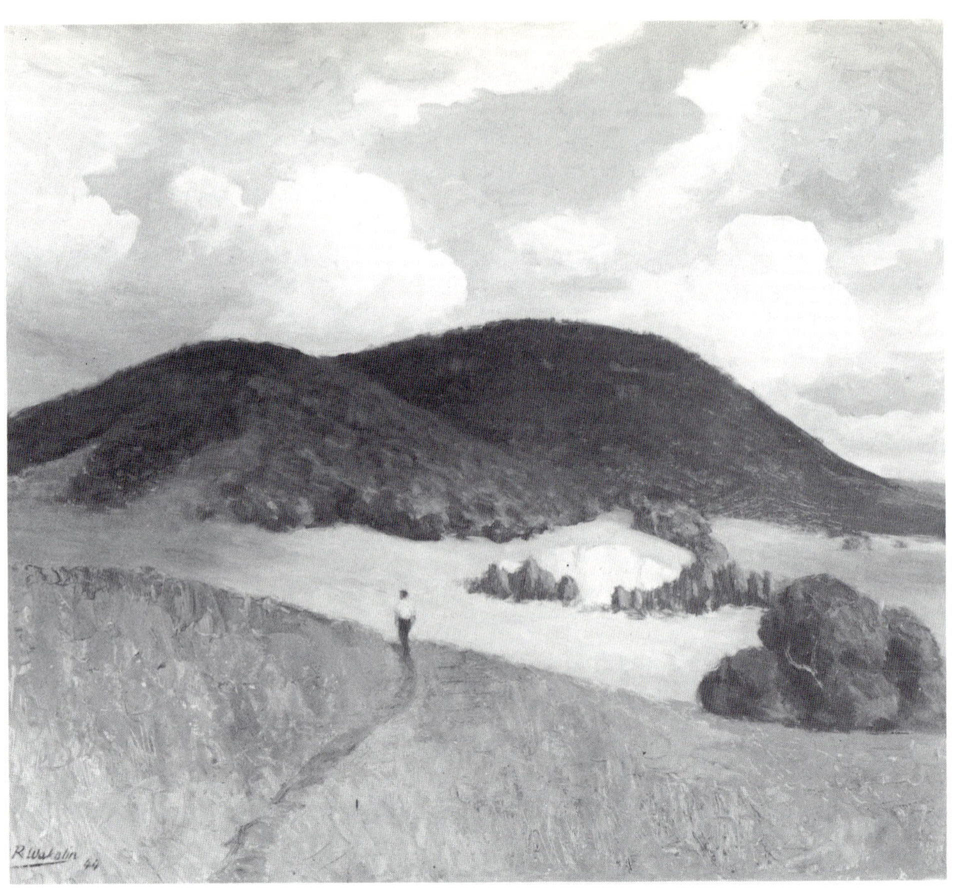

57
Roland Wakelin
b. New Zealand,
1887–1971
**Black Mountain,
Canberra** 1944
Oil on cardboard
59.5 × 68.5 cm
Inscriptions. Recto: l.l.
"R. Wakelin 44"
Ex. Macquarie
Galleries, Sydney, 1944
Purchased 1946
1611.4

painters which seems to have impressed him most. Though a painter of the sparsely settled parts of Australia, he does not paint the wide expanses of the pastoralist's paradise that Streeton encompassed. His theme is the life of the small outback town, and of the selectors of the drought-plagued areas of the west.

Though Drysdale's subject matter is realist, his manner is romantic. Through each individual he suggests the type. Drovers, rabbiters, jackeroos, and the wives and children of the outback are presented in formal compositions of rich dramatic colour. **Moody's Pub,** with its group of lounging men, is the essence of every remote pub in the dry plains. Drysdale's strong dramatic sense is saved from the merely theatrical by an ironic sense of detachment. It is with a harsher note, and in much richer scale, that he treats those subjects of everyday pioneering life first introduced to Australian art by S. T. Gill.

A. P.
(1961)

57

Roland Wakelin, b. New Zealand, 1887–1971
Black Mountain, Canberra. 1944
Roland Wakelin, one of the first artists in Australia to be influenced by post-impressionist theories, came to Sydney in 1912. He studied for some years at the Royal Art Society's classes, but it was in the company of Sydney's younger

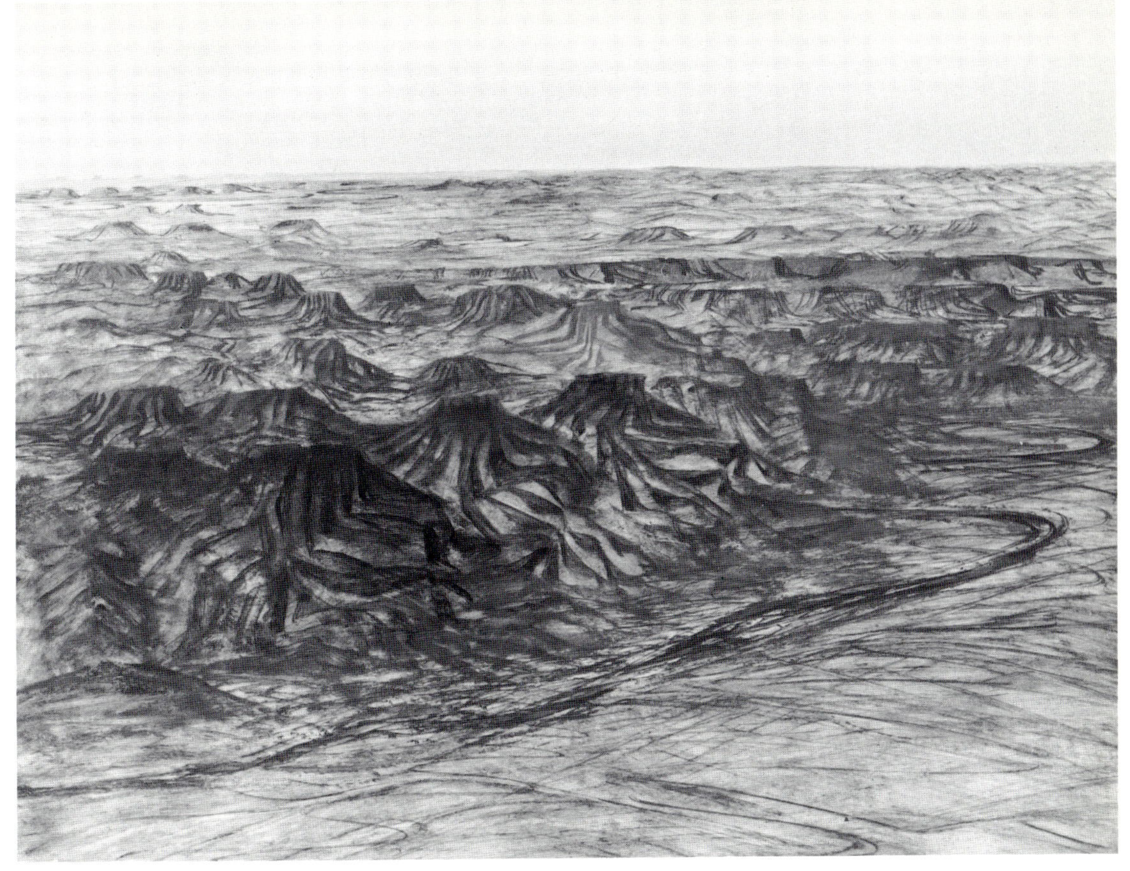

experimental artists, seeking a new approach to replace the accepted impressionist manner, that he discovered the post-impressionist masters—Van Gogh (1853–90), Gauguin (1848–1903) and Cezanne (1839–1906). During the 1914–18 war, working with Roy de Maistre and Grace Cossington Smith, he simplified the structure of his painting with a bias towards cubism, and developed that personal limited palette which still characterizes his work. Though their experiments now seem mild, the young artists were much criticized. After the war they went abroad, Wakelin returning in 1924.

Primarily a landscapist, Wakelin always emphasizes the weight and design underlying the impressionist surface of his painting. His palette lends his work an overall gold-yellow hue, particularly in its higher register, and a spontaneous physical delight in the outdoors breathes through the formal concentration of his work. In this boldly composed picture, mountains, clumps of trees and clouds share an air of equal solidity, while the broken rhythm of light and dark areas creates the sense of a brisk wind blowing across the rolling landscape.

A. P.
(1961)

58
Sidney Nolan
Australian, 1917–
Central Australia
1949
91.5 × 122 cm
Ex. no. 19, David
Jones Gallery, Sydney,
1950
Purchased 1950
2241.4

58

Sidney Nolan, Australian, 1917–

Central Australia. 1949

Though now living abroad, with London as his headquarters, Sidney Nolan was born in Melbourne. He first studied at various Technical Art Schools and subsequently at the National Gallery School. Meantime he worked in various industries practising crafts associated with glass painting, lacquer, and silk screen techniques. Largely a primitive and self-taught painter, he was an early member of the Contemporary Art Society. From 1940 he exhibited regularly in Melbourne and Sydney. Since going abroad he has held successful exhibitions of his work in Rome, Paris, London and New York.

Nolan tends to paint in series—groups of pictures upon a single theme. These range from one aspect of landscape to subject pictures like the "Ned Kelly" series of 1946 or the "Leda and the Swan" series of 1960. He is best known in Australia by his paintings of the harsh, eroded landscapes of central Australia. Here he discards the fertile countryside of the impressionists and presents a bird's eye view of desert. The countryside is laid out like a vast contour map in the brilliant colours of the enamels he prefers to use. This aerial vision is familiar to his fellow countrymen, who are constant air travellers. In those series which incorporate figures, Nolan attempts to fuse landscape with historical anecdote to create national myths. These latter pictures have won him much fame in Europe.

A. P.
(1961)

59

Arthur Boyd, Australian, 1920–

Irrigation Lake, Wimmera. 1949–50

Arthur Boyd is mainly self-taught, though he began painting under the tutelage of his grandfather, Arthur Merric Boyd (1862–1940). In pursuit of ideals inspired by his own imagination and the example of European masters, whose work he has studied in reproduction, he has developed a style and technique of his own.

Boyd works in two manners, as a landscapist and as a figure painter of symbolical subjects. This landscape reveals his interest in the half-tamed aspect of the Australian countryside—the juxtaposition of barren land and the endeavours of man. The small scale of the inhabitants, the wide expanse of land and sky, reflect his study of the Netherlands painter Pieter Breughel (1525/30–1569). Opposed to this aspect of Boyd's work is his allegorical painting best exemplified in his series, "Love, Marriage and Death of a Half-Caste" exhibited in 1958.

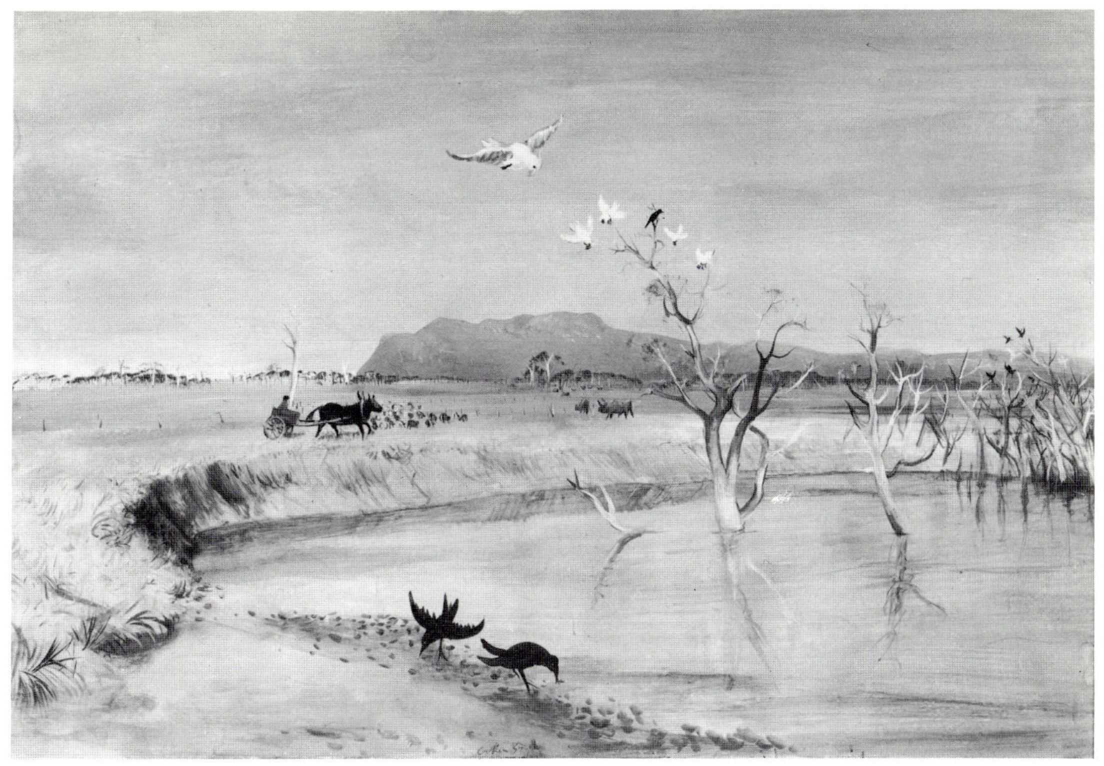

Like Sidney Nolan, Boyd attempts a fusion of romantic poetic representation
with the historic scene and local landscape.

His work is well represented in all State galleries, and he also works in an
expressionist form of ceramic sculpture. He has been living in England since
early in 1960, and is a leading member of a group of artists known as "Anti-
podeans".

A. P.
(1961)

59
Arthur Boyd
Australian, b. 1920
**Irrigation Lake,
Wimmera** 1949–50
Resin and tempera
on hardboard
82 × 121.9 cm
Inscriptions. Recto:
l.c. "Arthur Boyd"
Backed
Purchased 1950
2331.4

60

Ralph Balson, b. England, 1890–1964

Constructive Painting. 1950

Balson is one of the key figures in the development of non-representational
painting in Australia. His work in Sydney with Miss Grace Crowley and Mr Frank
Hinder is part of the history of Australian Art. No public collection can afford
to be without a collection of works by this artist who was not only influential,
but whose works are of fine quality. His example as a precursor of some
current attitudes is self evident. This painting is widely regarded as the best
picture Balson painted in this style. Its provenance from the collection of the
fellow artist with whom he operated Sydney's only school of "Modern" art
guarantees its quality. It was exhibited in the retrospective exhibition "Balson,

60
Ralph Balson
b. England, 1890–1964
Constructive Painting 1950
Oil on hardboard
122.2 × 122 cm
Inscriptions. Verso: "Constructive
Painting Ralph Balson 1950"
Ex. Balson, Crowley, Fizelle, Hinder
Art Gallery of New South Wales, October 1966
Purchased 1969
96.6

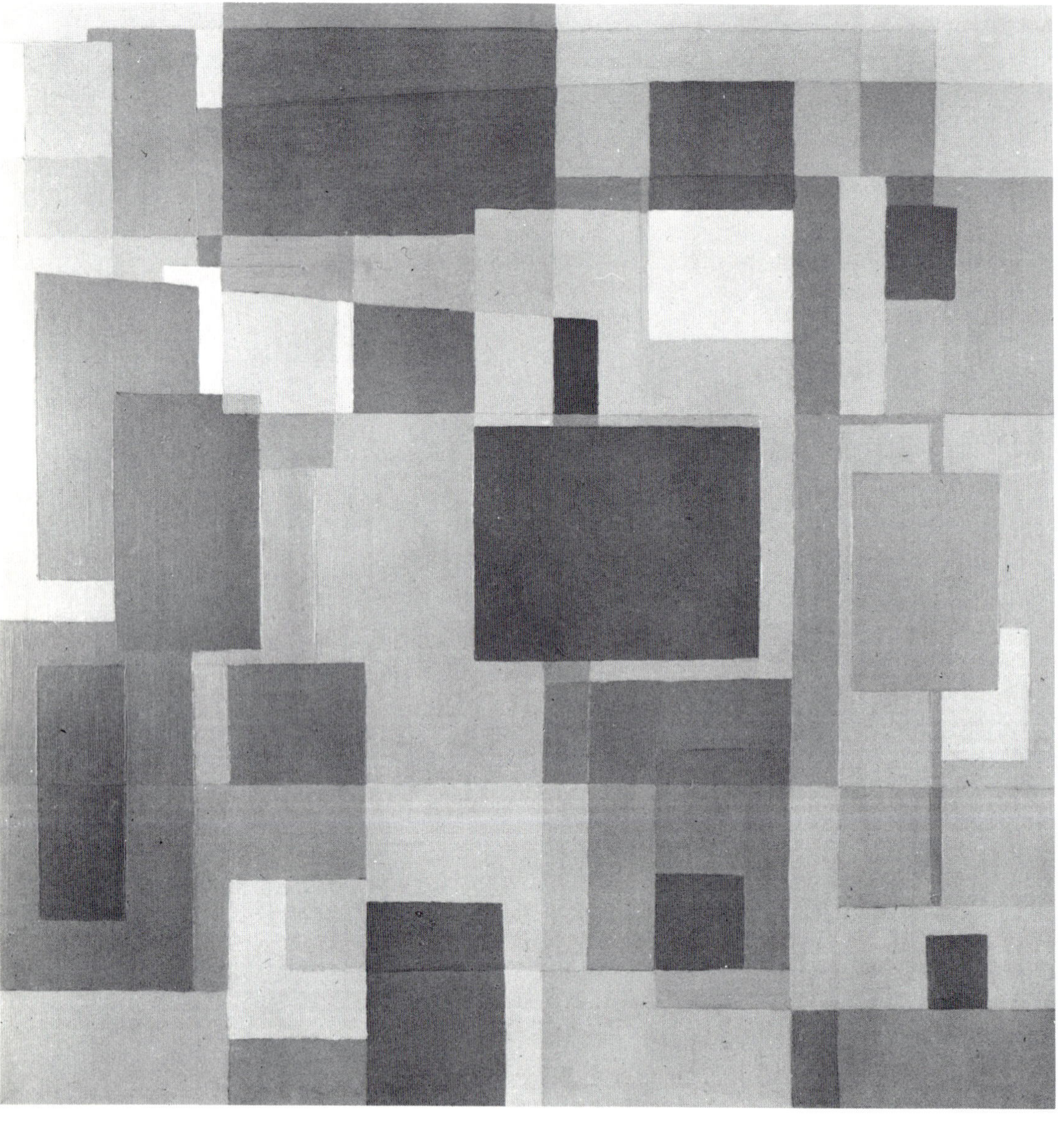

Crowley, Fizelle, Hinder" compiled by the Art Gallery of N.S.W. in 1966. It is reproduced in colour in *Art and Australia* Vol. 2 No. 4 (1965). It was offered to us in friendship by Miss Crowley.

(1969)

Footnote: Ralph Balson was born in England in 1890 and came to Sydney in 1913. He painted part-time while he worked as a house painter until his retirement in 1956. He took formal painting lessons at the Julian Ashton School, where he attended night classes for a few years in the 1920s. About 1934, Balson worked with Grace Crowley, Rah Fizelle and Frank Hinder, painting on Saturday mornings at the Crowley-Fizelle Art School which taught modern art, and after the school closed, with Grace Crowley at her studio. His interest in cubist and abstract art grew from his fellow artists and from his own wide reading. After a group exhibition of cubist art, held at David Jones Gallery in 1939, Balson held the first one-man exhibition of entirely non-figurative painting seen in Australia at Anthony Hordern's in 1941.

With Grace Crowley, Frank Hinder and Gerald Ryan, he held a Constructive Paintings Exhibition at the Macquarie Galleries in 1944. By 1955, he considered Mondrian the greatest single influence on his work. From 1949 to 1959 he taught abstract painting part-time at East Sydney Technical College, and in 1960 and 1961 left Australia to visit England, France and America. At this time he was working with a poured technique, flowing paint across the picture's surface. He died in Sydney in 1964, when he was again preparing to travel abroad.

J. P.
(1976)

61
Lloyd Rees, Australian, 1895–
Omega Pastoral. 1950
Lloyd Rees was born in Brisbane, and commenced his art training at the Technical College there. In 1917 he joined the Smith and Julius Studios in Sydney. He met the younger eclectic artists around Roland Wakelin, who were discussing everything from post-impressionism to the tonal theories of Max Meldrum. Though Rees joined the discussions, he did not identify himself with the group. In 1923 he went to Europe, studying both in Rome and in London. Returning in 1924, he spent some years perfecting his draughtsmanship by constant pencil drawing from nature.

Rees is not a controversial artist. He has pursued his romantic vision of the landscape undeterred by current fashions. Though he works directly from nature, his pictures have an air of artificial formality rather than spontaneity. His favourite subjects are wide vistas of rolling hills or the expanse of a valley. These scenes he portrays not in the high key of Arthur Streeton (1867–1943) but in muted tones and sombre colours. The browns and greens of **Omega Pastoral** typify his palette. By a lack of focus in the foreground and a lightening of tone

61
Lloyd Rees
Australian, 1895–
Omega Pastoral 1950
Oil on canvas
79.3 × 107.6 cm
Inscriptions. Recto:
l.l. "L. Rees '50"
Backed
Ex. Soc. of Artists,
Sydney, 1950
Felton Bequest 1950
2338.4

in the reflections of the meandering stream, Rees here concentrates interest on the middleground of his picture. It is a handsome, ordered composition evoking a mood of nature rather than visually describing a landscape. The Art Gallery of New South Wales has a particularly fine collection of his work.

A. P.
(1961)

Plate XX
Justin O'Brien, Australian, 1917–
Still Life. 1950–1
Justin O'Brien studied painting with Edward Smith, the Sydney portraitist, and later taught the craft of painting. He served with the 2nd A.I.F. and was taken prisoner of war in Greece. During his imprisonment in Poland for two and a half years, he contrived to paint whenever possible. Upon his return to Australia, these works were exhibited at the Macquarie Galleries, Sydney. Since then he has travelled in France, Italy and England, while developing a personal style of great originality.

62
Justin O'Brien
Australian, 1917–
**The Virgin
Enthroned** 1951
Oil on canvas
Tryptich
113 × 49.2, 113 ×
81.2, 113 × 49.2 cm
Backed
Winning entry First
Blake Prize for
Religious Art, 1951
Felton Bequest 1951
2901.4

Here the art of a contemporary Australian reflects the culture of past eras in Europe. O'Brien's work refers both to the splendour of Byzantium and to the intellectual elegance of fourteenth century Italy, while remaining firmly his own. As an object, this painting excites our sense of delight by its colour and brilliance, as does a jewel, yet we remain conscious of the intellect controlling the design. The real landscape glimpsed through the window challenges the painted image upon the wall; the flagon, flowers and fruit (the traditional objects of still-life painting) challenge both landscapes by the vividness—yet all is held in a vital equilibrium. This capacity to stylize, combined with an innate Irish sense of devotion, has made O'Brien a fine painter of religious subjects. In 1951 he won the first Blake Prize for a religious painting, a triptych **Virgin Enthroned (62)** now in the collection of the National Gallery of Victoria.

A. P.
(1961)

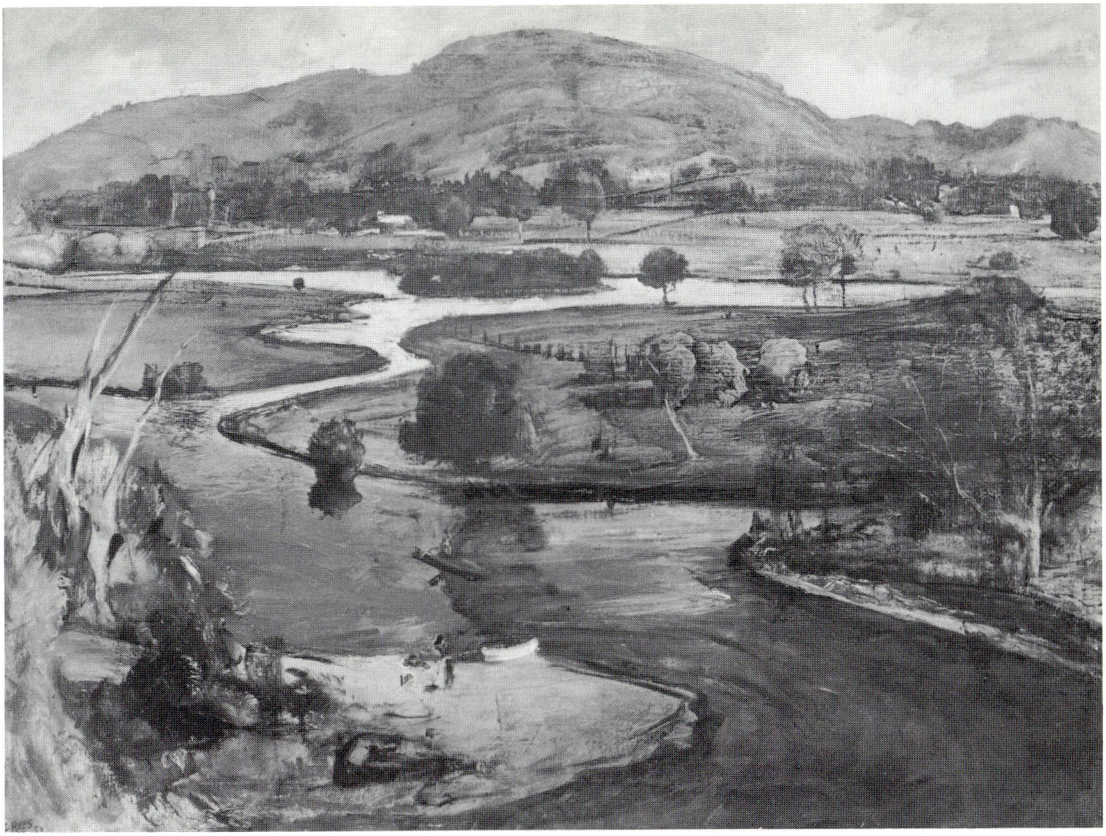

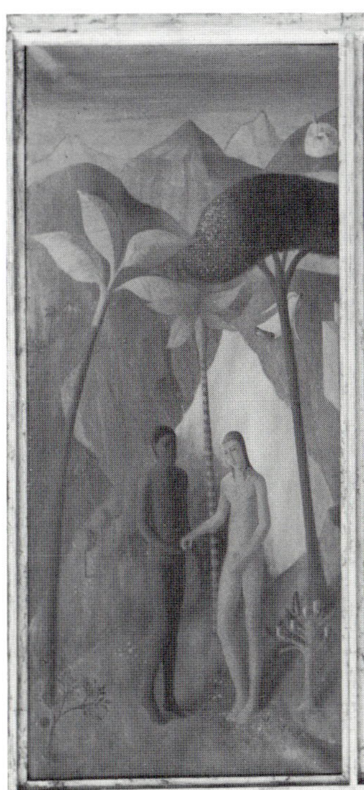
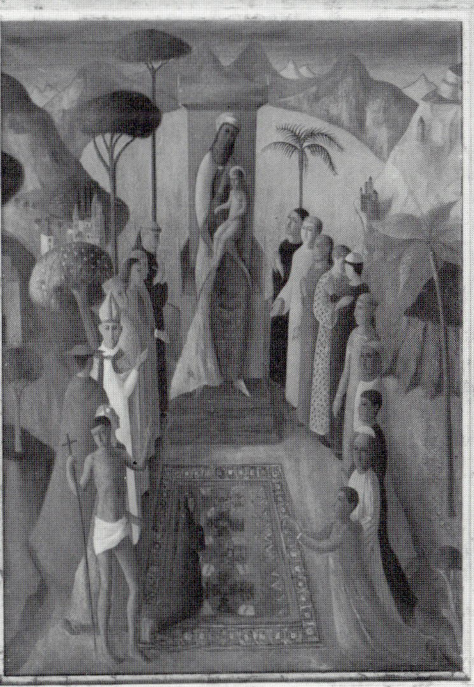
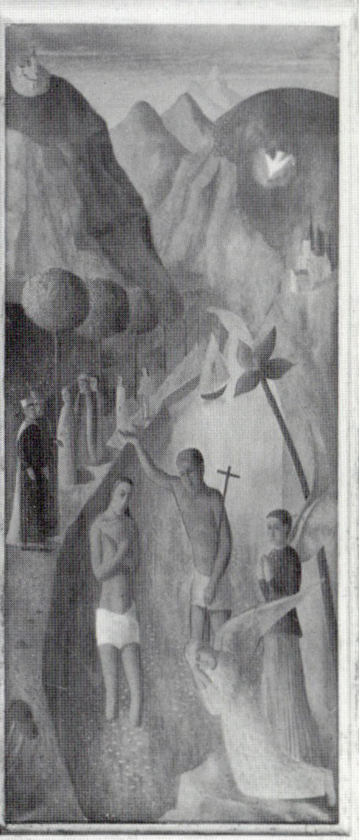

63
Danila Vassilieff
b. Russia, 1899–1958
Expressive Female Nude 1950
Lilydale limestone
45.9 × 31 × 27 cm
Inscriptions. On base of left foot: "D. V. 1950"
Purchased 1969
73.6

62

Justin O'Brien, Australian, 1917–
The Virgin Enthroned. 1951
This painting remains one of the outstanding religious pictures by the artist. In it are displayed to their fullest extent a capacity for formal structural design and for graceful arabesques of decorative linear surface patterns deployed upon that structure. Here also is evident his unrivalled sense of rich and resonant colour.

Justin O'Brien always commences his work with a series of drawings; these becoming more detailed and finished as the concept moves through the modification of the creative process towards its final form.

Then upon transferring his cartoon to the canvas, there begins the actual painting. O'Brien works slowly and meticulously building up his jewel like surface by semi-transparent glazes of colour one upon the other, enriching each area in relation to its juxtaposed local colour. The artist inherits the Hellenistic tradition of Byzantine Art, an art of elegance and craftsmanship.

One must regard this triptych as an altar piece telling in vivid visual form its religious story. The central panel **The Virgin Enthroned** is a glory where the Madonna presents to an encircling group of saints and martyrs the Christ Child, the Saviour. On the left is sin—Eve passes the apple to Adam. On the right is Salvation. John baptises Christ in the Jordan. Central is the resolution and triumph of these polarities. The individual panels are linked by the decorative curvilinear forms of the trees, and the blue lake which makes an auriole behind the enthroned Virgin.

While relating its pious story in shining light this painting itself is a precious object offered as part of an act of religious devotion.

N. G. S. B.
(March, 1973)

Footnote: Further biographical details accompany Plate XX. on p. 90.

63

Danila Vassilieff, b. Russia, 1899–1958
Expressive Female Nude. 1950
Danila Vassilieff was an active force in the emergence of the Contemporary Art Society in 1938 in Melbourne. His street scenes, and expressionist paintings are said to have influenced the early work of Perceval and Boyd. However, his finest artistic achievement is doubtless to be found in his carvings in Lilydale limestone which he commenced in 1950.

(1969)

Footnote: Born in Russia, Vassilieff escaped from the Russian Revolution into Persia in 1922. He travelled through Asia to Northern Australia, starting to paint in 1929 whilst living in Queens-

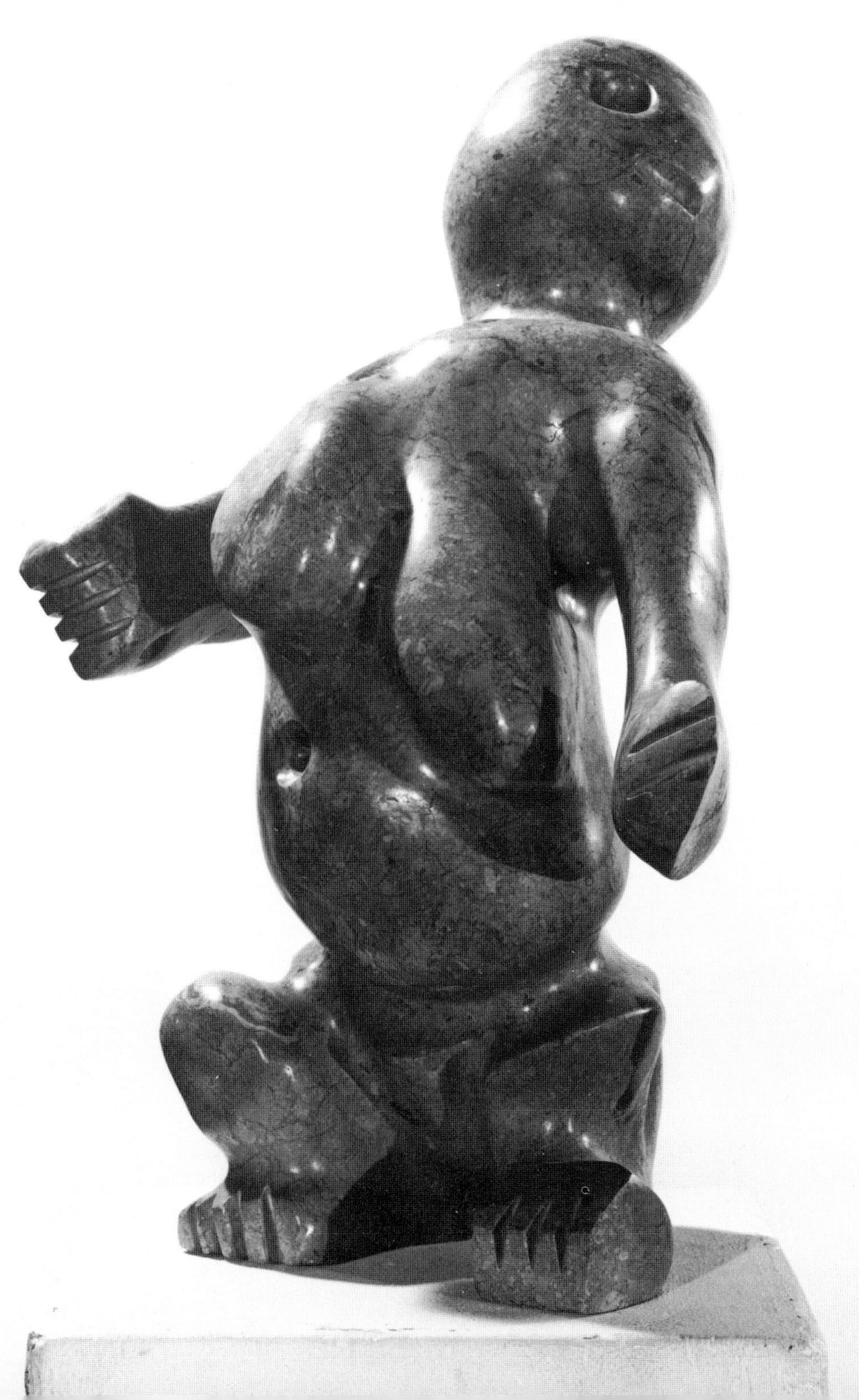

land. He then studied academic painting for a short time in Rio de Janiero where he was working as a draughtsman, but developed his own expressive style. From 1930 to 1936, he lived, painted and exhibited in Brazil, British and Dutch Guiana, Venezuela, the West Indies, Spain, Portugal and London. Back in Australia in 1936, he lived first at Fitzroy and then Warrandyte. He held many exhibitions of his work in Melbourne, and was encouraged by John Reed, a President of the Contemporary Art Society and founder of the Museum of Modern Art and Design of Australia, Melbourne.

J. P.
(1976)

64

Sir William Dobell, Australian, 1899–1970
Portrait of Helena Rubinstein. 1957
Born at Newcastle, N.S.W., in 1899, William Dobell studied at the Julian Ashton School, Sydney, 1924–9. Winning a travelling scholarship, he spent the following ten years in Europe, returning to Sydney on the eve of war in 1939. Two years were spent at the Slade School, London, studying under Henry Tonks and Wilson Steer with some private assistance from Sir William Orpen. A year was spent at The Hague studying the Dutch masters. During the war he was an official artist with the Allied Works Council. His paintings of the men of the Civil Construction Corps, which include some of his finest work, are housed in the Australian National War Memorial, Canberra. Thrice winner of the Archibald Prize, Australia's highest award for portraiture, he lives at Wangi Wangi, N.S.W.

William Dobell is the most famous of living Australian artists. Undeterred by, but not disinterested in, the experiments which have occupied many of his generation, he pursues a classical tradition. He devoted himself largely to portraiture, though his occasional landscapes are of a rare lyrical beauty. As a portraitist he does not work from the model, but, having made various sketches assessing his subject, he works from these gradually seeking the pose, expression and style which best typifies his reaction to the personality of the sitter.

In 1957 Mme Helena Rubinstein visited Australia: whilst in Sydney she granted Mr Dobell two sittings. He was much impressed by Mme Rubinstein and is reported to have said of her, "She was a good sitter, but oddly enough, rather diffident and shy—a very nice person with a strong personality".

Since then, apart from studies, he has painted three major portraits in an attempt to resolve the complexity of Mme Rubinstein's character as he saw it. The portrait here reproduced is the first complete work of the series and is a major addition to the Melbourne collection. A vigorous piece of painting of most lively surface, it displays an almost baroque richness in its tawny reds and honey yellows. It emphasizes the intelligence, self sufficiency and authority of the sitter.

64
Sir William Dobell
Australian, 1899–1970
Portrait of Helena Rubinstein 1957
Oil on hardboard
97.8 × 99.1 cm
Inscriptions. Recto: l.l. "Dobell"
Ex. Women's Weekly Portrait Prize,
Art Gallery of New South Wales, 1962
Felton Bequest, 1964
1391.5

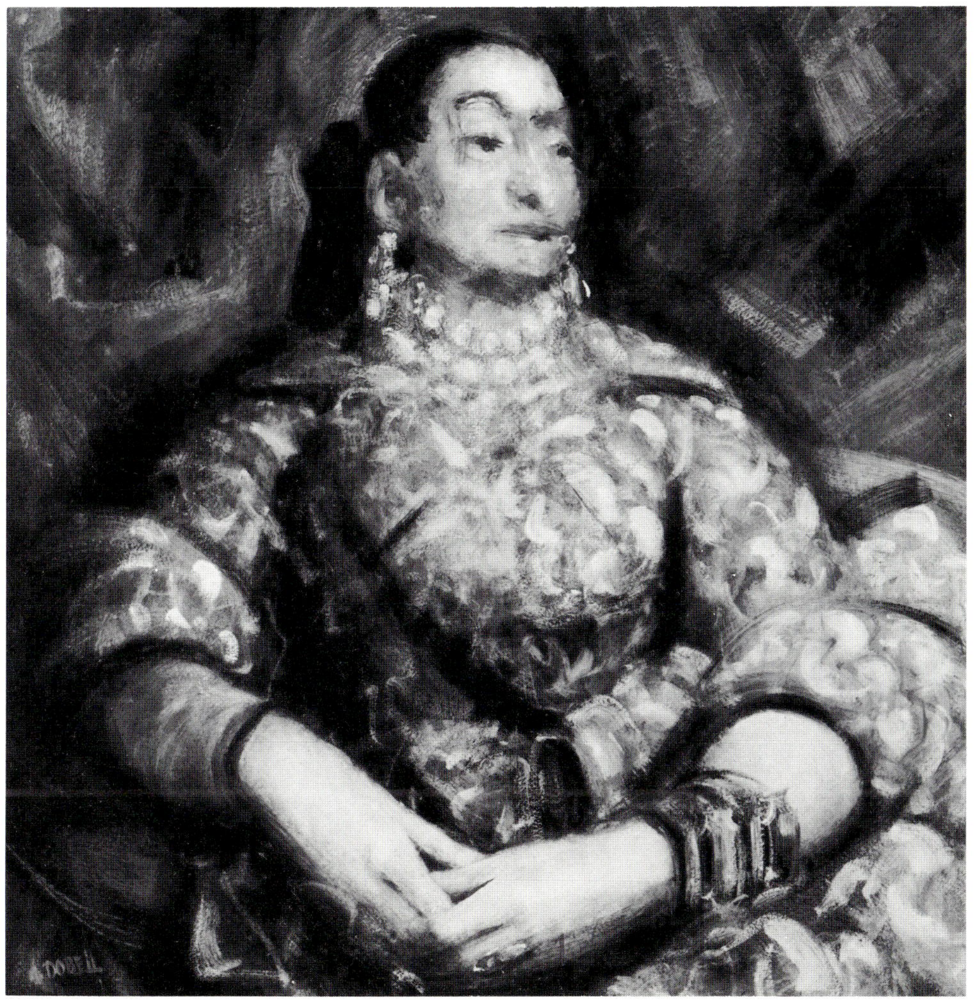

It is particularly happy that this picture comes to Melbourne for it was in this city that Mme Rubinstein humbly commenced the now world-wide cosmetic business which bears her name.

A. B.
(1964)

Footnote : Sir William Dobell died in 1970.

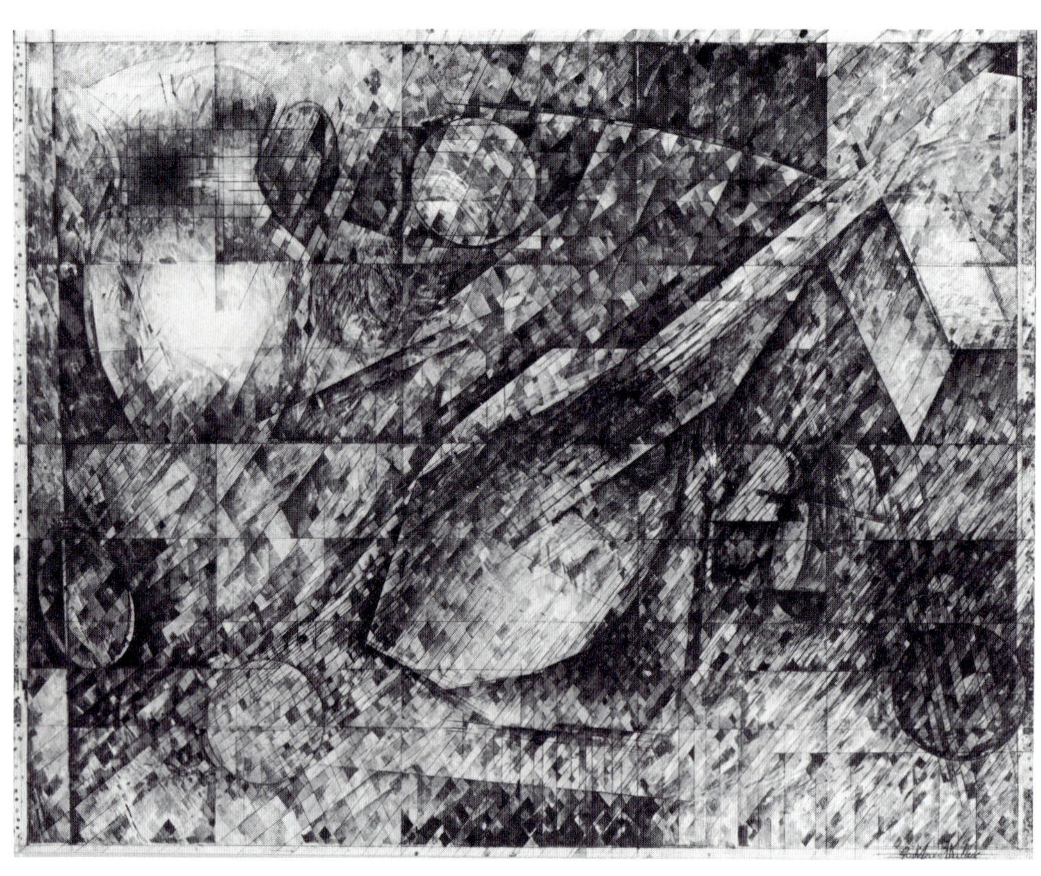

65
Godfrey Miller
b. New Zealand, 1893–1964
Still Life with Musical Instruments
Oil on canvas on board
65.5 × 83 cm
Inscriptions. Recto: l.r. "Godfrey Miller"
Verso: label "Still Life with Musical Instruments. G. M."
Backed
Felton Bequest 1963
1263.5

65

Godfrey Miller, b. New Zealand, 1893–1964
Still Life with Musical Instruments.
Born at Wellington, New Zealand, in 1893, Godfrey Miller studied at the Slade
School, London. He served in the First World War, then travelled extensively,
particularly in the East. He settled in Sydney where he taught drawing at East
Sydney Technical College for a time. Though of a solitary nature and reluctant
to exhibit he was honoured by a retrospective exhibition at the National Gallery
of Victoria in 1959. His work is represented in most Australian State Galleries
and in the Tate Gallery, London. He died in Sydney in 1964.

It is difficult to describe the work of Godfrey Miller. He was a man of intellectual
detachment about his pictures. He takes the traditional themes of nude, still life
or landscape and reconsiders them in the light of artistic problems posed by the
masters of post impressionism and early abstraction, Cézanne, Seurat and Braque.
No mere decorator, he seeks a mode of visual thought to convey the mystical idea
of permanence within perpetual flux. In this painting he takes the typical objects
of still life and encases them in small diamond facets of colour as in a net. The
surface glitters and vibrates but the objects preserve an impassive solidity and
tranquillity within their atmosphere of trembling mosaic fragments. Rarely
exhibiting, leading a life of seclusion, spurning publicity, he nevertheless exercised
a profound influence. This influence did not take the form of a school of followers
or imitators. Rather it was the example of his single minded life-long pursuit
of a classical idea which was an inspiration to the younger generation of artists,
particularly in Sydney.

A. B.
(1964)

Considering the enormous size of this continent, internal communications within the visual arts have generally been good, with artists moving about extensively not only within Australia but abroad, particularly in Europe and, of late, also in Japan and the United States. The "wanderlust" is as typical of the pioneers Martens, Von Guerard and Buvelot as of our contemporary artists—Fairweather, Nolan, Tucker, Olsen, French, Reddington, Redpath, Williams, Sellbach, Johnson and Leach-Jones. Consequently, though in our major outposts (Sydney, Melbourne and Adelaide), recognizable styles of painting might have evolved, there is sufficient interrelationship for us to justify directions that may be described as "national" rather than "regional". The Impressionists—Roberts, Streeton and Conder—were equally at home in Victoria and New South Wales and currently it would be difficult to select an exhibition in any given style without representing at least three states (as was found with the directional exhibition "The Field" with which we opened the new National Gallery of Victoria in August, 1968). Isolation is far from typical of even our most "stay at home" artists—Balson **(60)**, Kemp **(45)** and Miller **(65)** have travelled abroad and the recluse Fairweather **(66)** is one of the most widely travelled of all our artists.

Expatriate artists such as Rupert Bunny, Phillips Fox, and today Nolan **(58)**, Boyd **(59)**, Meadmore **(67)** and Whiteley **(68)** have maintained a strong influence on a national scale because Australian collectors go to such pains to import examples of their work. Their influence is also felt through the younger artists, who if not directly and stylistically influenced by them can at least be bracketed in broad terms of attitude, as again was obvious in "The Field". To observe the outcome of all this exchange it is necessary neither to analyse motivation nor debate whether "walkabout" is purely OZ phenomenon.

Though it is fashionable to regard internationalism as a new concept in art, clearly most movements which have flourished in Australia, with a few exceptions such as Meldrum's Tonal Impressionism and the "Antipodean" have been international manifestations simply tinged with some local colour.

Trends currently thriving irrespective of state barriers are no exception. "Texture" painting has its roots in the work of contemporary Spaniards and is known at source to our most notable exponents Peter Clarke, Elwyn Lynn **(69)**, Ignacio Marmol, Thomas Gleghorn and Frank Hodgkinson. Kinetics have been pioneered in Sydney by Frank Hinder, Mike Kitching and Ken Reinhard, in Melbourne by Frank Eidlitz and in Adelaide by Ostoja Kotkowski.

A kind of metamorphic figuration is still prevalent, derived largely from the English painter Francis Bacon but also incorporating the discoveries of the English and American pop artists. A variety of organic abstraction is also prevalent exemplified by Coburn **(78)**, Olsen **(70)**, Walker, Daws **(75)** and Last. Recent purchases by the National Gallery of Victoria have concentrated around the area of geometric abstraction earlier clarified in "The Field" exhibition. All seven

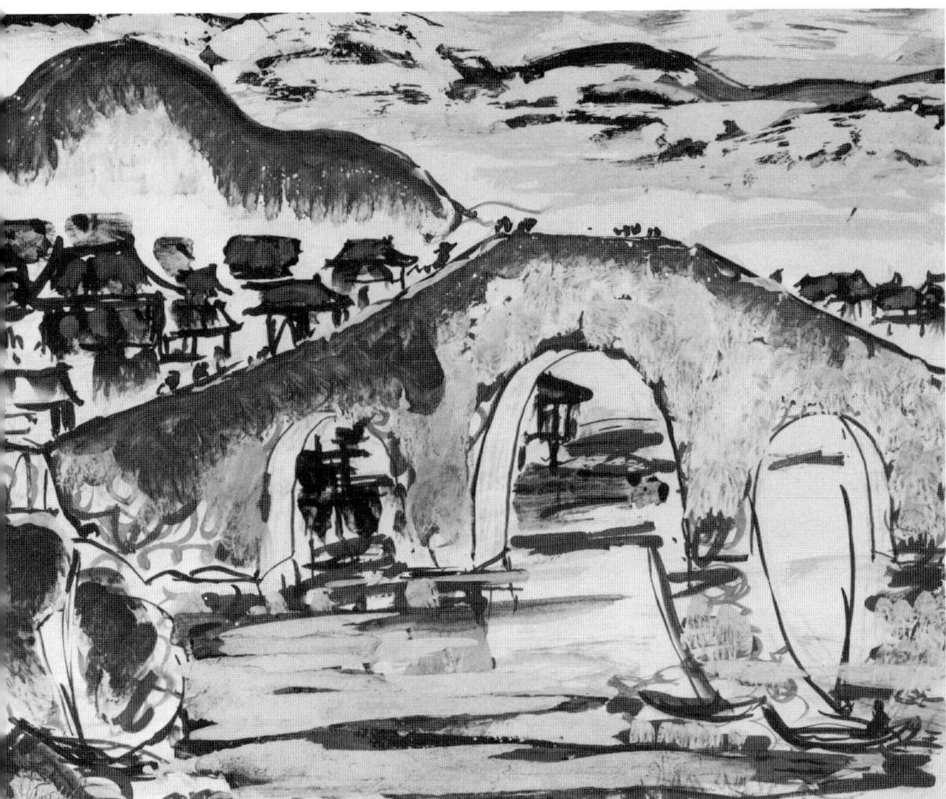

66
Ian Fairweather
b. Scotland, 1891–1974
The Bridge
Gouache on paper
44.1 × 56.5 cm
Inscriptions. Recto:
l.l. "I. Fairweather"
On edge of paper
"Bridge Huchow"
l.r. "I. Fairweather.
C5"
Purchased 1949
1958.4

of the young artists acquired, Ball **(47)**, Coleing **(85)**, Doolin **(Plate XXI)**, Hickey **(82)**, Hunter **(83)**, Lendon **(71)** and Partos **(84)**, invite comparison with the stars of the international firmament, Stella, Poons, Newman and Reinhardt, scorning the local teacup in which the Antipodean storm raged. This style is not indigenous but the conditions attendant upon its birth in New York are now characteristic of any western twentieth century metropolis, and there is no reason to suppose that the universal truth found in acknowledging the flatness of the picture plane should be any less valid in the Melbourne work of Dale Hickey than in the paintings of his American mentors.

In all of the areas discussed to date we have been dealing primarily with painting and to a lesser extent sculpture. Both of these forms are a media convention, for a painting—no matter how revolutionary its design may appear—remains a flat surface bounded by a perimeter, always to be hung on a wall, and all sculpture exists in space as a three-dimensional object around which the viewer is obliged to orientate himself. Parallel to their evolution over many centuries we have also established basic criteria of design such as proportion, balance, rhythm and articulation, with which we have learnt to evaluate the colour, tone, line, texture and form in both painting and sculpture. It is on these qualities that we base much of our critical assessment and as a yardstick we expect them to remain constant irrespective of fashion. Now, during this decade we have witnessed in Australia the growth of works of art which no longer quite conform to these canons.

99

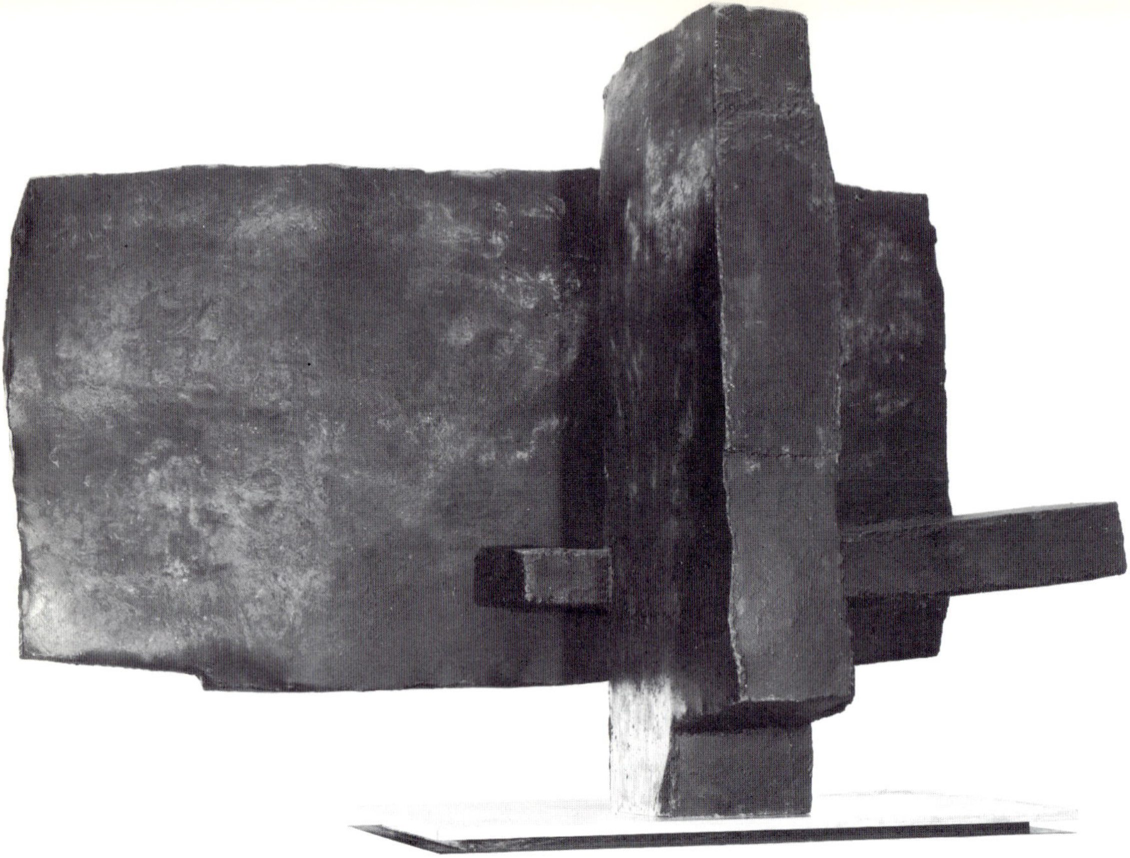

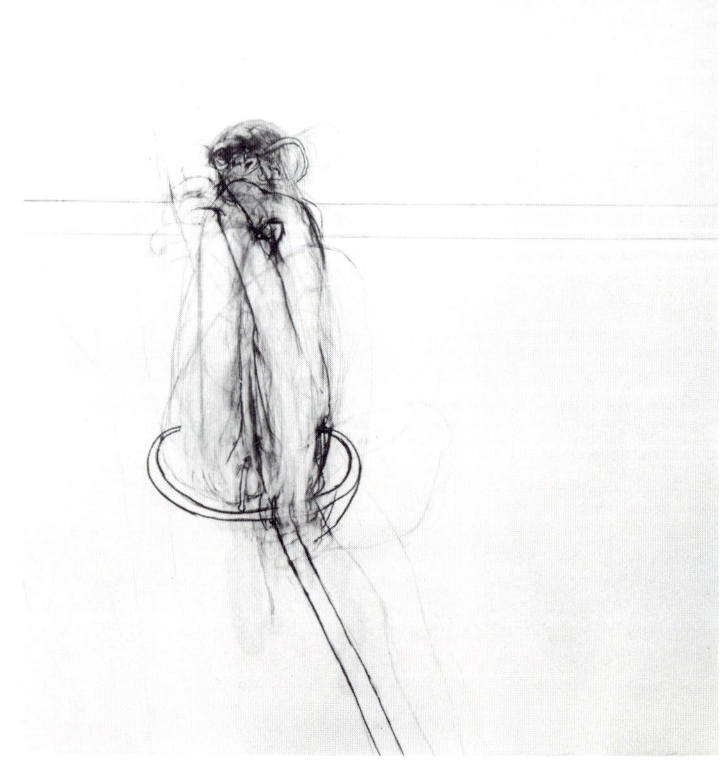

67
Clement Meadmore
Australian, 1929–
Duolith III 1962
Welded steel
125 × 198.5 × 108.5 cm
Purchased with the assistance of a
donation from Colonel Aubrey Gibson,
1962
470.5

68
Brett Whiteley
Australian, 1939–
Drawing of an Ape
Perspex, pencil, charcoal on paper
on hardboard
120.5 × 104.5 cm
Black arrow originally painted on
outer surface of perspex
Purchased 1966
1689.5

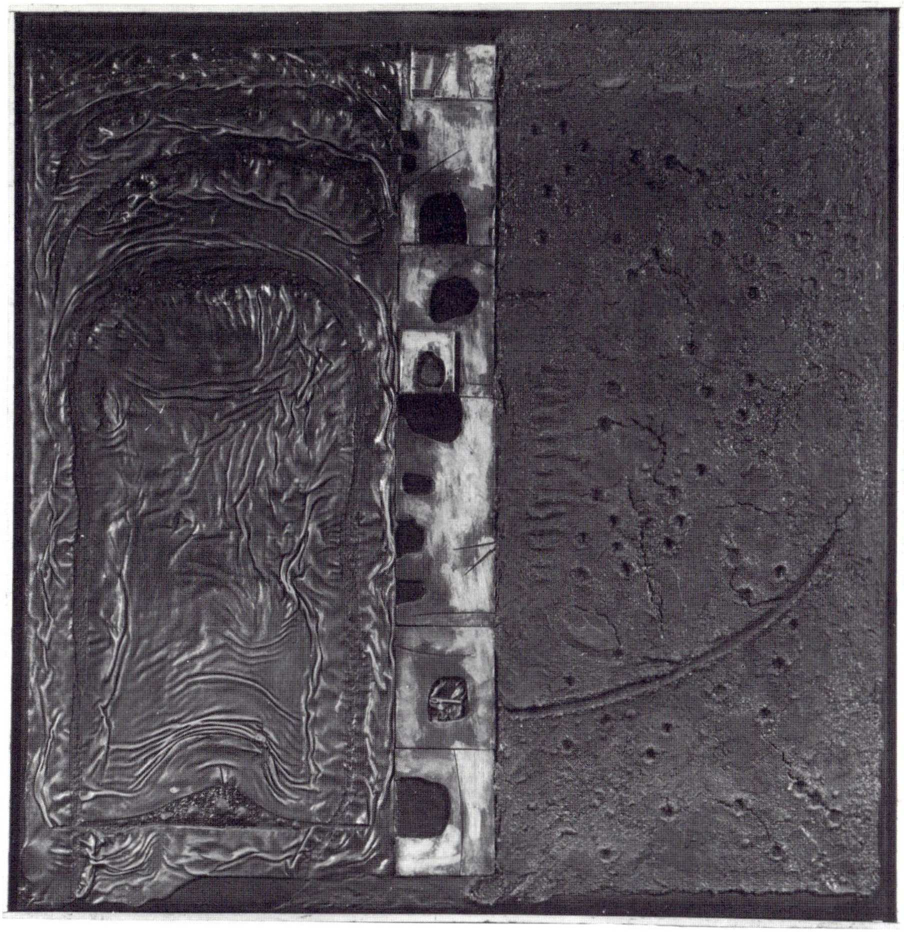

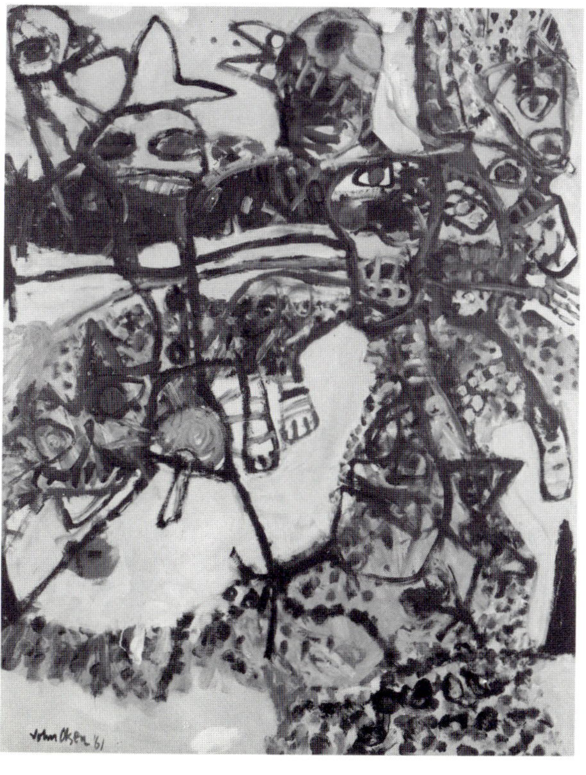

69
Elwyn Lynn
Australian, 1917–
The Dividual 1962
Mixed media: wood,
resin, sand, oil paint
on canvas
102 × 102 cm
Purchased 1963
1304.5

70
John Olsen
Australian, 1928–
Journey into You Beaut Country 1961
Oil on hardboard
152 × 121.5 cm
Inscriptions. Recto: l.l. "John Olsen 61"
Purchased 1961
918.5

71
Nigel Lendon
Australian, 1944–
Painting 68-1 1968
Acrylic on shaped
board
83 × 163 × 4.5 cm
Inscriptions. Verso:
" 'Painting 68–1'
Nigel Lendon '68"
Purchased 1969
152.6

72
Ti Parks
b. England, 1939–
The Tent II 1968
Mohair, painted wood,
metal
304.8 × 609.6 × 91.4
(size varies with
installation)
Presented anonymously
1969
76.6

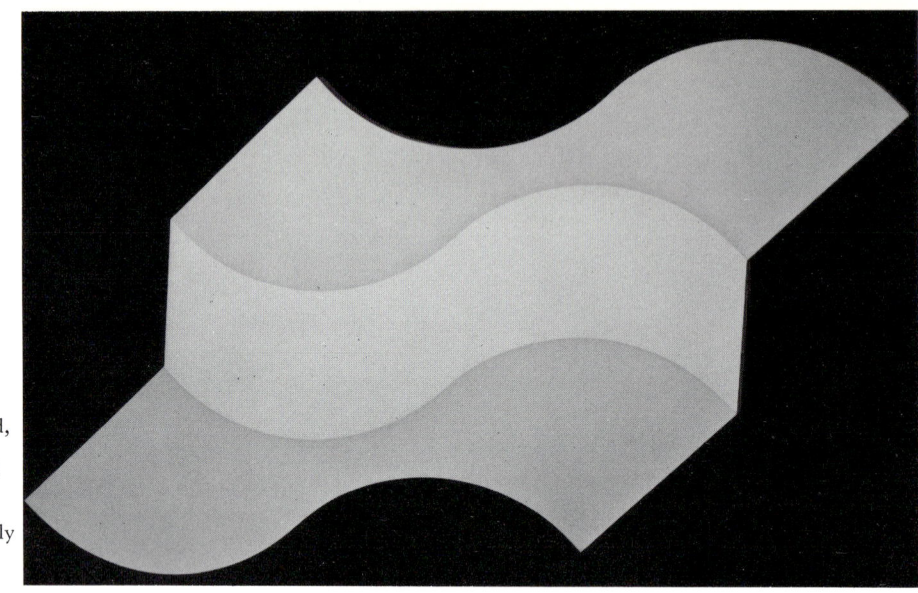

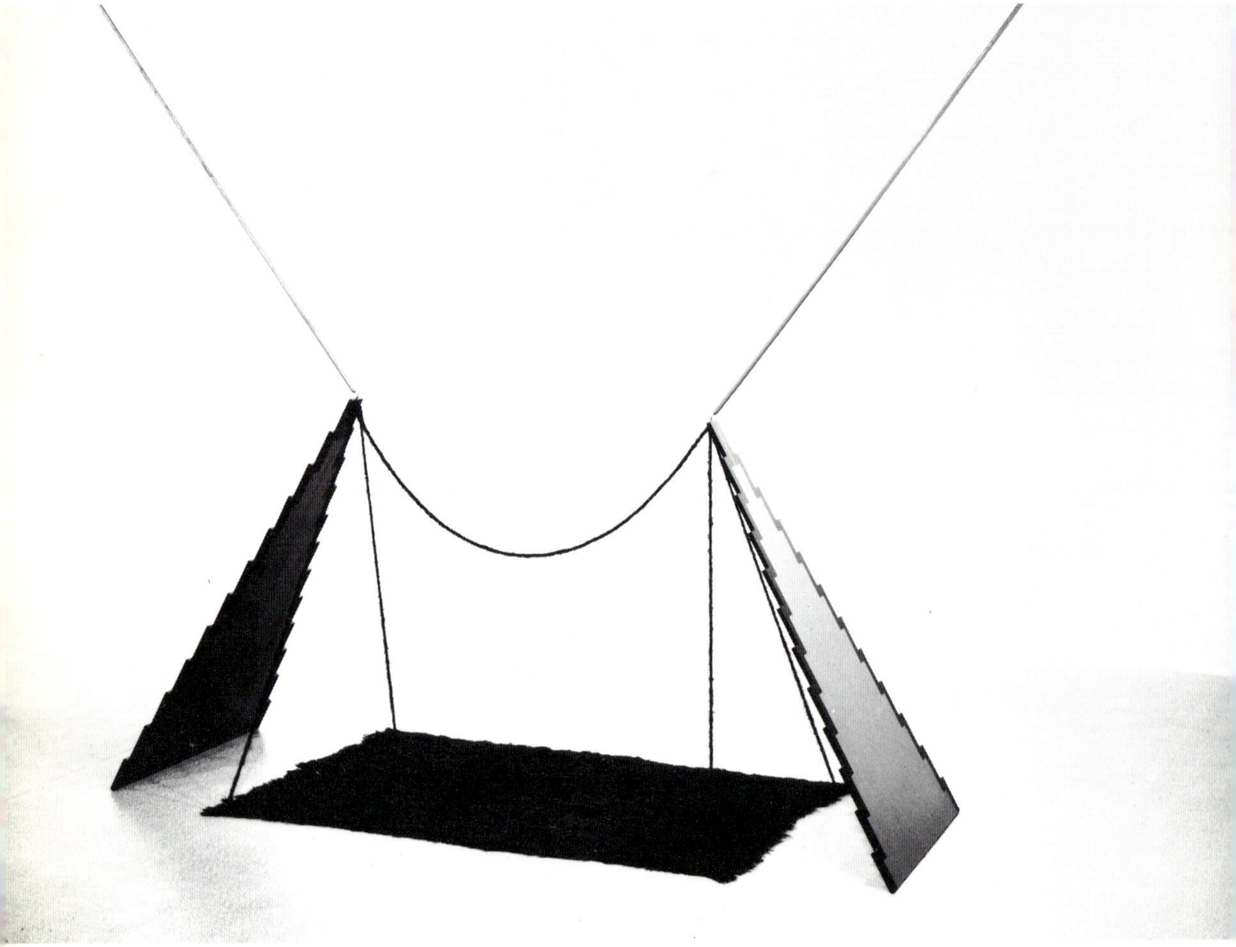

The work exhibited in Melbourne during 1962 by three young Sydney artists call-ing themselves the Annandale Imitation Realists—Colin Lanceley (**Plate XXII**), Mike Brown (**79**) and Ross Crothall—parallels earlier departures from con-ventional painting and sculpture by European, American and Japanese artists, but its naivety must be given credit for the original and spontaneous gesture which it represented. It was with the Annandale Imitation Realists that we first became aware of the art of assemblage: pictures embellished with discarded objects and physically intruding into the three-dimensional realm of sculptures—the sculptures in turn, fabricated from junk then finished with brush and pigment. The Imitation Realists also worked with a great degree of anonymity, combining their talents in certain items and failing also to explain to the visitor the authorship of the individual pieces. Their works were remarkably similar and difficult to distinguish from one another in marked contrast to the painters Salkaukas, Olsen (**70**), Coburn (**78**), Hessing and Rose who preceded them.

All this of course is chaos and insurrection to the Gallery curator who, though himself a comparatively recent product of the twentieth century, has his terrain staked out strictly in terms of media and, as a public servant, is obliged always to provide full documentation on the collection entrusted to his keeping. It is a further assault on Gallery attitudes in that most assemblages defy preservation and we have been bred to believe that a National Gallery, apart from being a centre for viewing is equally a repository for preservation.

None the less, it was still possible to apply our established aesthetic measures to the Annandale Imitation Realists (a test which they passed with flying colours) and even to certain of the Environments which were the next media mix-up to develop. It is in fact not until the art-object turns itself inside out and the spectator is completely enveloped inside it, or the object becomes so vast that it is no longer possible to take it all in from a particular view point—in other words with the collapse of the framing edge or boundary—that our aesthetic principles become outmoded.

The only Environment in the collection of the National Gallery of Victoria is small enough still to be evaluated as a sculpture. It is by Ti Parks, a young English artist resident in Melbourne, and belongs to his series **The Tent (72).** Designed to fit into a corridor-like space, a red lacquered wooden rod reaches down from each of the lateral walls to support a pair of flat triangular red boards whose serrated edges are outlined in blue; between both of these elements an open tent-like volume defined with blue mohair rope reaches down to a small rectangular carpet, again of knitted blue mohair. This is a sculpture situation and when analysed in terms of volume weight and interpretation, ignoring the levity and originality of the artist's comment, it is a most successful piece. Practising with equal accomplishment as a painter, there is no feeling of con-trivance or self consciousness in Parks's oscillation between these two art forms:

he is simply using the tools at his disposal, and this happens to be the twentieth century.

It is perhaps inevitable that the earlier generation of abstract expressionists so violently involved in the "act" of making art—flinging, pouring and directing paint in wild gestures with little respect for either convention or preservation—should presage a style based entirely on action, situation and participation. In Australia we can shortly expect to witness the media-expansion taken to further extremes and ultimately into the area of Happenings where audience reaction, response and participation are programmed into the work of art as an integral part of its fabric. Happenings have already occurred in Sydney and there is considerable ferment here in Melbourne with many artists ambitious to collaborate in a manifestation, while our most distinguished practitioner, Jeffrey Shaw, is central to the movement in London as one of the three members of a group called Eventstructure. The Eventstructure group have already completed successful commissions to conduct public manifestations in both England and Holland—their programme generally centres about some inflatable polythene construction of monumental scale, geared to public involvement or response. One proposal, **Sandquake,** incorporates about 200 yards of polythene tubing buried in a beach. Compressed air is fed into the tube and as inflation takes place the tubing erupts through the sand involving the spectators who, unaware of its precise location, are unable to predict its behaviour. Jeffrey Shaw is yet another example of what we have previously observed in Clement Meadmore, Brett Whiteley and Colin Lanceley—a gifted local artist passionately involved in a certain movement, going abroad and, depending upon his degree of talent, becoming central to a new departure.

Another young Melbourne artist Ian Burn, at present resident in New York, has become involved with Serial Art, an emerging movement which as yet, seems to have no counterpart in his home country.

Though Burn's works are still concerned with the picture format, in examining an individual painting one must be aware that it is in fact only part of a series, hanging in a row with identical (or near identical) companion pieces—the work is incomplete if the series is broken, since the art situation partially exists in the relationship and interaction of the component parts **(73).** Once again the importance of interval and sequence coupled with the absence of a finite boundary relate the conception to that of the "environment" for which we must discover a new aesthetic.

Perhaps the most significant of the new aesthetic factors is "chance"—an element previously frowned upon because in some way it implied loss of control and without "control" incorporating the will and direction of the artist we understand that there would be no art. To take a finite example Ian Burn exhibited two works in "The Field" entitled **2 Glass/Mirror Piece (74)** and

73
Ian Burn
Australian, 1939–
Yellow Premiss 1965
Acrylic on cotton duck
6 panels each 81.2 ×
81.2 cm
Inscriptions. Verso:
Each panel signed
at top "Ian Burn
Yellow Premiss $\frac{1}{6}$ (to)
$\frac{6}{6}$ 1965"
Purchased 1976
A22/1976

74
Ian Burn
Australian, 1939–
Mirror Piece 1967
Assemblage
(a) Glass, mirror,
wood and
(b) 14 pages of notes
(a) 57.4 × 39.3 cm
(b) 27.5 × 21.3 cm each
Inscriptions. Signed
"Ian Burn" on second
sheet of paper
Purchased 1972
A20/1972

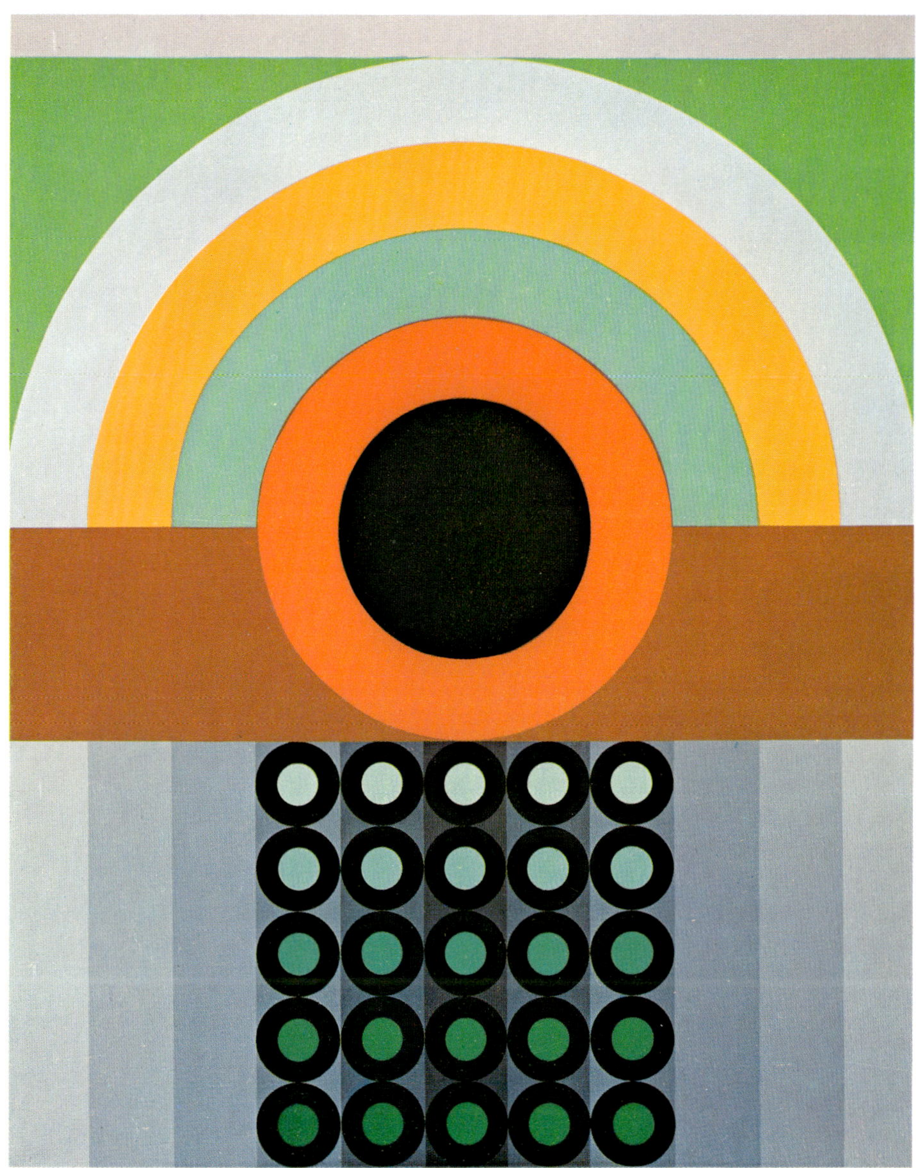

Plate **XXI**
James Doolin
b. U.S.A., 1932–
Artificial Landscape 67–5 1967
Acrylic on canvas
129.6 × 101.9 cm
Inscriptions. Verso: "James Doolin 1967 Los Angeles"
"Note: Hang with bottom of painting approximately 30 inches from floor so that top of Red circle
is at normal eye level."
Purchased 1969
87/6

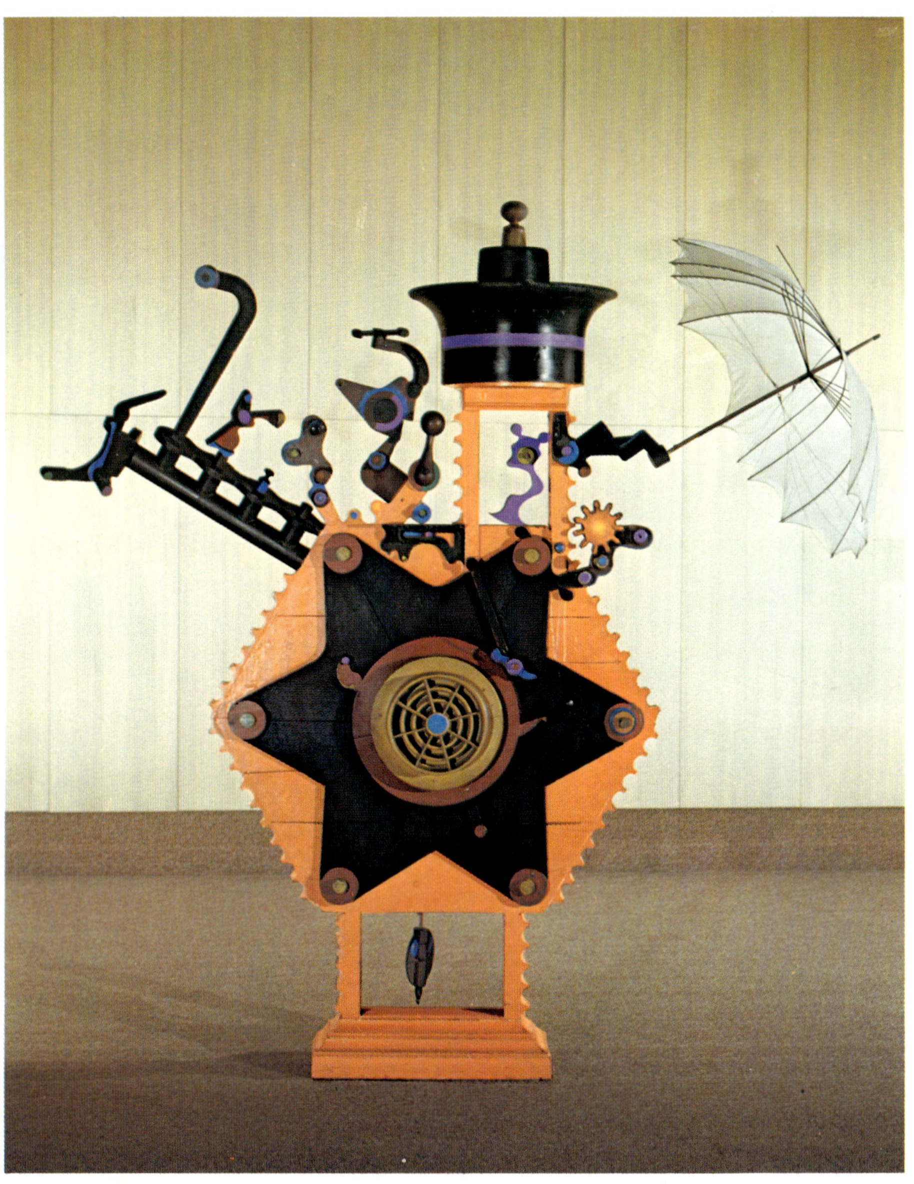

Plate **XXII**
Colin Lanceley
b. New Zealand, 1938–
The King is in His Counting House 1964–5
Assemblage: painted wood, paper, umbrella frame, wire
h. 258.5 × 246.4 × 99.1 cm
Inscriptions. Verso: "Defender of the Cities"
Purchased 1976
A9/1976

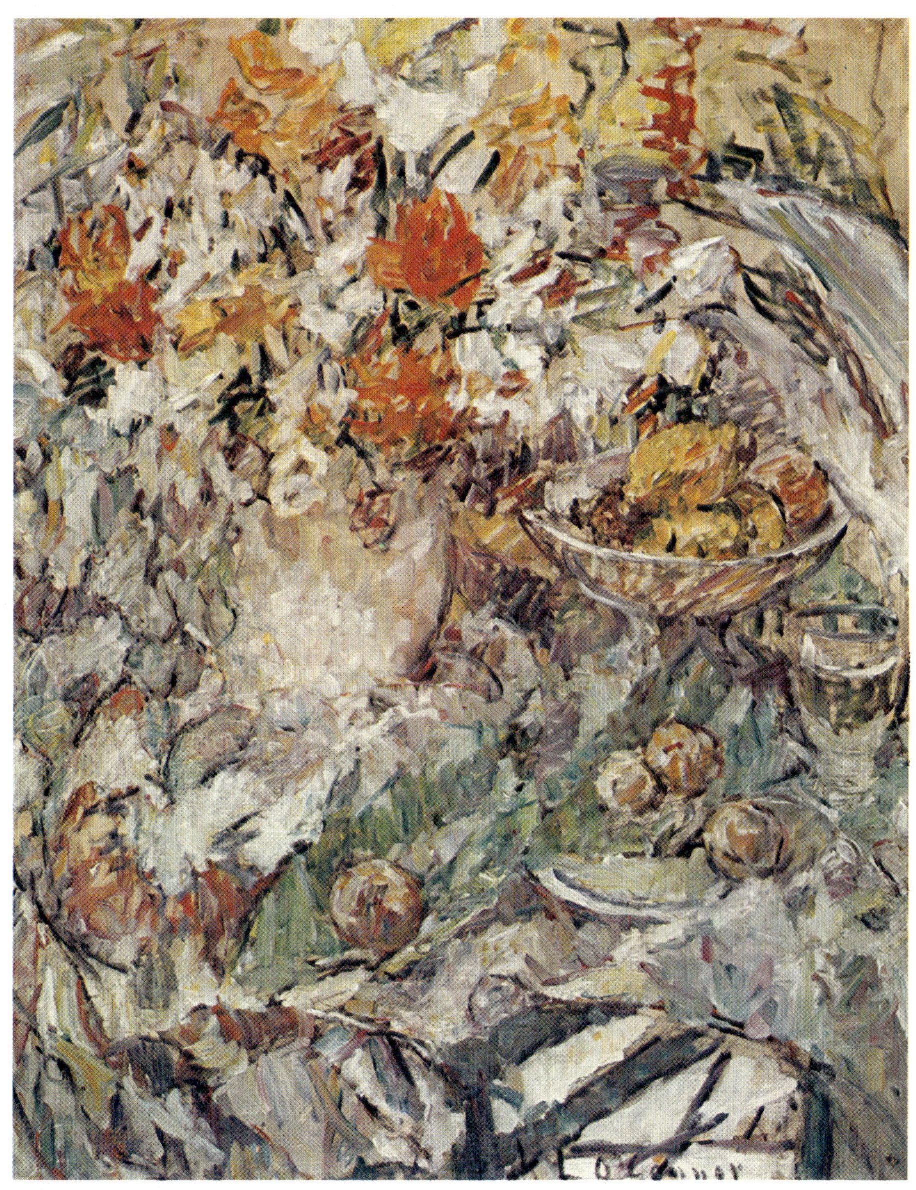

Plate **XXIII**
Kate O'Connor
b. New Zealand, 1886–1968
Verging on the Abstract c. 1962
Oil on canvas on board
91.5 × 73 cm
Inscriptions. Recto: l.r. "K. L. O'Connor"
Ex. Perth Prize For Commonwealth Games, 1962—prizewinner
Purchased 1966
1581.5

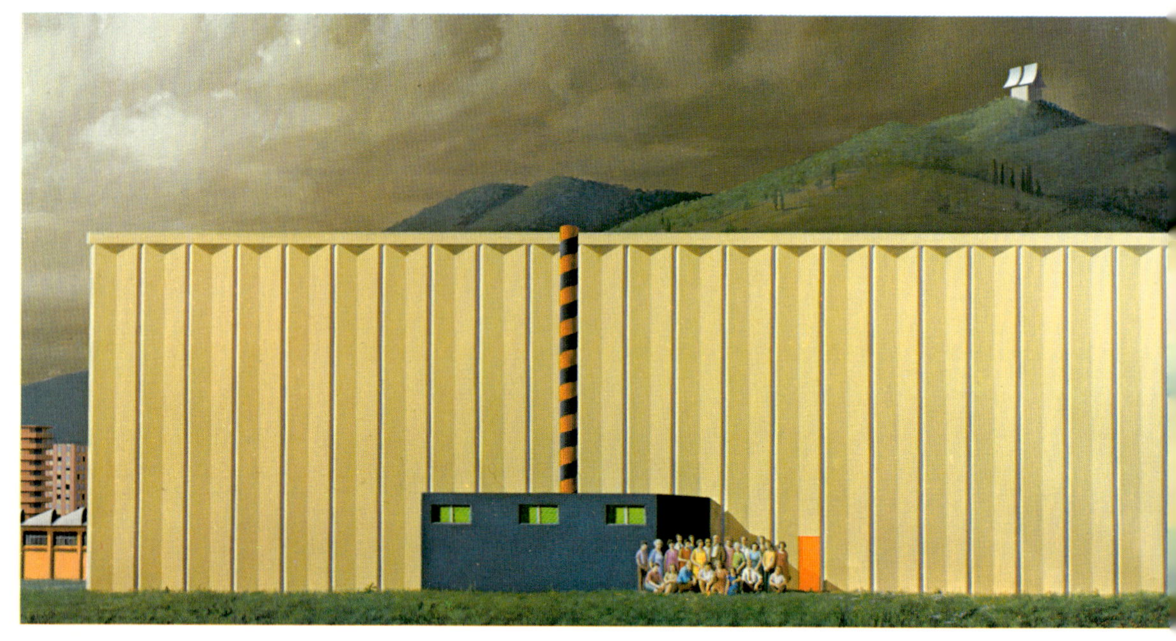

Plate **XXIV**
Jeffrey Smart
Australian, 1921–
Factory Staff, Erehwyna 1972
Oil on canvas
100.4 × 200.2 cm
Inscriptions. Recto: l.r. "Jeffrey Smart"
Ex. Sth Yarra Gallery, Melb., 1972
Purchased 1972
A26/1972

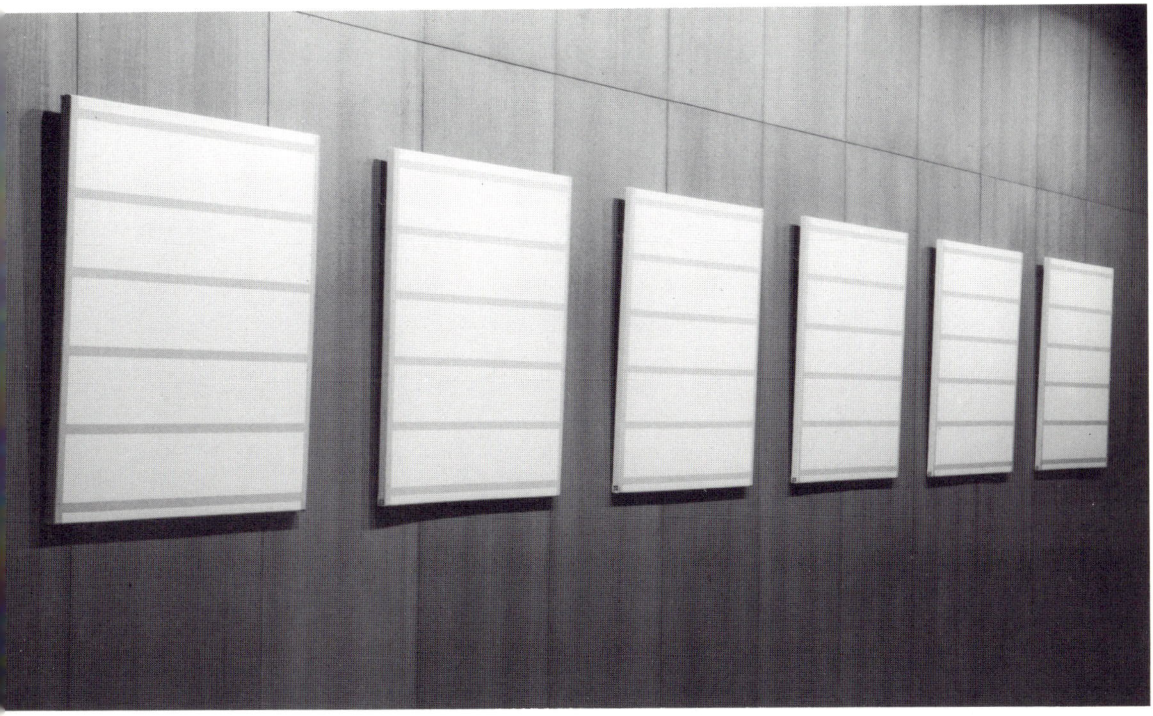

4 Glass/Mirror Piece which betrayed no evidence of the artist's hand—they were in fact made in Melbourne to specifications which he mailed us from New York. The **2 Glass/Mirror Piece** was simply a mirror framed so that two thicknesses of glass completely covered its surface while the **4 Glass/Mirror Piece** was an identical construction except that the face of the mirror was this time buried beneath four sheets of glass. As anybody knows, glass is an imperfect material and the slight distortion, imperfection and discolouration in a sheet of glass therefore became twice as apparent in the **4 Glass/Mirror Piece** as it was in the **2 Glass.** The distortion inherent in the glass is a characteristic outside the artist's control but the artist is aware of this phenomenon and programmed this feature into a series actually conceived to run from a single glass/mirror piece through to a maximum twelve glass/mirror piece. Thus it is illustrated that the artist is still in control since the whole progression depends upon his power of selection. The appreciation of such a work comes partly in the knowledge of how it is achieved.

To finally clarify the National Gallery's position in relation to these developments: in the absence of Melbourne's Museum of Modern Art which went into recess during 1966, we have a clear duty to inform our public of the art of their era by showing the best original examples available. Where such works defy addition to our permanent collection we may at least be host, sponsoring temporary exhibitions and at the same time recording and documenting "transient art" in the best means at our disposal. To the artists we owe the rewards of recognition and encouragement.

(1969)

Plate XXIII
Kate O'Connor, Australian, 1886–1968
Verging on the Abstract. c. 1962
The National Gallery of Victoria had long wished to acquire a work by Kate O'Connor, but her extreme age, reluctance to exhibit and sell, and the remoteness of her residence in Western Australia, had delayed its fulfilment. Miss O'Connor has spent most of her life from the turn of the century in Europe, mainly Paris. She is a first-rate painter, little known in the Eastern States, because of her long residence abroad, and her Western Australian allegiance. The March, 1966 issue of *Art and Australia* has an illustrated article which reintroduces her work to the public. This painting won the Western Australian section of the Perth Games Prize in 1962 and can hang happily with either the Australian or European collections. The quality of this work derives both from native ability and a direct drawing from the stylistic source in Paris. To compare it with the work of Shore

(50,51), Isabel Tweddle **(Plate XVIII),** Lina Bryans **(Plate XIX),** Ada May Plante **(53)** and Teresa Vigano is instructive.

(1966)

Footnote: Miss O'Connor died in 1968.

75
Lawrence Daws, Australian, 1927–
Mandala IV. 1962

Lawrence Daws was born in Adelaide in 1927. For three years he studied architecture and geology at Adelaide University and School of Mines. He then spent two years in New Guinea on field survey work. Coming to Melbourne he concentrated his activity on painting, undertaking the full four years' course of study at the National Gallery School from 1950 to 1953. For the following eighteen months he did geological field work in the north of Australia, painting the while. An exhibition in 1955, "A Group of Four" (Lawrence Daws, Donald Laycock, Clifton Pugh and John Howley) first brought him critical acclaim. In 1957 winning the Italian Flotto Lauro-Dante Alighieri scholarship enabled him to study in Europe. He now resides in England, returning for brief visits coinciding with Australian exhibitions of his work.

Since first coming to critical notice in 1955 Lawrence Daws's work has reflected the changing interests of Australia's younger painters. He has moved from figurative to non-figurative painting, from intellectual cubist tendencies to a romantic symbolic abstraction. His early work relates to his survey mapping journeys in the more remote and arid regions of Australia. **Oenpelli** of 1955 in the National Gallery of Victoria shows a group of Aboriginals, elongated and silhouetted against a background of simple segmented planes enclosing areas of flat local colour. He thus handled a constant motif of Australian painting, "figures in the landscape", within an idiom ultimately derived from cubism.

His contact with contemporary Italian painting led to a more painterly manner and denser, richer colour shown in **Mandala,** here reproduced. This picture belongs to a series of paintings incorporating the mandala form in its Jungian sense of archetypal unifying image. These paintings were exhibited in London in October, 1962. Lest one incline to a doctrinaire psychological interpretation of the works, Daws wrote in 1963: "In my case the symbols in the paintings came instinctively, i.e., is just instinctive shape making. I decided to call them

75
Lawrence Daws
Australian, 1927–
Mandala IV 1962
Oil on canvas
137 × 137 cm
Inscriptions. Recto: l.r. "Daws '62"
Verso: "L Daws"
Ex. no. 16, Mathieson Gallery,
London, 1962
Purchased 1964
1433.5

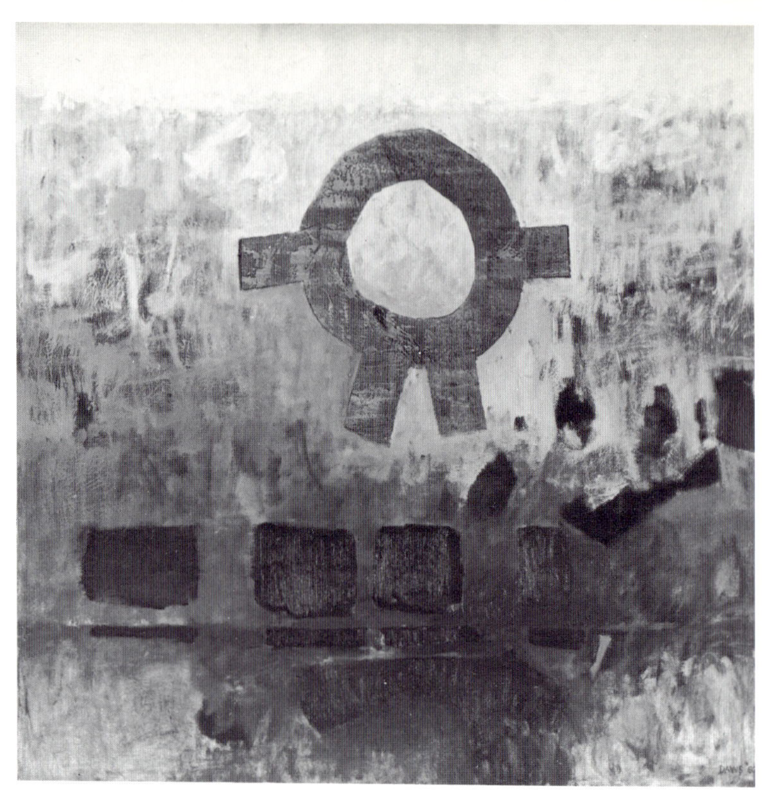

76
Jeffrey Smart
Australian, 1921–
Cahill Expressway
1962
Oil on plywood
81.2 × 111.7 cm
Inscriptions. Recto:
l.l. "Jeffrey Smart"
Purchased 1963
1306.5

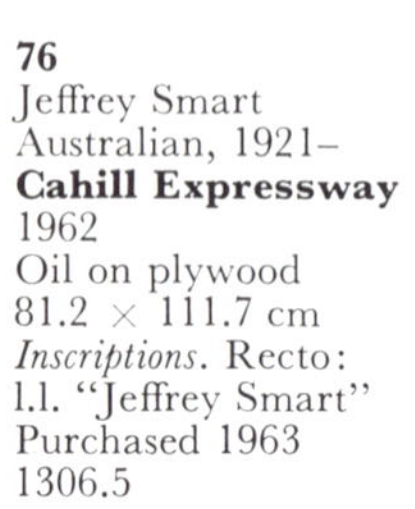

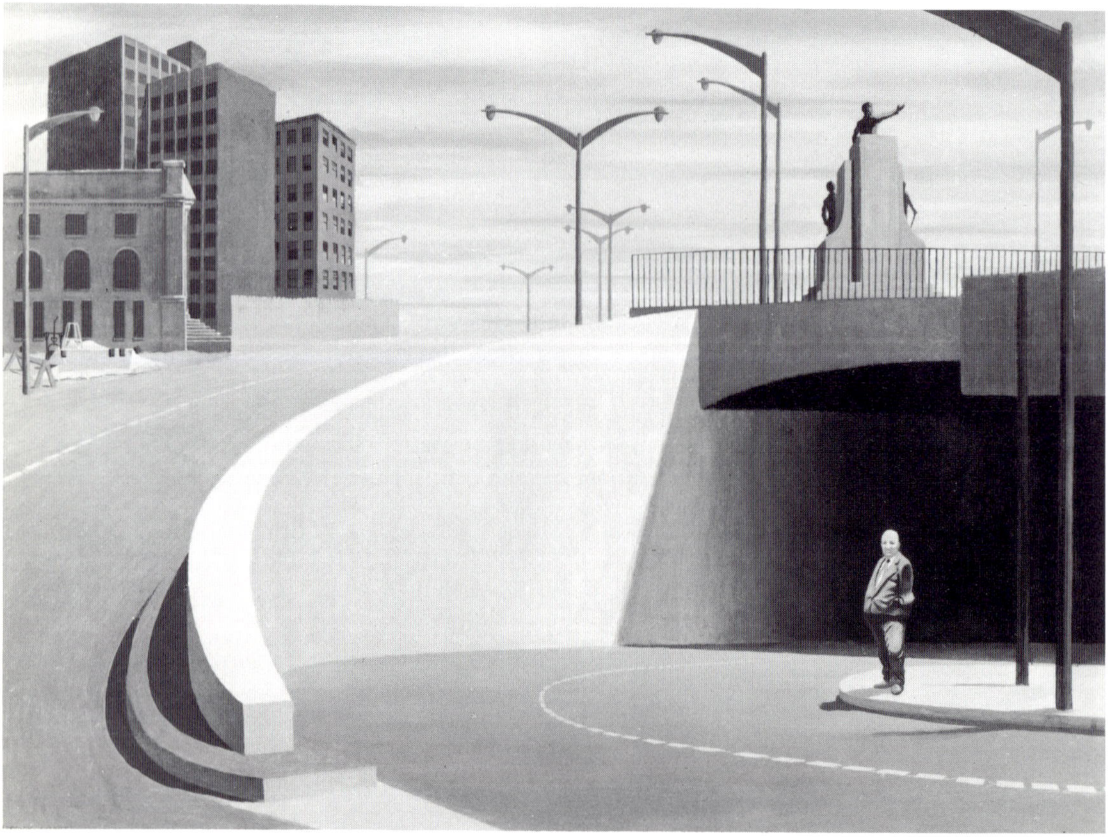

mandalas later and after I had read about mandalas in the works of Jung and other sources. It just seemed the best thing to call them".

The most recent work of Lawrence Daws shows a return to a more figurative manner. The unifying and continuing quality of his work is a strong sense of rich and resonant colour which European critics have considered typically Australian.

A. B.
(1964)

Footnote: In 1976 Lawrence Daws was living in Brisbane.

76

Jeffrey Smart, Australian, 1921–
Cahill Expressway. 1962

Jeffrey Smart was born at Adelaide, South Australia, in 1921. He first studied at the South Australian School of Art. Then for three years he travelled in Europe. During 1949–50 he studied in Paris at La Grande Chaumiere and at the Academie Montmartre under Fernand Leger. On his return to Australia he settled in Sydney where he is widely known both as a painter and a lucid artistic commentator on television. In 1951 he was awarded the Commonwealth Jubilee Open Art Competition. In December, 1963, he left for Italy where he plans an extended stay.

Jeffrey Smart's painting lies apart from the mainstream of contemporary Australian art. He paints the landscape and townscape of urban Australia. He reveals to Australians his view of what Australia is like. It is a highly personal image, always tinged with some unnerving hint of isolation, of threatening change, of mortal man imprisoned in his environment. These imaginative constructions are painted in the studio, but they are based on factual observation. In his wanderings about Sydney, watching its people in the city streets, or in their playgrounds, or on their beaches he notices the bizarre, almost macabre juxtaposition of man and his city. Sometimes on a beach ablaze with light he sees one solitary youth, vulnerable in isolation, looking out to sea where in the dark sky is the hint of coming violence in a whirlwind forming. Or in his painting here reproduced the great concrete highway is contrasted with the rhetorical gesture of a Victorian statue and the lone one-armed man.

These imitations he paints with a close focus realism reminiscent of surrealism, and a minute linear rendering of particularities akin to pre-Raphaelite practice. It is the vision of a highly literate and speculative mind that he offers without apology to his generation. A period of critical neglect during the last decade of general enthusiasm for the development of romantic abstract expressionism in Australia has in no way deterred Jeffrey Smart from his chosen subject and figurative manner.

A. B.
(1964)

Plate XXIV
Jeffrey Smart, Australian, 1921–
Factory Staff—Erehwyna. 1972
Factory Staff—Erehwyna sums up a lot of Smart's attitude towards man in his technological environment against a background of nature, and a threatening symbol of "godlike" communication on the mountain top against a lowering sky.

The expressive detail of the group of workers, in "snapshot" composition reveals a humane and somewhat ironic observation of man in his social and age group environment. Man whose rabbit warren uniform housing development is seen on the left, is dwarfed by the monumental presence of the FACTORY. Smart is one of the few Australian artists who maintains a presence which can be judged on international standards.

(1972)

Footnote: Further information accompanies illustration number **76** on p. 109.

Plate XXV
William Frater, b. Scotland, 1890–1974
Mount Bogong. 1963
Frater is a stained glass artist, painter in oils of landscape, still life, the nude and figure compositions. In the 1920s he was a central figure in the emergence of the first "modern art" movement in Victoria. Born in 1890 in Ochiltre, Linlithgow, Scotland he migrated to Melbourne in 1910 having already trained under Legros, Greiffenhagen and Anning Bell at the Glasgow School of Art. Apart from a brief return to Scotland 1912–13 he has lived in Melbourne without interruption since 1914. Frater first worked as a stained glass artist at Brooks Robinson's Studio where in 1911 he met the young Arnold Shore (**51** and **52**) who was apprenticed to the same firm. Their life-long friendship commenced in a mutual questioning of the direction of contemporary art. Turning away from the tonal principles expounded by Max Meldrum they found guide lines in Cezanne and Van Gogh through coloured reproductions, periodicals like the *Dial* and Orpen's

Outline of Art. In 1931, at the annual exhibition of the "Twenty Melbourne Painters", one wall of the Athenaeum Gallery was given over to the work of Frater, Shore and Isabel Hunter Tweddle **(Plate XVIII)**. Amid a bitter controversy Frater emerged as a combative proponent of "modernism".

In February 1932 George Bell **(41)** and Arnold Shore opened the influential and now legendary school of modern art, Frater being a party to their discussions and finding the premises. Frater's main stylistic inspiration has been Cezanne though he paints in the Impressionist *plein air* tradition and is a worker with a prodigious production. In the 1950s he found a new source of inspiration in the landscape of Central Australia. In the 1960s he painted the brilliant opalescent sunlight of Mount Bogong. He lectured to the life class at the Royal Melbourne Institute of Technology and taught at the Victorian Artists' Society. He has been President of the Victorian Artists' Society from 1963.

(1970)

Footnote: William Frater, President of the V.A.S. till 1972, died in 1974.

77

Helen Marshall, b. Ireland, 1918–
To Awakening. 1965
Helen Marshall was born in Ireland, came to Australia in 1935 and studied for several years under George Bell. In 1950 she left for Europe where she has exhibited regularly—1951 Galleria Numero, Florence; 1952 Galerie Les Mages, Venice; 1953 Kunsthalle, Bern (with Vieira da Silva and Philip Martin); 1955 Galleria Schneider, Rome; 1962 Galerie Librairie Anglais, Paris; 1966 Palais des Beaux-Arts, Brussels, Retrospective (with Phillip Martin); 1968 Galerie Kontakt, Antwerp.

To Awakening is essentially "Ecole de Paris" and is in marked contrast to the sonorous utterance of the colourists of "The Field" exhibition. The accession of this painting helps to make the contemporary collection more catholic and less parochial and is a notable addition to the Gallery's holding of works by Australian women. This is a visionary work utilizing colour as a poetic associative medium. It is an amalgam of varied experiences of the Indian bazaar, the lotus pond and seeming fruitfulness. In brief, it is a romantic vision of India filtered through memories.

(1970)

77
Helen Marshall
b. Ireland, 1918
To Awakening 1965
Tempera on canvas
122.3 × 175.4 cm
Inscriptions. Recto:
l.l. "H.M. 1965"
Verso: "Helen
Marshall 'To
Awakening' 1965"
Purchased 1970
A18/1970

78
John Coburn
Australian, 1925–
Primordial Garden
c. 1965–6
Liquitex on hardboard
3 panels, each
157.6 × 122.3 cm
Inscriptions. Recto:
right panel, l.r.
"Coburn"
Felton Bequest 1968
1825.5

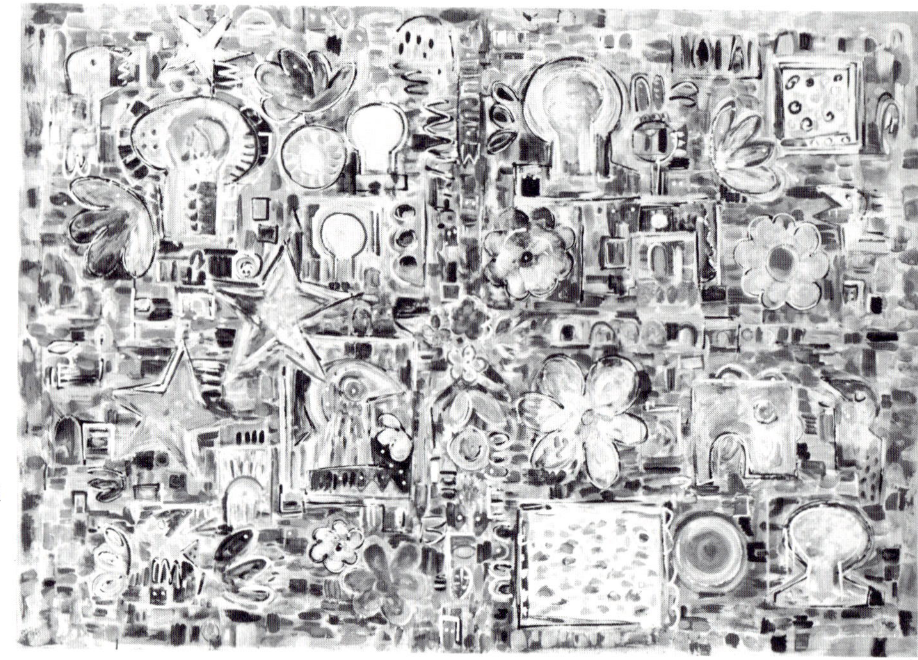

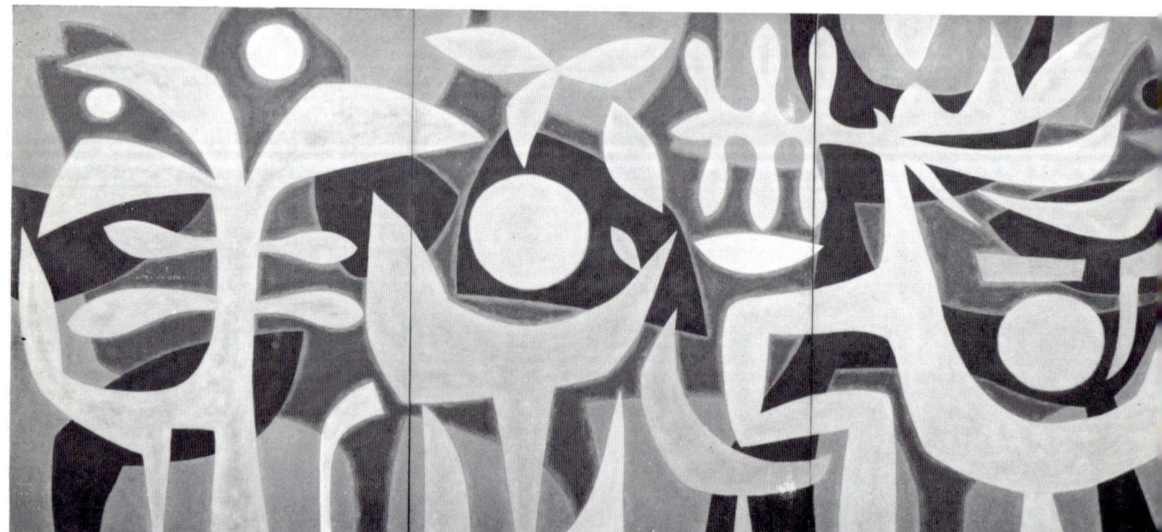

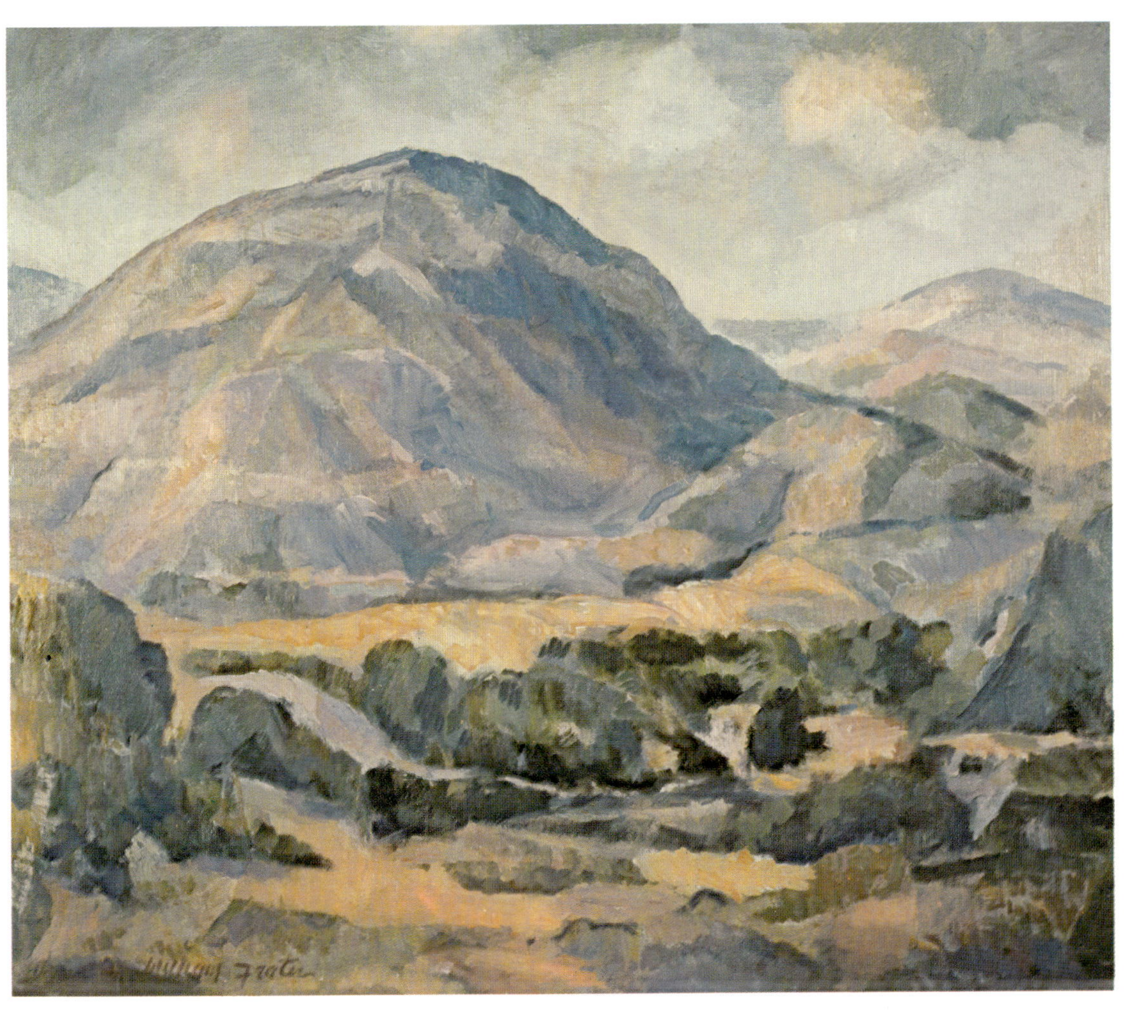

Plate **XXV**
William Frater
b. Scotland, 1890–1974
Mount Bogong 1963
Oil on canvas
130.5 × 151 cm
Inscriptions. Recto: l.l. "William Frater"
Purchased 1964
1436.5

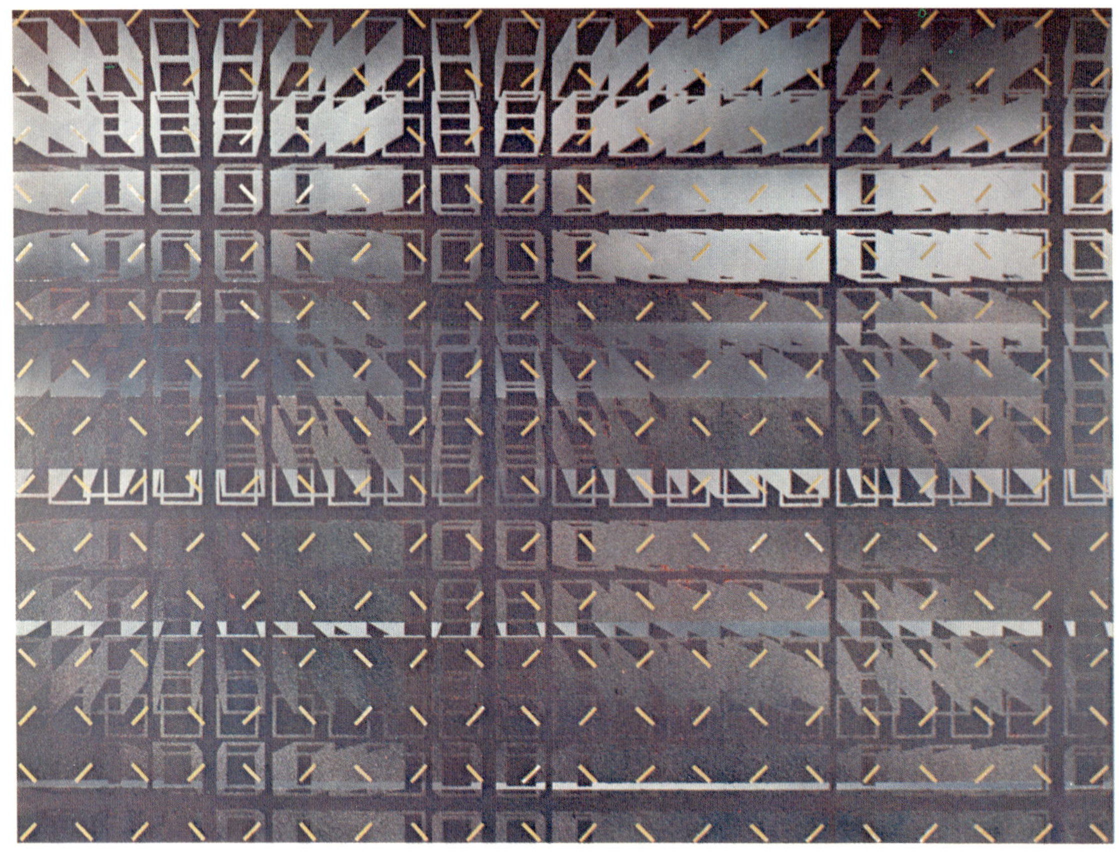

Plate **XXVI**
Jonas Balsaitis
b. Germany, 1948–
Metron 11 1971
Acrylic on canvas
304.8 × 345.6 cm
Inscriptions. Verso: "Metron No. 2 J. Balsaitis 1971"
Ex. Pinacotheca Gallery, Melbourne, 1972
Purchased 1972
A5/1972

78

John Coburn, Australian, 1925–

Primordial Garden. c. 1965–6

John Coburn has pursued a solitary course of painting organic abstracts. His integrity has won admiration and his work critical praise. This painting shows him at his finest, as a controller of large decorative areas. He has himself in a private letter described it as the best of his "garden" series. The Art Gallery of New South Wales owns the important **Tree of Life** from this series but it pales beside this work.

(1968)

Footnote: John Coburn studied art at East Sydney Technical School, from 1947 to 1950. He held his first one man exhibition in Melbourne in 1957, and has since had a distinguished career, exhibiting widely in Australia, and also abroad. He has taught art at the Canberra Technical College and the National Art School, East Sydney Technical College of which school he was the Principal from 1972 to 1974. From 1969 to 1972, Coburn lived in France, designing tapestries for the Aubusson workshops. His tapestries hang in the Sydney Opera House and the John F. Kennedy Centre for the Performing Arts in Washington.

J. P.
(1976)

79

Michael Brown, Australian, 1938–

Omega. 1966

Early in 1962 the Museum of Modern Art, Melbourne, staged an exhibition by the Annandale Imitation Realist group who had formed the previous year, basing themselves in the Sydney suburb of Annandale. The three artists who made up the group were Michael Brown, Colin Lanceley **(Plate XXII)** and Ross Crothall. The group had an enormous impact on the Sydney scene when they exhibited there as the Subterranean Imitation Realists with a similar show to their first Melbourne appearance.

This work painted in 1966, the year after Colin Lanceley left for England, bases itself on the traditional theme "Omega" with all its references through the title, to the Final End or Last Judgement, as opposed to Alpha, the Beginning or Awakening. But the title, and perhaps, the use of the diptych and the overall grey tones are as far as the artist goes in drawing on the traditional for his theme. This painterly "Omega" for the mid-1960s is a frozen "pop" explosion. There almost appears to be a certain type of aggressive resistance going on between the brush and the hardboard surface. The brushwork which is raw and obvious

113

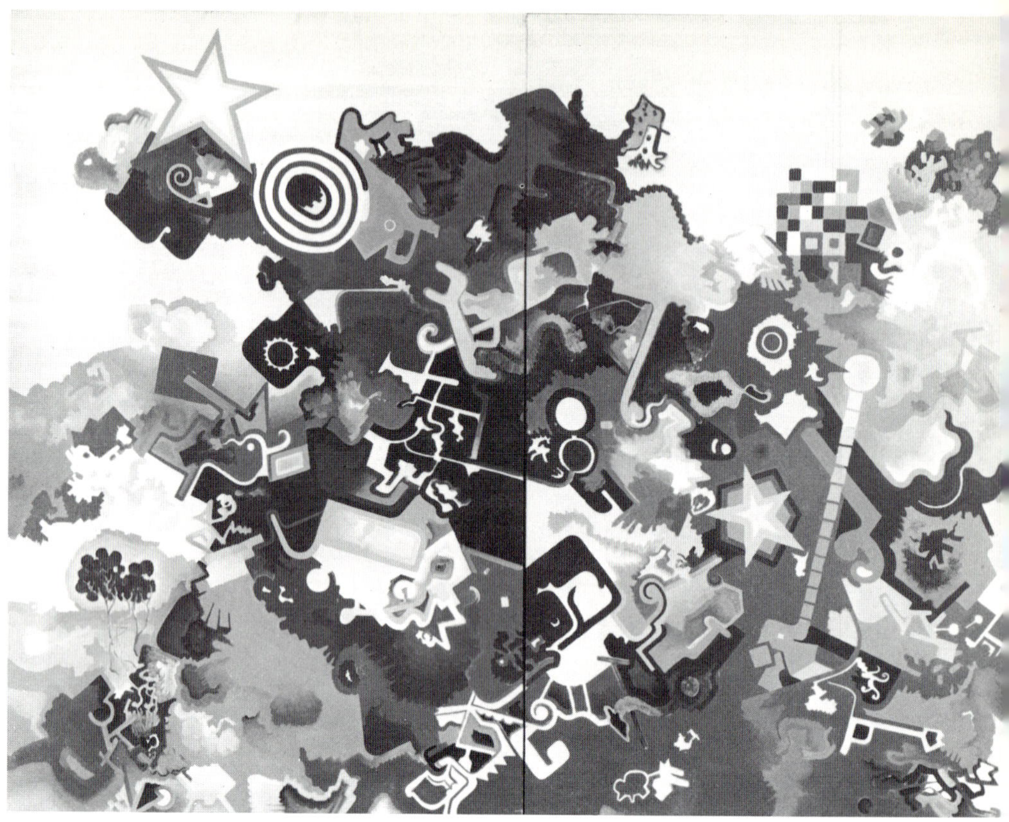

in some areas and highly finished in others adds to the certain chaotic effect and feeling. The vague reference to landscape in the bottom left of the painting gives way to the crazy assemblage of stars, targets, mandala forms and other uncontained commercial images that have "zap-pow-crashed" their way into existence, more like an episode from a Captain Marvel or Dr Strange comic-book than any aesthetical counterpart that comes to mind.

Michael Brown has continued to exhibit works which, like the assemblages of the Annandale Imitation Realist days, have broken with a definite tradition and moved away from the lyrical Australian image.

G. B. in *N. G. S. B.*
(April, 1971)

80

Dick Watkins, Australian, 1937–
Pilot. 1967
A travelling exhibition from the Museum of Modern Art, New York, entitled "Two Decades of American Painting", was presented to the Australian public in 1967 at the National Gallery of Victoria (June/July) and the Art Gallery of New South Wales (July/August). Large sections of the local "art world" and "viewing public" were thereby given their first opportunity to familiarise themselves with and become aware of the various contemporary movements and their

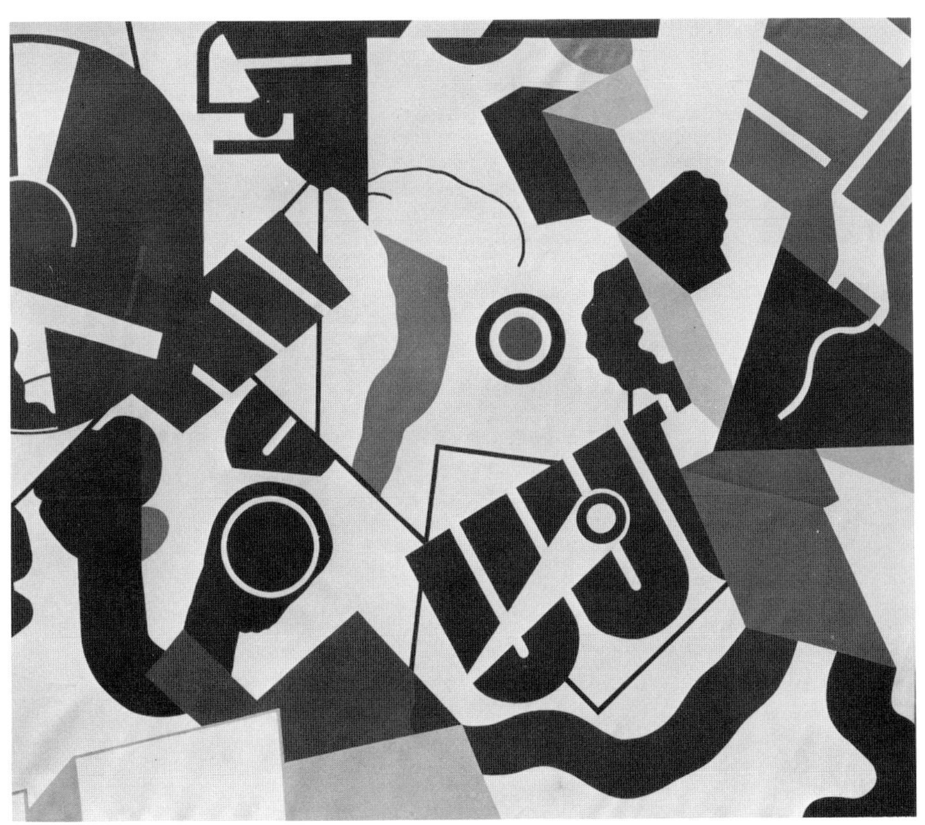

developments—the emphasis being placed almost solely in the exhibition on the abstract expressionist, pop and hard-edge schools. *Studio International* in June the same year stated that the centre of the art world had moved from Paris to New York. August 1968 saw the National Gallery of Victoria open in its new building with "The Field", an exhibition devoted to the local development of the international movement of hard-edge painting. Perhaps one of the main uses of such information is that it makes the general public aware that such international re-assessings and developments of "art" are in fact occurring. No matter how many forums that come together to discuss such occurrences or how many critical essays are written, it always occurs that they follow after the movement itself has already taken root and is flourishing in certain sections of, usually, the younger artistic community. It was in this atmosphere that Dick Watkins worked and **Pilot** was painted.

Dick Watkins was born in Sydney in 1937. Besides the various jobs he held between 1955–8 he also began to occasionally attend classes at the East Sydney Technical College and the Julian Ashton School of Art. 1959 saw him at the age of twenty-three in London. Before he returned to Sydney in 1961 he was also to visit Paris, Madrid and New York where the artists he specially interested himself in, apart from the obvious contemporary movements, were Titian, Goya, Manet, Monet and that destroyer of the tradition of western renaissance illusionism, Matisse. Having his initial training in the '50s as well as the '60s Watkins has been able therefore to maintain that "painting is" the ideas of abstract expressionism and hard-edge. His early works from 1963 were also showing an awareness of Malevich

80
Dick Watkins
Australian, 1937–
Pilot 1967
Polyvinyl acetate and oil on canvas
156 × 180.9 cm
Inscriptions. Verso:
"Pilot, 1967, Dick Watkins"
Ex. Central St. Gallery, Sydney, N.S.W.
Purchased 1969
124.6

and a very definite interest in the British and American Pop movement, particularly Rauschenberg and Johns, and the hard-edge school of New York. It was in 1963 Watkins held his first one-man show at Barry Stern's gallery. He has continued having regular exhibitions moving to Central Street Gallery in 1967, the then centre of Sydney's "new school", and exerting a considerable influence with Tony McGillick, the co-founder of Central Street Gallery, on the establishment of the new ideas of what "art" could be. Watkins through his regular exhibitions has not allowed himself to become too entrenched in any particular movement or style but draws from wherever he feels appropriate to achieve the completion of a particular work. The olive, brown, green, dull red tones of **Pilot** are no guarantee that another work by the artist will not be pure "fauve" colour structure.

Perhaps the artist could have been referring to his own **Pilot** when he is quoted in Horton's *Present Day Art in Australia* 1969: "There's not much point talking if the picture is saying something—even less if it isn't—or, a flight from reality at a low altitude is better than never taking off at all".

G. B. in N. G. S. B.
(Jan./Feb. 1975)

81

Mel Ramsden, b. England, 1944–
Secret Painting. 1967–8
One of the major foundation blocks for practically all art produced up to the mid-point of this century has been: what you see is what you know. When presented with a work of art that overrides this major assumption the area tends to become uncharted and possibly quite confusing. **Secret Painting** (1967–8) by Mel Ramsden is an example of one of these uncharted areas, although it is certainly not necessary to warn people off with signs of "here be dragons".

Familiar means of judging and relating to the work under "art history" and "art theory" terms of aesthetics, composition and technique become irrelevant. All we are given is a small all-black canvas and a slightly larger board with the information "the content of this painting is invisible; the character and dimensions of the content are to be kept permanently secret, known only to the artist". We know what "is" but we will never know what "was". And from the information supplied there definitely "was" a time when the character of the work was more in line with the traditionally accepted standards of what "art" can be. The artist overrides the usual method of gathering information about a work of art which is the range of the five sense fields—the most common methods employed being sight and touch. Here he forces the viewer to directly employ the mind itself.

81
Mel Ramsden
b. England, 1944–
Secret Painting 1967–8
(a) Enamel on canvas
(b) Xerox sheet on board
(a) 45.8 × 38.8 × 7 cm
(b) 86.4 × 86.4 cm
Inscriptions. On verso of each piece signed:
"Mel Ramsden". "Secret Painting". "1967–8".
Purchased 1972
A21/1972

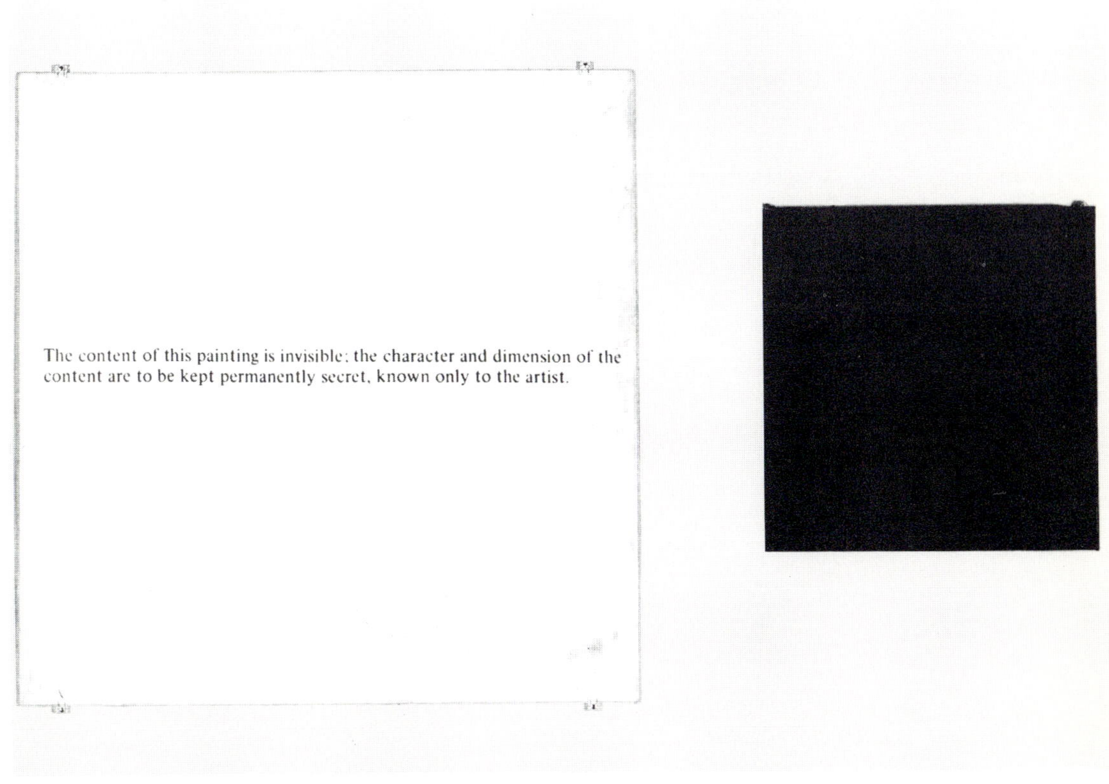

Specific visual information is irrelevant to considering this work. To do this would place it in an "art history" line with Malevich's **Black Square** (1915); or Ad Reinhardt's **Abstract Paintings** which began about 1953 and culminated in 1960 in the series of identical near-black squares. And to apply progressive or structure imagery concepts such as: from white plain canvas to a type of imagery to an all-black canvas, or small raised black canvas contrasts with large flat white board, would be regarded as "flashy" or "ultra attractive theory" by the artist and in no way relevant to the work.

If such mapping is necessary closer areas would be John Cage's **4′33″ (tacet) for any instrument(s)** (1952) a piece which is four minutes thirty-three seconds of silence by the musician(s), the non-playing allowing any "incidentals" to become the performance; or Robert Rauschenberg's **Erased de Kooning Drawing** (1953), an actual drawing by de Kooning, although we are not informed exactly which drawing it is that Rauschenberg has erased.

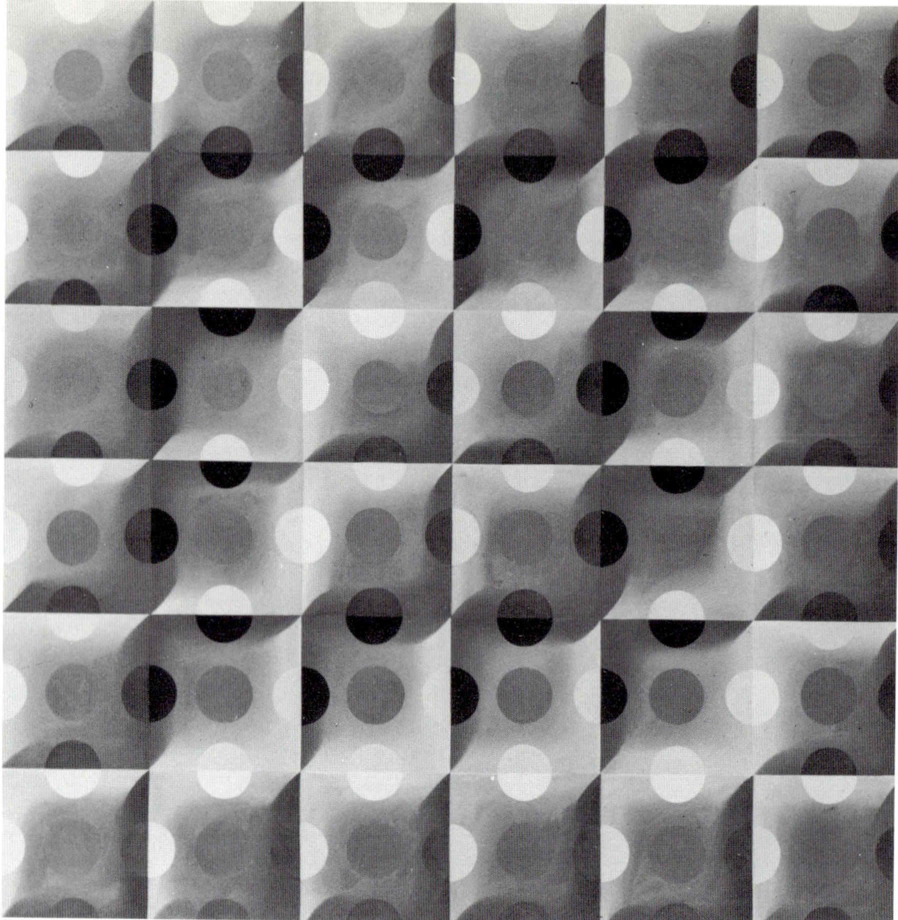

Mel Ramsden was born in 1944 in Nottingham, England and studied at the Nottingham School of Art and National Gallery School, Melbourne. He has participated in Art — Language shows in England, Europe and U.S.A. and has lived in New York since 1967.

G. B. in *N. G. S. B.*
(August, 1975)

82

Dale Hickey, Australian, 1937–
Untitled. 1967–8
From an uncertain start this artist has shown a most amazing advance. Fully in command of his unusual work which allies conceptual painting with elements of "op" illusionism he seems likely to be an outstanding artist of this decade.

(1968)

Footnote: This painting is similar to works exhibited in "The Field". It does not have the hard vibrating luminous qualities commonly associated with American Op Art although it was painted in 1967 when the American artist, James Doolin—a friend of Dale Hickey's—was living in Australia. It shows the characteristics of all Dale Hickey's work—strong painterly qualities, with soft brush strokes and colour, despite the tensions between colours and shapes. The greatest tension is where dark and light blue meet in the circles, and deflect the straight lines running on the edges of the squares. The painting reverses itself, whichever way you look at it. The conception behind this painting is related to visual contradiction and the question of how to simplify art—this particular work is painted in values of blue and yellow only.

Other artists who worked with Dale Hickey at this time, and who reacted against the pervasive "softness" of those artists upheld by the American critic Clement Greenberg were Doolin (**Plate XXI**), Robert Rooney, and Robert Hunter (**83**). At the same time that Robert Rooney was painting hard-edge, luminously refractive works based on clothes pegs and plastic corn-flake packet toys, Dale Hickey did this painting, based on a quilt.

Dale Hickey's work in the three years following included fences built against walls at Pinacotheca Gallery, Melbourne, and a photographic piece which explored blank images—**90 White Walls.** In 1971 he visited U.S.A., where he again met James Doolin, and Europe. He is now painting realist landscapes and still-life.

Dale Hickey had exhibited from 1964 onwards at galleries in Melbourne and Sydney. From 1954 to 1957, he attended Swinburne Technical College as a graphic design student, and, after working in advertising, began teaching. Now a lecturer at Preston Institute of Technology, Dale Hickey's influence as a teacher is widespread amongst younger artists.

J. P.
(1976)

83

Robert Hunter, Australian, 1947–
No. 8 Untitled Painting. 1968
Robert Hunter was born in Melbourne in 1947. He studied and worked at Preston Technical College under Dale Hickey in 1964–5, and studied industrial design and later painting at the Royal Melbourne Institute of Technology in 1966–7.

In 1968 he was invited to participate in "The Field", at the National Gallery of Victoria, and in August the same year he left to tour the United States of America and Europe after his successful first one-man exhibition at the Tolarno Galleries. All the works in this show were based on the same circle/square/triangle grid combination, the earlier works employing pastel tones in the colour combinations, the later ones tending to the cool, white/off-white combinations. It is one of the works from this show that has entered the Australian collection, **Untitled Painting** 1968, a canvas in off-white patterns so closely related tonally that the camera cannot capture the image satisfactorily.

The different names, Hard Edge, Systemic or Minimal Art which cover this style, give hints of the aims of the artist. This particular work is also an example of a new cool style where subtleties are stated, rather than contrasts of local

83
Robert Hunter
Australian, 1947–
No. 8 Untitled 1968
Oil on canvas
158.5 × 158.5 cm
Inscriptions. Verso:
"No. 8 Untitled
Painting Robert
Hunter 1968"
Ex. Tolarno Galleries,
Melb., 1968
Presented by Mr N.
R. Seddon, 1968
1827.5

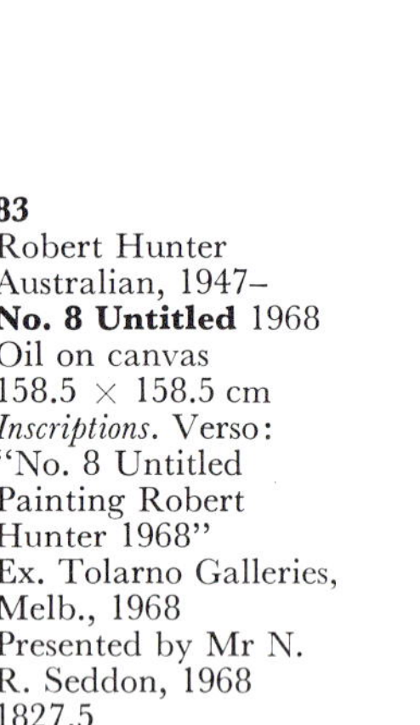

colour forced upon a viewer. This is painting in a classic manner, to be contemplated for some time before it begins to actually *work* for the viewer, and once this does occur the qualities of the painting become clear. As well as being an extremely competent work technically, with the delicacy of the thin raised lines tracing their way over the surface of the canvas in perfect geometric shapes, it is also a very aesthetically successful exercise. The circles balance calmly in their respective squares, while a tonal monotony is avoided through the introduction of the extremely subtle tones of white-cream/white colouration.

This is not a work in which to find hidden forms or meaning. It is an uncluttered piece of deceptively simple balance which is an excellent example of the beauty that exists in the simplicity and subtleties of a calm, quiet, rationally conceived object that is approached in a receptive frame of mind.

Robert Hunter has continued to maintain his concern "with specifics is as straight a way as possible: that is why the mathematical progressions are obvious". In 1970 at the opening of the new Pinacotheca premises he exhibited a group of grey acrylics on unmounted paper and masking tape—"because the paper was there and available" and later that year and in 1971 at the Second Indian Triennale of Contemporary Art, Lalit Kala Akademi, New Delhi, he painted grids directly onto the walls. He has also been included in "Recent Australian Art", 1973 Art Gallery of New South Wales and "Eight Contemporary Artists", Museum of Modern Art, New York, 1974.

G. B. in *N. G. S. B.*
(December, 1968)

Footnote: Quotations from *Australia 1971 Robert Hunter*, catalogue, Second Indian Triennale of Contemporary Art, New Delhi.

84

Paul Partos, b. Czechoslovakia, 1943–

Quantum. 1968

Perhaps among the most brilliant of the young painters, Partos has a tenacity and control quite remarkable in this very difficult area. From his early expressionist abstracts he has developed into a painter of great authority in the minimal manner. His paintings in "The Field" have won wide acclaim and the example of his work has been most influential in Melbourne.

(1968)

Footnote: The work of Paul Partos has always been exploratory and varied, and he has encompassed a rapid investigation of minimal and conceptual art in a highly personal manner. **Quantum,** which literally means sum, or amount, is a spray-painted constructed canvas, divided in two—the left side of three panels, and the right side of two panels. The artist aims to keep unity in the painting without asserting the structure and so the strong colour makes the divisions between the canvas units spaces rather than lines. The red surface has subtle tonal changes, and gains depth from the finely grained surface of minute bronze flecks. The control in the painting comes from the care with which the colours are applied, the change of tone with change of viewing angle, and the fragile surface shimmer so fine that it is discernible only on close examination.

Born in Czechoslovakia, Paul Partos came to Australia in 1950. He studied painting at the Royal Melbourne Institute of Technology, from 1959 to 1963, and began exhibiting in Melbourne and Sydney. By 1965, he had turned away from his expressionist style, and when travelling in Europe in 1965 and 1966, he became familiar with the work of the American Abstract Expressionists, particularly Frank Stella and Kenneth Noland. In 1969 he was spray-painting nylon screens, cutting them up and photographing them. In 1973, after two years living in New York, he exhibited cut up books and small painted panels with numbers and letters tied across them with black elastic. This work developed into large minimal paintings, of one cool colour, rich brush texture, and with numbers and letters at the edge of the canvas. The edge of the painting was extended by black elastic lines pinned to the wall beside it, or stretched across it. Since 1973 he has lectured in painting at the Victorian College of the Arts.

J. P.
(1976)

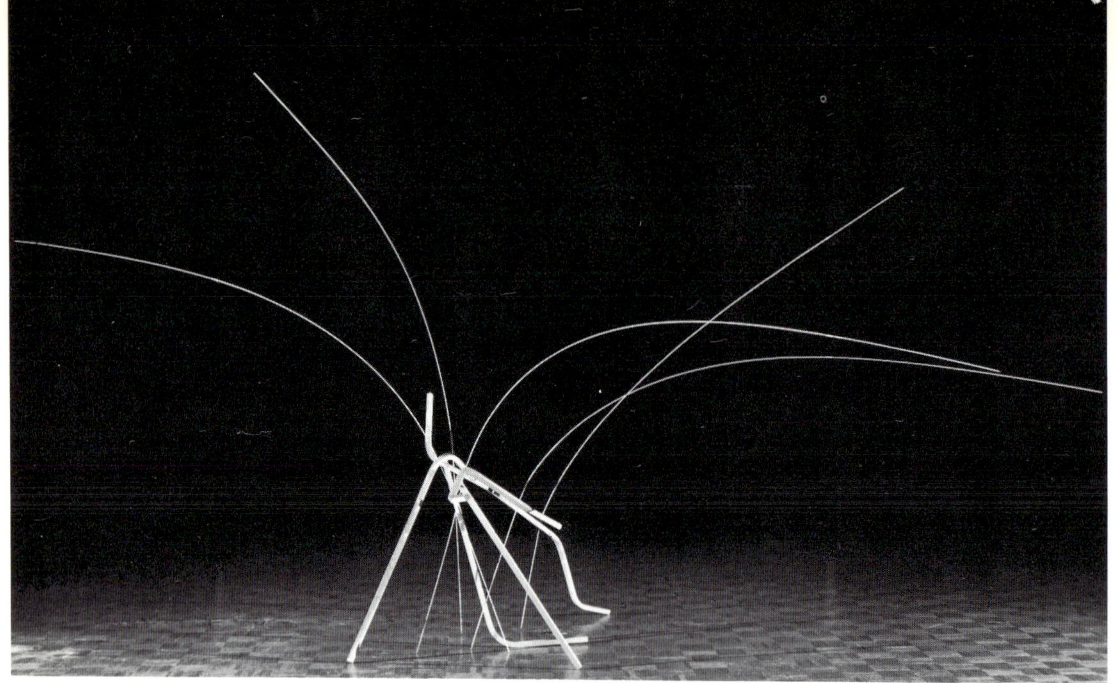

85
Tony Coleing
Australian, 1942–
**Untitled
(Frondescence)** 1968
Aluminium, painted
steel
175 × 446 × 285 cm
(size varies with
installation)
Ex. Gallery A,
Sydney, 1969
Purchased 1969
82.6

85

Tony Coleing, Australian, 1942–
Untitled ("Frondescence"). 1968

Tony Coleing was born in Warrnambool, Victoria, in 1942. He studied painting at the National Art School, Sydney, in 1958–9 and took labouring work throughout 1960–1 in Queensland, Victoria and New South Wales. He worked as a labourer in New Zealand in 1962, and in 1963 he left for England to study painting and sculpture. It was painting that was going to occupy him until 1968. While in London he participated in exhibitions at the Whitechapel Gallery, and Royal Institute Gallery, as well as doing theatrical décor work for the Royal Court Theatre, London and dealing in antiques and fine art. In 1965 he visited Iceland where he worked for three months on a fishing trawler. It was this same year that he became interested in plastics, developing and experimenting in small sculptures. Having travelled extensively throughout Europe, including Cairo, he returned to Sydney in 1968. He began to participate in a number of group shows, including "The Field" (1968) at the National Gallery of Victoria. In April 1969 he held his first one-man exhibition in Melbourne to be followed later that year by a Sydney showing. It was from this first exhibition, known collectively under the title of "Frondescence", that this **Untitled** sculpture was purchased.

Frondescence, as the title suggests, brings to mind the organic plant form, in particular the fronds of the large ferns found throughout the Australian bush. Although especially suited to outdoors where it is activated by the wind it does work equally well indoors where it takes just the slightest touch or air disturbance to set it in motion. Its movements range from the great, broad arcs traced out by wide, springing sweeps to the calm, rhythmic pulsations set up by the just barely moving wires. This actual springing, circular movement, that is so pleasant and soothing to watch, is completely different from the mechanical/optical jolts delivered by the works of people like Tinguely, Le Parc of Pol Bury whom one usually associates with the idea of Kinetic art—the word Kinetic here referring to a work of art that does in fact actually move or appears to move. The soft natural curves of the wire are emphasised by the angular, obviously man-made movement the metal base is forced through.

Tony Coleing's sculpture gives the Australian collection an extremely good example of the type of interests the new generation artists hold and the directions their experiments are taking them.

G. B. in N. G. S. B.
(September, 1969)

86

David Wire, b. England, 1934–
Abstract Construction. 1969

David Wire, an Englishman, was born in 1934 and studied at the Royal College of Art, London between 1955 and 1959. He came to Australia in late 1966 bringing with him the experimental form/dimension concepts that are already establishing themselves in the Continental traditions. The work in question was purchased from David Wire's first one-man show at Central Street Gallery, Sydney, held in July, 1969.

The concepts employed have their origins in the works of people like Vasarely and Albers but a new set of values are experienced through the introduction of a third dimension, that being depth. In this case we are still looking at a painting but through the use of this added dimension of depth it is probably easier to consider the work as a construction, the term here implying a three-dimensional activity. This then becomes an exercise in not only the disintegration but also the reality of the existence of each square and circle and its depth relationship. Through the use of this depth the harmonies and shapes are therefore able to flow not only across and up and down the picture plane, but also "into" it. The restricted use of colour heightens this visual illusion and lets the construction work through its own "cool" beauty without any strong irrelevant visual interference that additional colour would introduce.

This work makes its impact through its questioning of certain realities and the playing down of the result.

In 1970 Wire was invited to participate in the Transfield Art Prize. He exhibited a work called **No Survivors,** a tableau of bodies under a sheet—again exploring reality/illusion.

G. B. in N. G. S. B.
(1969)

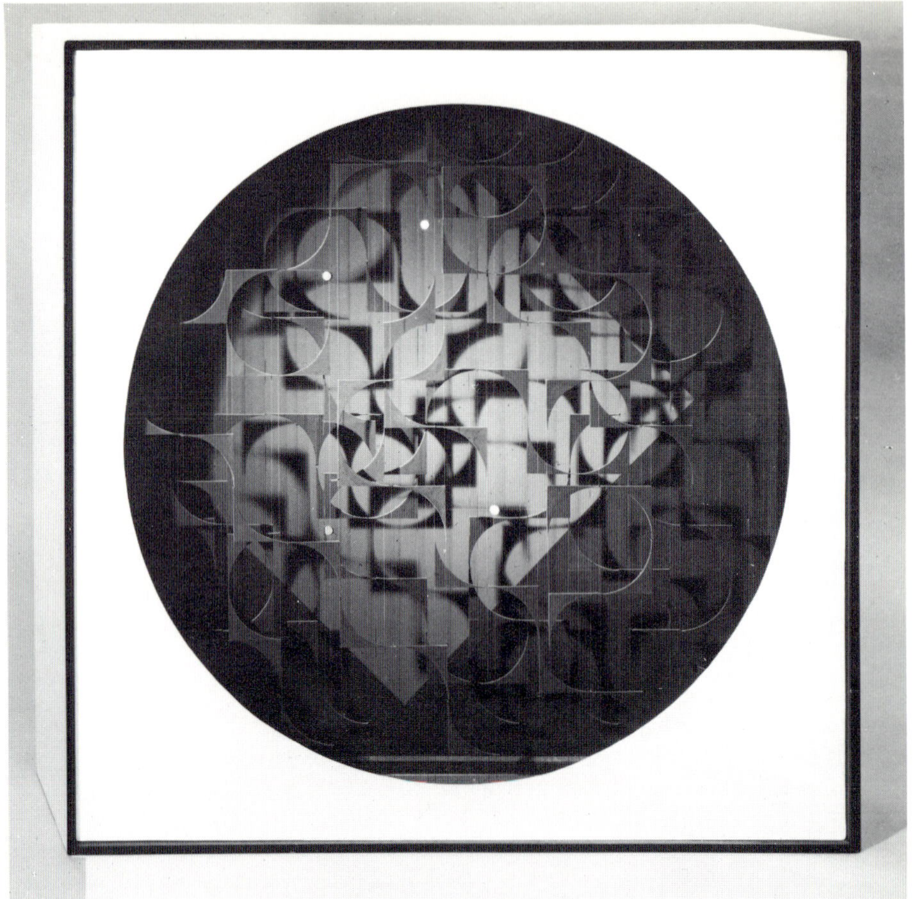

87

Richard Havyatt, Australian, 1945–

Untitled. 1971

This **Untitled** acrylic on canvas is the third example of the young Melbourne artist Richard Havyatt to enter the collection of the National Gallery of Victoria. The two earlier works, a 1966 **Untitled** coloured inks on paper and a 1969 watercolour and indian ink on paper, from the series "Without Contraries Is No Progression"*, give good indication of the artist's technical ability and sense of colour and balance which comes to full bloom in this large acrylic. Through its addition to the collection we are able to follow the development of the style of the artist and admire the painting as the single entity that it is in itself.

Richard Havyatt was born in Melbourne in 1945. He attended Melbourne Grammar School where John Brack was his art master. He studied architecture at Melbourne University from 1962. It was also in 1962 that Janet Dawson started a workshop/art school at the old Gallery A, Melbourne, an activity she would be involved in until the end of 1964. Richard Havyatt "hung around" the studio working as "casual labour" and was allowed the use of a small studio at the back of the premises as part payment for his efforts. He was involved with this until the end of 1965. At the end of 1964 he dropped his architectural studies to concentrate on painting, exhibiting in numerous group exhibitions and holding

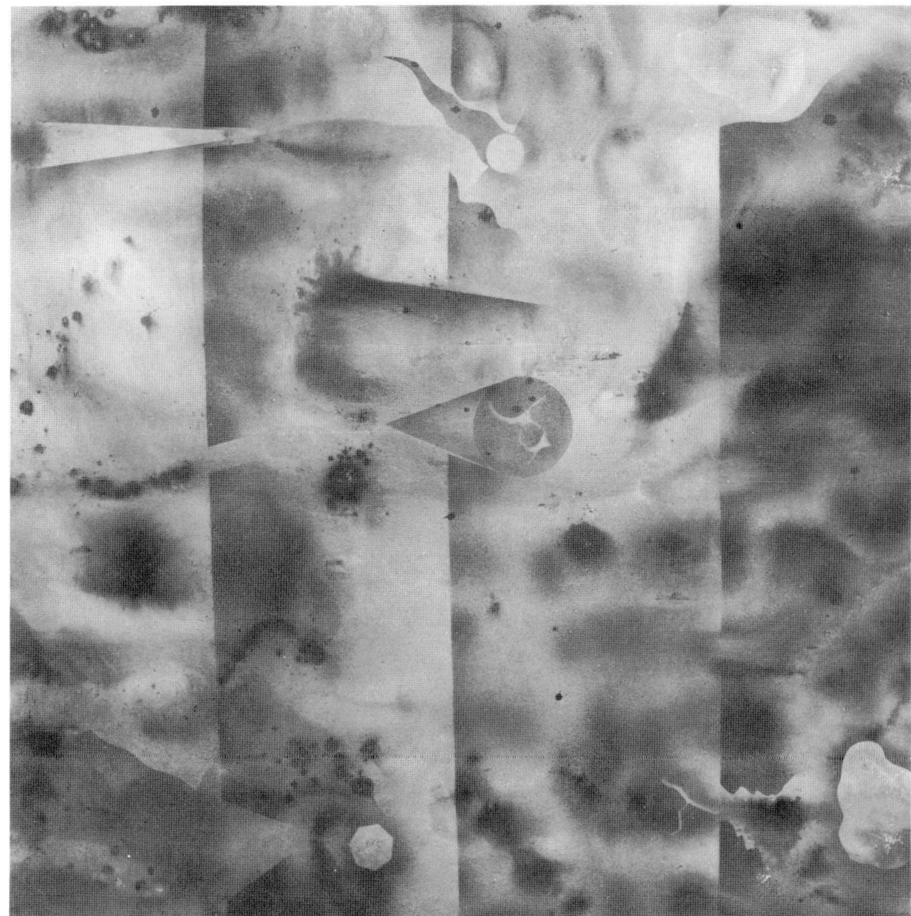

one-man shows in Melbourne, Sydney and Ballarat from 1964 onwards. In 1968 and 1969 he was awarded the Minnie Crouch Prize for watercolours, Ballarat.

The painting itself must be admired for its technical and lyrical romantic qualities. The overall red stain movement quarters itself vertically as it fades, strengthens and pulses within the canvas. This initial movement then supports within itself a whole range of amorphous or small solid geometrics that take up carefully balanced positions. The yellows and blues of these intrusive shapes glow, mix and luminesce as they complement and add to the vibrant deep reds. Taking shape within the clouds of red stain they outline their own solid little movements and boundaries across and through the work. Small areas of raw canvas create further contrast or appear as tiny echoes of areas of pigment. The effect of the whole is a movement and flow within a carefully worked and controlled area of activity.

G. B.
(1976)

* William Blake.
   "The Marriage of Heaven and Hell".
   "The Argument" Plate 3.
   "Without Contraries is no Progression. Attraction and Repulsion, Reason and Energy, Love and Hate, are necessary to Human existence."

88

Peter Booth, b. England, 1940–

Painting. 1971

Born in Sheffield England, Peter Booth studied at the Sheffield College of Art before emigrating to Australia in 1958. In Melbourne he studied painting at the National Gallery School.

He has held several one-man shows and participated in major group survey exhibitions.

Peter Booth's paintings of the late sixties were typically hard-edge and impersonal in style, but by 1970 his work had begun to reveal a significant interest in surface painterly qualities.

Painting 1971 is a work which represents the beginning of a mature phase in Booth's art—the commencement of a series of black "doorway" paintings, often over-life size, which present the viewer with a direct confrontation. With its rich glossy surface, **Painting 1971** is essentially a meditative contemplative work, concerned not only with surface painterly qualities but also with inward reflection.

The surface is rich and fluid with movement, there is no central axis or focus, the whole of the painting is articulated by the relationship of tension which exists between the solid black rectangle and the dull pink border.

The dominance of black is significant not only for its effect upon the viewer, but also because for Peter Booth it represents an emotive condition—it cannot be disassociated from his youth spent in a blackened industrial environment. The pink of the border which frames the block and underlies the black skin is like the flash from a furnace on a dark night.

Peter Booth is an artist who responds with absolute directness to the techniques and materials which he uses. The depth and intensity of his paintings results as much from a highly charged emotional involvement as from his delight in the sensuous and expressive use of paint.

F. McC.
(1971)

Plate XXVI
Jonas Balsaitis, b. Germany, 1948–
Metron II. 1971
Born in Germany, 1948, and arriving in Australia in 1950, Jonas Balsaitis is a Melbourne artist who studied painting at Preston and Prahran Technical Colleges and finally at the Melbourne National Gallery School. During this time he came into contact with Dale Hickey, Alun Leach-Jones and the artists of the Pinacotheca group. He has had two one-man exhibitions. **Metron II** was purchased from his second exhibition at which it was one of the three large canvases that were exhibited.

His paintings contain the lyrical and romantic enjoyment of colour which is associated with the Sydney painters and the inquiry into spatial relationships which is a deep concern of many Melbourne artists. They have spectacular impact and command immediate attention. Allied to the visual excitement is a compelling investigation of the ambiguities posed by this subtly conceived work.

The complexity of the painting is derived from the results of a series of xerox sheets made from the structure of a radio astronomy telescope that has been cut out and collaged over ploughed fields. The lowest grey tone line indicates the base of the radio telescope. Balsaitis uses an unusual and inventive technique of overall linear design of incised surface together with a chromatic decoration of miniature nature. This enables the work to be commanding when viewed at a distance and appreciated for the intricate colour variations at close range.

The dark, heavy stippled bands and blocks move across the surface of the canvas in a definite rigid movement creating the impression of film and film frames. Also from these areas, perspectives are created which move to the various centre points which lose themselves in the pulsing cloudy "background" areas of colour ranging from smoky pinks and blues in the upper areas of the canvas to the heavy blue/indigo/purple areas of the middle areas and downwards. Over the whole of this an incised series of broken diagonal yellow lines make their way creating another contrast of colour, movement and direction. At the moment Jonas Balsaitis is carrying his experiments in movement and colour into the range of experimental film which he has been working on and developing while exploring the possibilities of spatial illusion on canvas.

G. B. in *N. G. S. B.*
(Jan./Feb. 1973)

89
Patrick O'Carrigan
b. Ireland, 1918–
Rooftop Calligraphy
1972
Watercolour
55.5 × 75.5 cm
Inscriptions. Recto:
l.r. "P. J. O'Carrigan
1972"
Ex. Munster Arms
Gallery, Melbourne,
1973
A9/1974

89

Patrick O'Carrigan, b. Ireland, 1918–
Roof Top Calligraphy. 1972
Patrick O'Carrigan was born near Belfast in Northern Ireland. His first formal art training was in the studio of the Sydney artist Edward Smith, (a portraitist who was the first mentor of Justin O'Brien whose work is so vastly different). In 1962 he held his first one-man exhibition at the Hamilton Art Gallery, Victoria—later exhibitions have been at Canberra, Hobart, Adelaide and Melbourne. In 1969 he studied at the Accademiadi Belle Arte in Rome and the "Scuolo del Nudo" under Gutilini. He later spent some time in Japan where he fell under the fascination of the ancient art of calligraphy.

This watercolour, which shows great dexterity, reveals the influence of both these traditions. The Italian watercolourists are of unbelieveable skill.

(1974)

90
John Peart
Australian, 1945–
Somerset Blue 1972
Acrylic on canvas
230.5 × 428.4 cm
Inscriptions. Verso:
"John Peart,
Somerset Blue, 1972"
Ex. Powell Street
Gallery, Melb., 1972
Presented by the
National Gallery
Society 1972
A22/1972

90

John Peart, Australian, 1945–
Somerset Blue. 1972
The concept of letting paint on canvas, in large, simple areas of flat colour, act of its own accord making reference to no deeper meaning other than its own inherent physical and optical properties, was the primary aim of the Hard Edge School. John Peart first achieved acclaim as a practitioner of the Hard Edge style. He soon left the hard, geometric approach behind to develop his own more personal style. Indeed when he exhibited the two large, shaped, segmented canvases **Cool Corner 11** (1968) and **Corner Square Diagonal** (1968) in

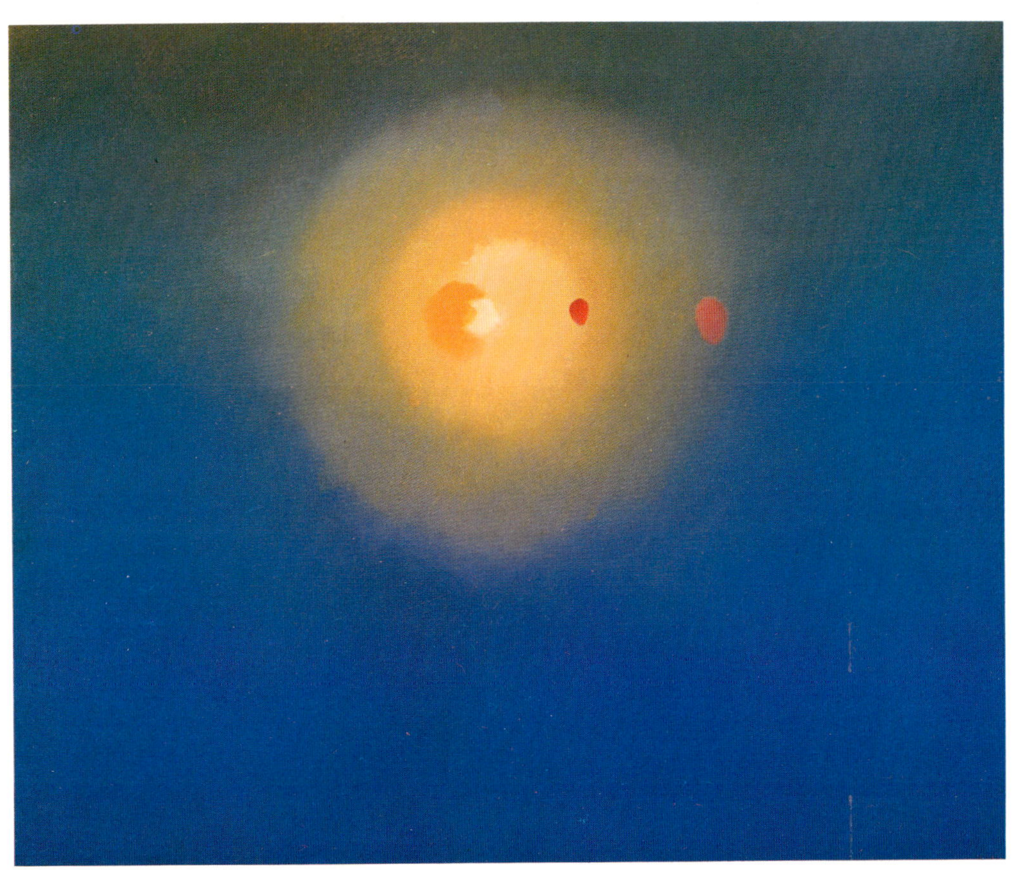

Plate **XXVII**
Donald Laycock
Australian, 1931–
Star Cycle 1972
Oil and acrylic on canvas
152.3 × 182.9 cm
Inscriptions. Recto: l.r. "D. L. 72"
Awarded the John McCaughey Memorial Prize, 1972
Presented by the National Gallery Society of Victoria 1972
A24/1972

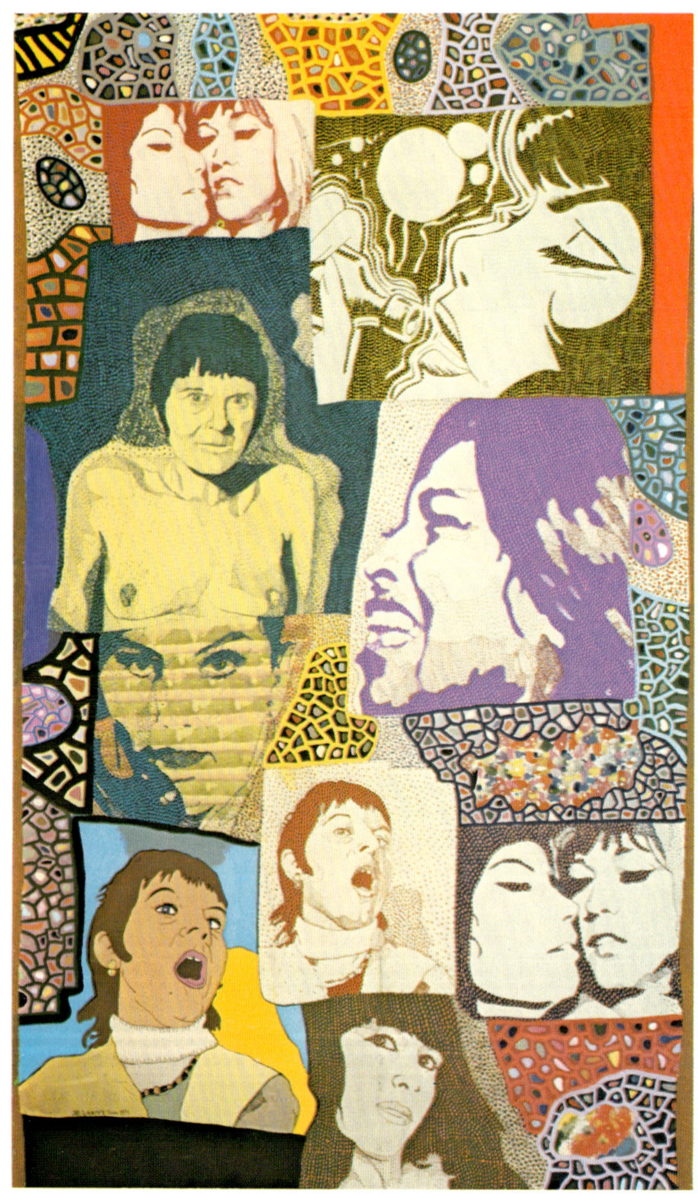

Plate XXVIII
Richard Larter
Australian, 1938–
Root Ripples Stocks 1975
Acrylic on canvas on hardboard
189.3 × 110.4 cm
Inscriptions. Recto: l.l. "R. Larter, June, 1975"
Ex. The John McCaughey Memorial Prize, 1975
Presented by the National Gallery Society of Victoria 1976
A2/1976

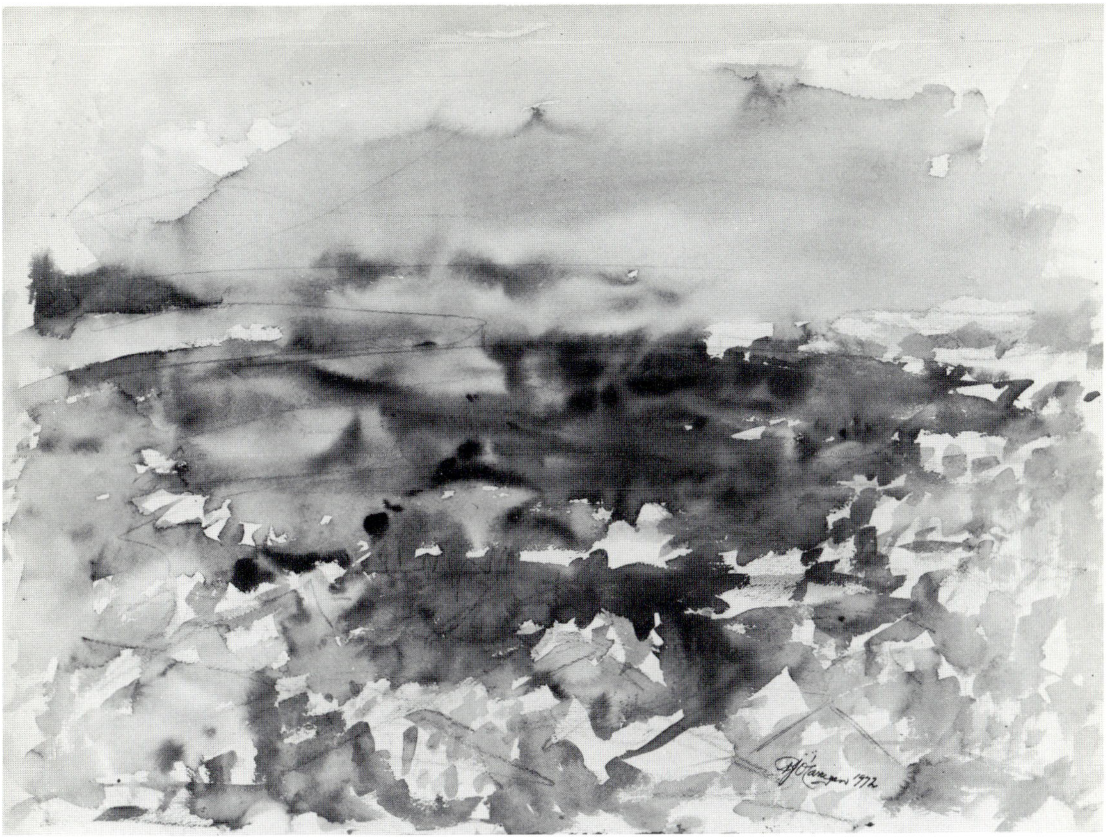

"The Field" exhibition he had already been working and experimenting with dots and dabbing of colour stain on raw canvas. The earlier **Blue Square, 1–69** (1969), which entered the collection in November 1969, is an outcome of this experimentation and a result of the breakaway from the then more "fashionable" Hard Edge style. **Somerset Blue** is a further development of the individualization of John Peart's personal approach to the qualities of paint on canvas.

Born in 1945 in Brisbane, John Peart studied at the Brisbane Technical College Art School before moving to Sydney in 1964. He participated in a number of group shows and has held successful one-man shows from 1965. In 1968 he was awarded the Pacesetter Award for overseas travel, the Mirror-Waratah Prize, the NBN Channel 3 Newcastle Prize and the Transfield Prize. With the award of a Myer Foundation grant in 1969 he left Australia to travel through the U.S.A. and Europe to England where he settled and is at present working. He returned to Australia briefly in 1972 and held one-man shows in Melbourne and Sydney.

Somerset Blue was purchased from the 1972 Melbourne exhibition of the paintings John Peart worked on while in England and it is initially an obviously worthwhile exercise to compare it to and note its development from **Blue Square, 1–69.** Abstract expressionism and lyrical colourfield both hold the originating concepts for this painting and are employed in it. Awareness of the various qualities of paint and its application are an integral part of the work. The flat surface gains a new dimension through the application of paint as staining "into" the canvas as well as painting "on" the canvas. The lyrical pastel colours are used in an almost unconscious placement of a controlled splash and running technique which results in intricate webs and networks of fine, running lines. Contrasting with this fine network of lines other colour shapes are broken and spread across the canvas as though with a heavy overloaded brush. All this is applied over a block/grid structure which is seen as the large squared and rectangular stained areas of the basic colours of pink, green, blue and orange. Peart has used these colours in the disintegration of this underlying structure so that the whole becomes an exercise in the controlled, and also chance, application of paint to give the work the all-over lyrical movement and contrast of colour and application. Texture, colour and structure are all brought into obvious contrast and subtle interplay in this example of the young Sydney artist's work.

G. B. in *N. G. S. B.*
(July, 1970)

91
Ron Robertson-Swann
Australian, 1941–
Cyclops 1971
Rusted steel
121.9 × 221 × 149.9 cm
Ex. Rudy Komon Gallery, Sydney, 1972
Presented by the National Gallery Society
with the assistance of Containers Ltd, 1972
A12/1972

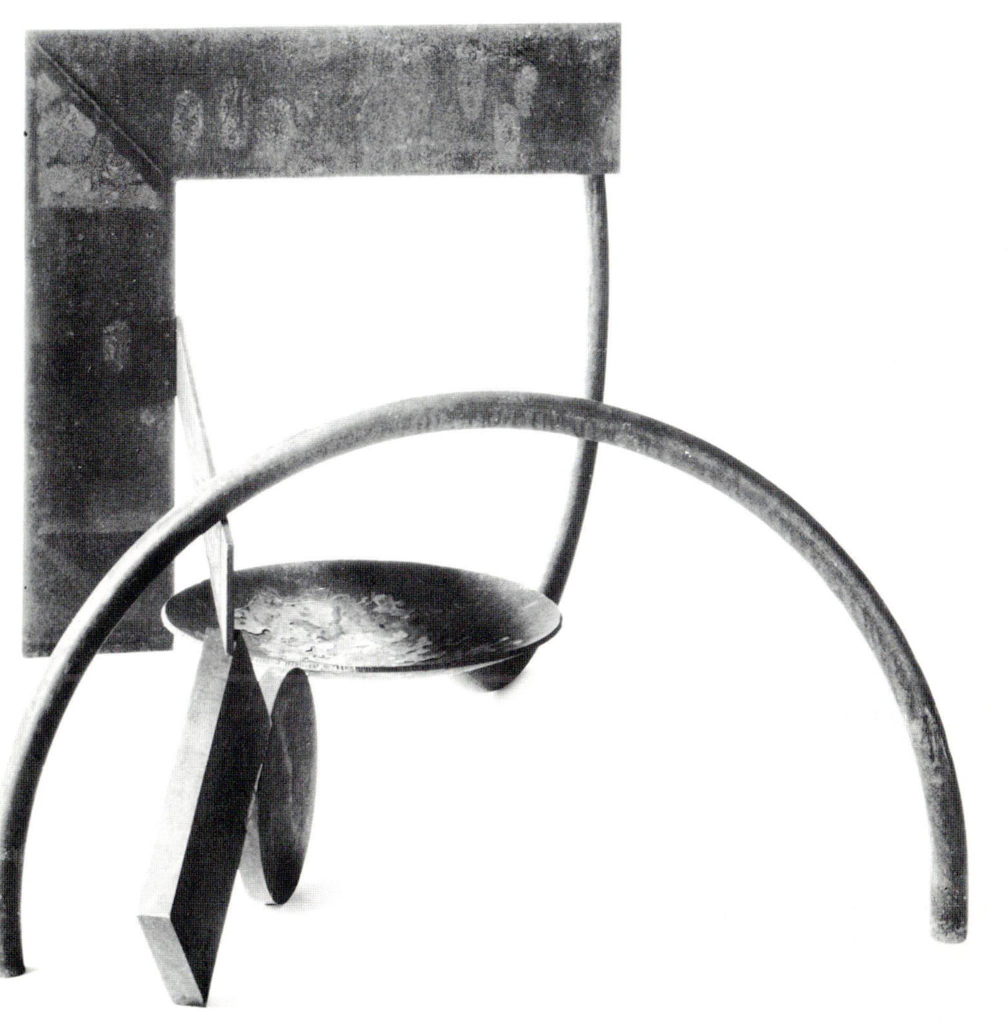

91
Ron Robertson-Swann, Australian, 1941–
Cyclops. 1971
Robertson-Swann is the most distinguished Australian sculptor working in the idiom of the St Martin's School of Art. The master of that style is Anthony Caro, (whose **Piano** is in the Gallery collection), and two of its prominent artists are Tim Scott and Philip King, whose **Peach Wheels** and **Span** are also in the Collection. It is rare for an Australian artist to work with the masters of a style; more often he is influenced by later followers. **Cyclops** is a striking illustration of fine work done by an Australian artist studying abroad who has developed a personal and individual accent within an artistic language.

Cyclops has been criticized for the material of its construction. A work of art is not assessed upon the intrinsic value of its component. The recently acquired Carracci drawing is made of a little paper and a little lead. The use of a rusted surface in contradistinction to the brightly painted works of his colleagues is a rejection of the blandishments of colour and finish, in favour of an emphasis on pure linear form. **Cyclops** explores open and closed space. In many ways it partakes of the nature of a drawing. It is not concerned with mass as is the Gallery's sculpture, **Balzac** by Rodin. It is a work of classical restraint appealing to the intellect rather than to the emotions. Yet it is a product of the mind working at a peak of intensity. At this late stage it should not be necessary to defend its non-representational nature. It deploys cubist geometric shapes. For that one needs no greater defence than Plato: "The beauty of the straight line and the circle and the plane and the solid figures formed from these is not like other things *Relative* but always *absolutely* beautiful".

N. G. S. B.
(December, 1972)

Plate XXVII
Donald Laycock, Australian, 1931–
Star Cycle. 1972
Star Cycle was the winning entry for the 1972 McCaughey Prize and was presented by the National Gallery Society of Victoria.

Donald Laycock is one of the most interesting painters to emerge in Australian art of recent years. Since his first joint shows of 1955 with Lawrence Daws, Clifton Pugh and John Howley, his work has developed consistently and very personally.

All his paintings are in a sense metaphysical. Though they are figurative they do not plan to tell us about the world of appearances, or of society but rather to comment on the innate mystery of life itself.

The strange 1968 paintings of fruit floating in space were a major breakthrough in his career. The finest of them is now in the Commonwealth Art Collection having been declined by Melbourne.

The great series of luminous nudes, painted in vibrant reds and orange excited all who saw them in 1971. But it is perhaps in the cosmic pictures of planets and stars that his evocative genius is most individually expressed. This picture of pulsing light, its planes merged and as it were moving and intermingling before our eyes, is a splendid example of which the Gallery is rightly proud and very grateful to the Society for its presentation.

Laycock studied for five years at the National Gallery School and his work is an admirable contribution to the history of that institution. His work was represented in the Whitechapel Exhibition of 1961, the Paris Biennale of 1963 and the Sao Paulo Bienal of 1969. He is now reaching the crest of a distinguished career.

N. G. S. B.
(December, 1973)

Plate XXVIII
Richard Larter, b. England, 1938–
Root Ripples Stocks. 1975
Richard Larter was born in Hornchurch, England. He studied part time at St Martin's School of Art in the late 1940s at Toynbee Hall, London; and graduated as an art teacher from Shoreditch Teacher's College, Surrey, in 1957. He came to Sydney in 1962.

While in England, Larter for a short while painted in the Abstract Expressionist style—knowledge of the New York painters of the 1950s, with their flat soft surfaces, is still clear in Larter's work.

Except for this brief period, Richard Larter's painting has always been figurative. He was influenced by the English artist Eduardo Paolozzi, one of the first to juxtapose photographic images, often on a random basis, in order to set up new visual and cultural associations for the viewer.

Root Ripples Stocks is painted as a collage of images taken from popular culture; the images are either that of pop figures—the head in the centre is the rock singer Tina Turner—or else depicted in flat magazine advertisement and comic book style. Despite the different colour saturations, the overall effect is one of flatness and surface glitter. This is achieved with bright colour and the vibrant, broken lines and dots that make up the images. Pat Larter, the artist's wife, is depicted three times; her image on the lower left is in bright flat coloured-comic style—blue eyes, pink lips, blue sky behind. Immediately to the upper right is a smaller but compelling second image of her; this is painted in shimmering "newspaper photograph" dots, a deep optical illusion created by chromatically opposed red on green. She is also the nude facing out of the canvas on the centre left, the largest of all the images, but softest in colour and outline.

The colours do give subtle recession, but the artist always counteracts this with dazzling patterns of coloured dots and mosaics that are painted between the irregular fields which hold the images.

No edge is neat in this painting; the pull the colour exerts on the eye is echoed in the rough edges of the image areas, and the rough stuckdown canvas. Flatness, bright colour, no brush texture and no strong emphasis to any one part of the painting are characteristics shared with abstract expressionism.

Richard Larter's paintings have been described as "Cultural Reportage". He uses television images, and has made prints from collages in a photocopying machine. Sydney is a city where figurative art and pop culture have had greater importance than in Melbourne—for instance, the Yellow House in King's Cross, started by Martin Sharp in 1969—and it is against this background that Richard Larter works and lives.

J. P.
(1976)

ARTICLES

"Three Self Portraits by John Bratby", 1957, *Annual Bulletin of the National Gallery of Victoria*, Vol. 1, Melbourne, 1959.

"Charles Blackman: Australian Painter", *Annual Bulletin of the National Gallery of Victoria*, Vol. III, Melbourne, 1961.

"Art is a Language", *The Rationalist*, Jan.-Feb., Melbourne, 1963.

"The Australian Collection: Some Recent Accessions of Contemporary Painting", *Annual Bulletin of the National Gallery of Victoria*, Vol. VI, Melbourne, 1964.

"Selected Accessions in Australian Painting", *Art Bulletin of Victoria*, 1967–68, National Gallery of Victoria, Melbourne, 1968.

"Australian Collection" *Art and Australia*, Vol. 6, No. 3, Sydney, 1968.

"Memo on the Transfield Art Prize Selection", *Art International*, Vol. 14, Nov., Switzerland, 1970.

"Painting in Victoria", *The Victorian Year Book*, Melbourne, 1973.

"Introduction", *National Gallery Society of Victoria Collector's Diary*, Melbourne, 1974.

OTHER ARTICLES APPEAR IN:

National Gallery Society of Victoria Bulletin, Jan., 1969. Aug., 1970. Dec., 1972. March, Sept., 1973. Dec., 1974. Dec., 1975.

Country Crafts, Melbourne, Aug. to Dec., 1959. March, April, June, July, 1960. Feb., May, Oct., 1961.

BOOKS AND CATALOGUES

Australian Painting, Longmans, Melbourne, 1961.

Max Meldrum, Catalogue, National Gallery of Victoria, Melbourne, 1961.

Australian Landscape Painting, Catalogue, National Gallery of Victoria, Melbourne, 1964.

Survey. Leonard Crawford, Leonard French, George Johnson, Roger Kemp, Jan Senbergs, Catalogue, National Gallery of Victoria, Melbourne, 1965.

Survey. Donald Friend, Justin O'Brien, Jeffrey Smart, David Strachan, Catalogue, National Gallery of Victoria, Melbourne, 1966.

William Frater, Catalogue, National Gallery of Victoria, Melbourne, 1966.

Lina Bryans, Catalogue, Georges Gallery, Melbourne, 1966.

John Rowell, Catalogue, The Block Galleries, Melbourne, 1967.

Australian Impressionists, Longmans, Melbourne, 1968.

The Field, Catalogue, National Gallery of Victoria, Melbourne, 1968.

Ambrose Patterson, Catalogue, Joshua McClelland Print Room, Melbourne, 1969.

Heroic Landscape, Catalogue, National Gallery of Victoria, Melbourne, 1970.

Object and Idea, Catalogue, National Gallery of Victoria, Melbourne, 1973.

Selected Bibliography

ASHTON, JULIAN ROSSI. *Now came still evening on.* Angus & Robertson, Sydney, 1941.
ASHTON, WILL. *Will Ashton; the life and work of artist Sir William.* Legend Press, Sydney, 1961.
Australian dictionary of biography. 4 vol. Melbourne University Press, Melbourne, 1966.
BADHAM, E. *A study of Australian art.* Currawong Press, Sydney, 1949.
BIRCH, ALAN & MACMILLAN, DAVID S. *The Sydney scene 1788–1860.* Melbourne University Press, Melbourne, 1962.
BONYTHON, KIM. *Modern Australian painting, 1960/1970.* Rigby, Adelaide, 1970.
BONYTHON, KIM & LYNN, ELWYN. *Modern Australian painting 1970/1975.* Rigby, Adelaide, 1976.
BOWDEN, KEITH MACRAE. *Samual Thomas Gill.* Keith Bowden, Maryborough (Vic.), 1971.
CHRISTENSEN, C. B. *The gallery of Eastern Hill; the Victorian Artists' Society centenary.* Victorian Artists' Society, Melbourne, 1970.
CLARK, C. MANNING HOPE. *A history of Australia.* 3 vols. Melbourne University Press, Melbourne, 1963–
COLQUHOUN, ALEXANDER. *Frederick McCubbin; a consideration.* Alexander McCubbin, Melbourne, 192 –
COX, LEONARD B. *The National Gallery of Victoria 1861–1968 A search for a collection.* National Gallery of Victoria, Melbourne, 1970.
CROLL, R. H. (ed.) *Smike to Bulldog; letters from Sir Arthur Streeton to Tom Roberts.* Ure Smith, Sydney, 1946.
DOCKING, GIL. *Two hundred years of New Zealand painting.* Lansdowne Press, Melbourne, 1971.
DUTTON, GEOFFREY. *Russell Drysdale.* Rev. ed. Thames & Hudson, London, 1969.
FAIRWEATHER, IAN, (trs and ill.) *The Drunken Buddha.* University of Queensland Press, Brisbane, 1965.
FREE, RENE. *Lloyd Rees.* Lansdowne Press, Melbourne, 1972.
FREEMAN, VIRGINIA. *Dobell on Dobell.* Ure Smith, Sydney, 1970.
GALBALLY, ANN. *Arthur Streeton.* Lansdowne Press, Melbourne, 1969.
GIBSON, FRANK & DODGSON, CAMPBELL. *Charles Conder, his life and work.* John Lane, London, 1914.
GILL, SAMUEL THOMAS. *The Australian sketchbook.* Lansdowne Press, Melbourne, 1974.
GLEESON, JAMES. *Colonial painters 1788–1880.* Lansdowne Press, Melbourne, 1971.
GLEESON, JAMES. *Impressionist painters 1881–1930.* Lansdowne Press, Melbourne, 1971.
GLEESON, JAMES. *Masterpieces of Australian painting.* Lansdowne Press, Melbourne, 1969.
GLEESON, JAMES. *Modern painters 1931–1970.* Lansdowne Press, Melbourne, 1971.
GLEESON, JAMES. *William Dobell.* Thames & Hudson, London, 1969.

GRANT, JAMES & SERLE, GEOFFREY. *The Melbourne scene 1803–1956*. Melbourne University Press, Melbourne, 1957.

HANCOCK, Sir WILLIAM KEITH. *Australia*. Benn, London, 1930.

HETHERINGTON, JOHN. *Australian painters; forty profiles*, (portrait drawings by Louis Kahan). Cheshire, Melbourne, 1963.

HOFF, URSULA. *Charles Conder*. Lansdowne Press, Melbourne, 1972.

HORTON, MERVYN (ed.) *Australian painters of the 70's*. Ure Smith, Sydney, 1975.

LAMBETH, AMY. *Fifty years of an artist's life*. Society of Artists, Sydney, 1938.

LINDSAY, LIONEL. *Conrad Martens; the man and his art*. Angus & Robertson, Sydney, 1920.

MCCUBBIN, FREDERICK. *The art of Frederick McCubbin*, (with an essay by James MacDonald). Lothian Book Publishing, Melbourne, 1916.

MCCULLOCH, ALAN. *Encyclopaedia of Australian art*. Hutchinson, London, 1968.

MCCULLOCH, ALAN. *The golden age of Australian painting; Impressionism and the Heidelberg School*. Lansdowne Press, Melbourne, 1969.

MACDONALD, JAMES S. *The art and life of David Davies*. Melbourne, n.d.

MACGEORGE, NORMAN. *The arts in Australia*. Cheshire, Melbourne, 1948.

MACINNES, COLIN. *Sidney Nolan*. Thames & Hudson, London, 1961.

MELDRUM, MAX. FOREMAN, RUSSELL (ed.). *The science of appearances as formulated & taught by Max Meldrum*. Shepherd Press, Sydney, 1950.

MOORE, WILLIAM. *The story of Australian art from the earliest known art of the continent to the art of today*. 2 vols. Angus & Robertson, Sydney, 1934.

NEWNHAM, W. H. *Victoria illustrated 1857 & 1862; engravings from S. T. Gill & N. Chevalier*. Lansdowne Press, Melbourne, 1971.

PHILIPP, FRANZ. *Arthur Boyd*. Thames & Hudson, London, 1967.

PRINGLE, J. M. D. *Australian painting today*. Thames & Hudson, London, 1963.

RIENITS, REX & THEA. *Early artists of Australia*. Angus & Robertson, Melbourne, 1963.

ROTHENSTEIN, JOHN. *The life and death of Charles Conder*. Dent, London, 1938.

SERLE, GEOFFREY. *From deserts the prophets come; the creative spirit in Australia 1788–1972*. Heinemann, Melbourne, 1973.

SERLE, GEOFFREY. *The rush to be rich; a history of the colony of Victoria 1883–1889*. Melbourne University Press, Melbourne, 1971.

SERLE, PERCIVAL. *Dictionary of Australian Biography*. 2 Vols. Angus & Robertson, Sydney, 1949.

SMITH, BERNARD. *Australian painting 1788–1970*, 2nd ed. Melbourne University Press, Melbourne, 1971.

SMITH, BERNARD. *European vision and the South Pacific 1768–1850; a study in the history of art and ideas*. Oxford University Press, London, 1960.

SMITH, BERNARD. *Place, taste and tradition; a study of Australian art since 1788*. Ure Smith, Sydney, 1945.

SPATE, VIRGINIA. *John Olsen*. Georgian House, Melbourne, 1963.
SPATE, VIRGINIA. *Tom Roberts*. Lansdowne Press, Melbourne, 1973.
STREETON, ARTHUR. *The art of Arthur Streeton*. Arthur Streeton, Melbourne, 1935.
THIELE, COLIN. *Heysen of Hahndorf*. Rigby, Adelaide, 1968.
THOMAS, DANIEL. *Grace Cossington Smith*. Art Gallery of N.S.W., Sydney, 1973.
THOMAS, DAVID. *Rupert Bunny 1864–1947*. Lansdowne Press, Melbourne, 1970.
TIPPING, MARJORIE. *Eugene Von Guerard's Australian Landscapes*. Lansdowne Press, Melbourne, 1975.

OTHER PUBLICATIONS:
Annual Bulletin. Vols 1959–1966/67. National Gallery of Victoria, Melbourne.
Art Bulletin of Victoria, 1967–8. National Gallery of Victoria, Melbourne.
Quarterly Bulletin. Vols 1945–58. National Gallery of Victoria, Melbourne.
The art and life of Walter Withers. Alexander McCubbin, Melbourne, 1925.
"The Herald Exhibition": exhibition of French and British contemporary art; paintings & sculpture. Exhibition catalogue. *The Herald*, Melbourne, 1939.
Two decades of American art; an exhibition from the Museum of Modern Art, New York. Exhibition catalogue. Museum of Modern Art, New York, 1967.